# BOOKS BY ADRIANA MATHER

HOW TO HANG A WITCH SERIES
*How to Hang a Witch*
*Haunting the Deep*

KILLING NOVEMBER SERIES
*Killing November*
*Hunting November*

STANDALONE NOVELS
*Mom Com*

# ADRIANA MATHER

**BLACK STONE**
PUBLISHING

Printed in the United States of America
Originally published in hardcover by Blackstone Publishing in 2023

First paperback edition: 2023
ISBN 979-8-212-87717-6
Fiction / Romance / General

Version 1

Blackstone Publishing
31 Mistletoe Rd.
Ashland, OR 97520

www.BlackstonePublishing.com

*For my beloved grandparents Claire and Frank Mather, who were married in 1953 and have been showing the world what true love is ever since.*

*Happy 70th Anniversary!*

When it's your ninth birthday and you're consuming indecent amounts of sugar, it's as if you've suddenly sprouted wings and found a natural source of laughing gas. Today, it just feels easy to be me, like I'm generating my own sunshine.

Wilder knocks my elbow with his, and I spill flour over the edge of my measuring cup. I immediately scoop it up and flick it at my best friend with a satisfied grin.

My dad glances at us. "Maddi," he corrects me, wiping the counter clear of the mess we've been making in the kitchen of my family bakery.

"What? He's cheating," I say, feeling justified.

"I'm not cheating," Wilder replies, his wavy hair flopping in his face, messy and dusted with flour. "I'm just helping myself win." He mixes his bowl of (what are sure to be) inferior cupcakes and grins. We've been in a constant bake-off since my dad bought me a toy oven for Christmas when we were four.

"Dad, my best friend's a total wanker," I say—a word Wilder picked up on one of his family trips to London.

Dad's eyebrows shoot up. "Madeline DeLuca!"

"What?" I stare at him with innocence, mixing spoon dripping yummy gingerbread batter into my bowl. "What does wanker mean?"

"It means—" my dad starts and stops, his cheeks taking on the color of Wilder's red velvet batter. "Don't worry about the meaning. It's a bad word."

Wilder's shoulders vibrate subtly with the laugh he's trying to contain.

"Oh," I say. "But what does it mean?"

"I have customers waiting," Dad says, and pushes through the door separating the kitchen from our family bakery.

As soon as the door closes, Wilder explodes with laughter. Needling our parents in good fun is one of our favorite hobbies. It's especially great when our families are having their weekly dinner together and we can get them all at once.

Wilder swipes a glob of maple frosting from my bowl and licks it off his finger. "Not bad."

I raise an eyebrow. "You mean best ever."

Wilder smirks mischievously. "I mean, maybe I'll let you work in my bakery when we're older."

I laugh. "Your bakery? No thanks. I'll be busy running this one. And maybe, just maybe, I'll hire you as my assistant."

Wilder's grin widens and his hair flops in his eyes. "Battle of the bakeries. You're on."

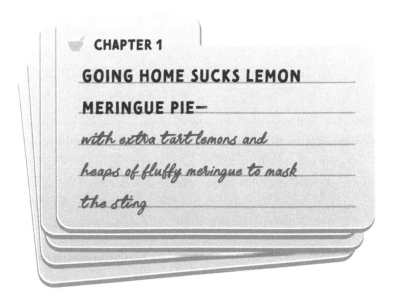

# CHAPTER 1

## GOING HOME SUCKS LEMON MERINGUE PIE—

*with extra tart lemons and heaps of fluffy meringue to mask the sting*

The only thing worse than being humiliated on national television in a baking show is having your disapproving mother call you up directly after it airs, forgo any words of comfort, and instead tell you there's an unsettled matter in your father's will that requires you to return home immediately. And that while you're coming you might as well stay for Christmas—not "it would be so great to have you" or "perfect timing for the season of lights and cookies," but a flat "Since you're currently unemployed, you might as well stay until the holidays have concluded."

I desperately wanted to refuse, wishing I could just spend the holiday in my LA apartment with my nine-year-old, piled in a sea of blankets on the couch, eating sweets and watching movies in our matching striped pajamas. Not to mention that my mother and I haven't spent more than a handful of hours together in the past ten years and even those were fraught with tension. But I also can't bring myself to let her spend the holiday alone the first year after my father passed. I'd like to see for myself that she's all right, and have her see me in turn—the deeply subtle and repressed version of support where I mumble, "You good? I'm good," even though neither of us probably ever will be. So here I am, headed for my childhood home with my son, pride obliterated and replaced with a couple of reindeer antlers strapped to the windows of my twelve-year-old Prius.

I shift in my seat, my butt numb from the long drive. We managed the frugal cross-country trek from Los Angeles in four days, staying with a friend in New Mexico, a friend of a friend in Missouri, and then using a buddy's travel points to get a motel room in Pennsylvania, which is not an option on the way back. My only hope is that this issue with Dad's will includes some long-lost family treasure.

"Seventeen minutes!" Spencer says from the back seat, reading the remaining travel time off my phone mounted on my dashboard. At this point, I don't need the directions, but I leave it up for him. A handful of seconds later he announces: "Sixteen minutes!"

I take a breath. "Spence, love of my heart, son of my everything, if you count down every minute we have left, Mom's head might explode. And in such a small space, brains are sure to get everywhere. You don't want brains on you, do you?" It's all I've got after nine hours on the road.

He grins at me in the rearview mirror. "Nobody likes sarcasm."

I chuckle. He's repeating something his teacher once said, but it gets me every time. "But my jokes are so good."

"They're not bad," he says, considering it for a moment. "But they're not great."

Leave it to a fourth grader to give you the cold hard truth. He recently read a book where the main character drank a potion that made him unable to lie. He told me that even though the boy's life was harder, he was happier because he no longer felt he needed to be what everyone wanted him to be, and was free to be his real self. Then he announced he was going to do the same. And he's been surprisingly committed.

"Haverberry Cove!" he exclaims as we drive past a hand-some wooden sign with black script.

I glance in my rearview mirror at Spence, who's pressed up against his window, one hand on the glass and his eyes illumi-nated by the white lights forming a canopy over Main Street.

"You haven't seen anything yet," I say, punching up my voice in an effort to convince myself more than him that being here won't be so bad. "They have a holiday market filled with every kind of hot chocolate and pecan pie. Horse-drawn sleighs, the whole nine."

He grins brightly, never taking his eyes from the window.

Haverberry Cove is Massachusetts' standard for elegance. It's three-quarters New England charm and one-quarter brine-scented driftwood, which is to say it's basically perfect—except for the fact that I can't stand being in it. Rambling historical houses with ocean views surround a postcard-worthy square where the aesthetic is handmade, hand-carved, and lo-cally sourced. The kind of small where everyone knows a little more than a little about everyone else, which is insufferable when you're the town scandal (me), but not so bad when a wait-ress brings you coffee without having to ask or the grocer saves you the last ripe cantaloupe because he knows it's your favorite.

"I'm gonna see Dad tomorrow?" he asks for the seventy-hundredth time.

"That's right," I confirm. Jake—my fertilizer, as my friends have nicknamed him—doesn't really deserve the title of "Dad" since he barely calls once a month and needs reminders to buy birthday presents.

"Do you think he'll take me to the holiday market?"

"I'm sure he will," I say with the utmost confidence, because if he doesn't, I'll happily key his truck.

The red light changes to green and I drive toward the square and my father's bakery. I use my last reserve of energy to redirect my thoughts away from all things Dad and baking, which works for shit. In half a second flat I'm picturing my utterly embarrassing performance on *Ultimate Bake Off*, where I not only revealed my financial woes but indulged in a sentimental rant that included my father's passing, something I promised myself I wouldn't mention on TV. Not only because my mother thinks reality competitions are vile perversions of the depraved, but because I do my very best not to spiral about my father—him, his bakery, or the fight we had the last time I saw him alive.

I train my eyes forward, death-gripping my wheel, and decidedly not looking at There's Nothing Batter Bakery. I don't want to know if the holiday window displays haven't been put up or if the door needs repainting—things we loved doing together every year of my childhood. It isn't mine, I remind myself. He didn't leave it to me; he left it to Mom, a woman who has less interest in bakeries than she does in reality television. And it wouldn't matter if he did, because I don't want it—a painful reminder of everything that went wrong.

"Mom!" Spence says, practically launching himself out of his seat, his pointer finger thudding against the window. "LOOK!"

I glance at the nine reindeer suspended over the green and the large menorah sculpture that resembles whimsical tree branches. There's a certain National Lampoon zealousness about holidays here. "Told you," I say.

"But are you seeing Grandpa's bakery?" he continues, giving me a start; I didn't realize he remembered what the bakery looked like, considering he's only been there once and was just five at the time. "Is that *chocolate*?"

Before I can reign in the compulsion, my eyes flit to There's Nothing Batter. But it's not the shabby, run-down heartbreak I envisioned. Twinkle lights and holly frame the window around an exquisitely detailed winter village scene replete with working lights in cottages and powdered sugar snow. And like Spence said, it's entirely handcrafted from chocolate—an insanely difficult task—and must have cost Mom a fortune. Unless maybe she hired a new manager who's a magical chocolate artist?

While I feel the sting of guilt I was expecting, there's also something else—a sense of not being needed. Now unable to look away, I lean toward the passenger seat window and slow down, trying to get a peek inside at the person behind the counter. But the guy has his back to me and I only catch a glimpse of his brown hair. *Come on, turn around so I can assess you and then not-so-secretly hate you for replacing me.* As if the dude heard me, he does turn, but just as a group of Friday night shoppers stops in front of the bakery to readjust their scarves and hats, obstructing my view.

"Move," I breathe, trying to shoo them with my hand, only my snooping is cut short by the distressed tone in my son's voice.

"MOM!" Spence yells and I whip my head toward the road, just as a fancy car cuts me off.

Getting cut off in Massachusetts is no surprise; there's a solid and justifiable reason the nickname for drivers in this state is Massholes. But what *is* a surprise is that directly after pulling in front of me, the car hits its brakes. It takes me a half second to realize what's happening and slam on my own. Only my worse-for-wear Prius doesn't jerk to a stop the way the new sports car did. Instead, it glides forward, hitting the silver bumper with a thud.

"Shit!" I say, cursing the silver car, myself, and my worn brakes.

"Mom?" Spencer says again, his worried eyes finding mine in the rearview mirror.

"Spence? You okay?" I demand, panic flaring. I yank my car to the curb and whip around in my seat, searching him for potential injury. It doesn't matter that we were gliding at approximately three miles per hour, my mind is screaming that my kid was just in a *car accident*.

"I'm fine," he says with a shrug. "It wasn't even as hard as bumper cars."

My lungs deflate, my heart rate slowing, as I register that he is indeed fine. But when I turn forward once more, all sense of relief vanishes. On the trunk of the fancy car are two small wings—the telltale logo of an Aston Martin. And there on the bumper is a hand-length scratch that I'm guessing matches up perfectly with the edge of my license plate.

I leap out of my car, moving toward it to get a better look.

"Shit," I mutter, running my hand along the groove in the cold metal, instantly aware that this is going to cost me more than I make . . . *made* in two months.

A car door clicks open and I stand up straight, furious at myself for the carelessness and at the bakery for existing at all.

Out of the driver's side door comes a woman in her late twenties. Her dark hair hangs just past her shoulders in a silky sheet outlining her face; her lipstick is red, and her clothes are impeccable—luxurious black gloves and shiny high-heeled boots highlighting the edges of a long herringbone coat.

My stomach sinks so low I fear it might retreat for good. *Liv Buenaventura*, Wilder's older sister, who not only owns her own internationally acclaimed line of beauty products but is also the face of the most recent campaign because she's *that* beautiful.

"Madeline DeLuca?" she says, the annoyance in her expression softening as her heels click toward me. "My God, is that really you?"

"It's me," I say, lifting my hands and then dropping them again, my grubby travel clothes painfully marking the contrast between us. She was my idol as a teen, a year older than me, and Haverberry's golden girl. I wanted to be her so badly that I practically had a poster of her in my bedroom. When I got accepted early decision to Vassar everyone in town kept saying: "We've got another Liv on our hands," and it was possibly the best compliment of my life. Of course, a week later I found out I was pregnant and Vassar never came to pass.

"It's been what? Ten years since I've seen you?" she continues.

"About that, yeah," I reply. I've been home exactly twice since Spence was born. Once about four years ago, when he wanted to meet Jake, and once right after my dad died. Both visits were brief and purposefully devoid of socializing.

"Have you seen Wilder yet?" she asks brightly, and I consider stepping into traffic as an alternative to answering.

"Uh, no," I say, biting back the urge to tell her that he's welcome to fall off a cliff for all I care. "I didn't know he was even here."

My parents (despite my resistance) have given me updates on Wilder over the years. How he studied business at Oxford and as a pastry chef at Le Cordon Bleu, how he then remained "abroad"—code for philandering socialite—visiting Haverberry only periodically to dazzle the commoners with his European-inspired charm (the child my parents not-so-secretly wished they'd had).

She gives me a surprised look. But all she says is, "Oh, he's here all right."

"Plus," I add, lightening my tone, "we just got in." I gesture to my car where Spence is staring at us with his window down. "I haven't even made it to the house yet."

She looks at my outfit as though seeing it for the first time. "Of course!" she exclaims, clasping her hands together. "And here I am chatting you up. You both must be exhausted."

And suddenly Spencer is out and moving to my side with a grin.

Liv looks from me to him. "You must be Maddi's son."

"Spence," he says, extending his hand.

"I'm Liv," she replies, shaking it happily.

"Wow. You're beautiful," Spence says in awe, then adds, "Not in an objectifying way, just, you know, as a fact."

Liv laughs and I can't help but do the same. We had a long conversation last week about reducing peoples' worth to their appearances and he really took it to heart.

"Well, aren't you my new favorite person," she says with a wink.

On the sidewalk behind us, I hear the buzz of whispers and feel eyes on my back, which I pointedly ignore. I don't want to know who's gossiping or draw Spence's attention to it.

Instead, I focus on Liv. "I'm sorry about your bumper. I feel awful," I say, moving the conversation to its conclusion so we can get back in the car. "Would it be all right if I paid out-of-pocket for the damage?" The words stick in my mouth. I have no idea how I'm going to accomplish that. But what I do know is that my insurance is so bad I'd wind up paying most of it anyway, and my rates would skyrocket for the next three years.

She stares at me for a moment and glances at my antlered car, probably registering the fact that it's the same one I was driving as a teen. She waves her hand through the air. "For a scratch? Nah. I'll just get it buffed out."

My intense relief turns to embarrassment. I hate that I can't insist on taking care of it. "That's so kind. Can I make it up to you in some way? Maybe with an obscene quantity of apology éclairs?"

"They're really good," Spence adds. "Like delicious."

"I bet they are, and I totally want to try them. *But*," she says, her red lips parting in a smile, "I was actually just thinking about my family's fundraiser tomorrow night. While it's a good cause and all, it's going to be about as fun as watching paint dry. Why don't you come with me, Maddi, and we'll call it even. You'll be saving me from death by boredom."

My heartbeat falters like a cartoon character that can't find its footing. The Buenaventura Annual Holiday Fundraiser—a lavish event akin to a high school reunion for all its posturing and bragging, and one that likely includes her brother. Selling my kidney on the black market is suddenly sounding like a preferable alternative. But in the face of her generosity, I'd hate to disappoint her. Not to mention that even though I haven't seen her in forever, she still feels like surrogate family.

"Sure," I manage. "I think I can swing that."

We say our goodbyes and Spence and I get back in the car, my stomach deeply unsettled by the plans I just made for Saturday night. This town isn't shy about being nosy, and I can't imagine for a second that the fundraiser guests are going to hold back their judgment just because it's been ten years. In fact, they'll probably be that much more insistent because they had to wait so long to put in their opinion.

I drive out of the square, leaving behind the bakery and the painful nostalgia. Two weeks, I tell myself. Two weeks until we can drive home to California.

## CHAPTER 2

## CHOCOLATE GIVE ME
## BOURBON CAKE—
*extra bourbon for all the reasons*

My car rolls to a stop in the driveway of my parents' house—a narrow two-story Victorian painted white with denim blue trim and a line of shaped shrubberies running along the side. Even though the property is small, everything on it is neat and tidy just like my parents, not a stray leaf on the lawn or a discolored shingle on the gray roof. I wince. My *mom's* house, I correct myself. Even though it's been almost a year, I still think of them as a unit. Charles and Eleanor, despite being distinct opposites—him a quiet baker's son from the country, her a socialite from a well-to-do Boston family—they found commonality in the small things, like their love of baked ziti and their impossible expectations for their daughter.

I hesitate, falling back in my seat and exhaling, resistance building inside of me. But Spence is out of the car in a half second, bouncing in the driveway and yanking his duffel bag out of the trunk. "We're here! Whoohoo!"

I desperately wish I could borrow his enthusiasm, and trade in my expectations of tension and inevitable disappointment for something less painful. But even in the best of times when I was a star student, my mother and I didn't have an easy relationship.

Spence opens my door. "*Mom*," he says like I'm holding up the fun.

For a split second, I consider pulling him onto my lap and throwing the car in reverse with a Harley Quinn celebratory getaway cackle. But instead, I find myself taking my coat and purse off the passenger seat and stepping into the chilled salty air that carries the scent of the ocean even in winter.

Spence yanks my cupcake-print suitcase out of the trunk with a plunk and drags both it and his duffel toward the door. I pluck it from his grasp, and he skips up the steps, pressing the doorbell two times fast. Unlike Jake's sparse communication, my parents have called every Saturday religiously these past few years. I'd spend about thirty seconds on the phone saying some version of *How's the weather?* and then Spence would take over. And while I'm glad that he has a relationship with my parents—*Goddammit*, I correct myself again, *with my mom*—that's enriching, I share no such bond.

Before I can steel myself for the inevitable, the door swings open, revealing my mother in a burgundy knee-length skirt suit, hair blown into fluffy waves around her rose-tinted ivory cheeks, a single strand of pearls around her neck—a debutante out of place in her middle-class backdrop like a crystal glass on an otherwise informal table.

Her eyes flit from Spence to me. "You're not wearing your coats," she says with a frown. "It's absolutely freezing."

I consider explaining that the proper-lady etiquette she attempted to instill in me didn't stick, but I don't get a chance because Spence is already inside and hugging her.

"Grandma, did you see the lights in town? They're *every-where*. And—" he stops short near the door of the living room. "Is that your tree? It's GIANT."

My mother smiles, satisfied by his reaction to her tree, impeccably decorated in red and white—all non-matching sentimental ornaments stashed away inside the branches where they can't muddy her aesthetic. It's not actually giant, but it appears that way because the living room is small and the thing pushes up to the ceiling and out like a Hershey's Kiss, exemplifying my mother's best skill—making her very average means appear more.

I close the front door behind me, hanging up my coat in the foyer closet and kicking off my boots while she shows Spence the stack of presents intended for him. I join them in the living room, and she looks from my cupcake suitcase to my jingle bell socks, her eyebrows knitting together. I can almost hear her thoughts: *Presentation is everything, Madeline.*

"You must be hungry," she says as Spence circles her living room ogling the monogrammed red velvet stockings hanging from the mantle.

"We ate on the way," I tell her, aware that it's hours past her designated dinnertime. She and my father have eaten promptly at 6:30 every day of my life.

"I saved you food," she replies. "It'll only take a minute to reheat."

"Thanks, Mom, I appreciate it, but I'm stuffed."

"You've had a long trip," she says, her tone betraying her annoyance that I drove instead of flew, which I justified as an adventure for Spence, purposefully omitting that I couldn't afford the last-minute holiday-adjacent tickets. "You should have something."

We stare at each other uncomfortably, the simplest of conversations somehow turning sour.

"I'll eat," Spence announces happily, and I find myself grateful for his bottomless kid hunger.

"While you guys do that," I start, "I'd love to take a quick—"

"You can sit with us, Madeline, even if you're not hungry," my mother says in a tone that leaves no room for disagreement.

"Sounds good," I reply, resisting the urge to engage in our usual verbal chess.

♥♥♥♥

I wheel my cupcake luggage into my little bedroom, exhausted from the drive, the worry, and the hour-long second dinner with my mother. Spence is still downstairs, giving Mom a detailed account of our recent trip to the aquarium. I figured it was best to exit before he got to the part where we reenacted *Jaws* so convincingly in the gift shop that one of the employees asked if we needed a medic.

I collapse onto the striped navy duvet, shoving a velvet accent pillow under my head. My room is like a time capsule of my life as a teen—outwardly perfect, a reflection of my mother's good taste with antique furniture and a spotless beige area rug, the sentimental things hidden away, shoved in a box in the closet or closed away in a drawer, the only exception being the picture frame on my vanity. It's one of me and my dad covered in flour in his bakery kitchen when I was eleven, our eyes practically squeezed shut from laughing so hard. As I stare at it, the memory hits me like an unseen wave, surprisingly forceful and disorienting. And before I realize I've made the decision to get up, I'm gravitating toward it, lifting the gold frame, my fingers grazing the velvet backing.

As reserved as my dad always was, he came alive in the bakery. Mostly, he was a man of few words; he'd state his piece and when he was done, he was done, so much so that I always wondered if his friends even knew him that well. But when he was teaching me the trick to pâte à choux or telling me the secret of his crème anglaise he could talk for hours, passionately rambling off the history of tarts and which piping tips yield the best flowers. And this was and is hands down my favorite picture of us, not posed like the others around the house, but real and messy. I immediately wonder if my dad saw it here, and if he thought about the fact that I didn't take it with me, the realization pricking me with unease.

I put the frame back in its place, about to turn away. But the hook of nostalgia keeps me planted there, staring at my vanity where I once stashed my most precious things.

And despite my knowing it's folly, a pang of anticipation zings through me. I carefully ease out the drawer with my stationery in it, and slide my hand to the back, popping out the false bottom. There, just where I left it ten years ago is my journal, chronicling my teen years with Wilder, the good and the bad. The leather cover is worn from being clutched to my chest in moments of high drama, and the pages are stuffed with pictures. When I left it, I cried big heavy hormonal tears. I even considered turning my Prius around halfway across the state and going back for it. But in time, I was glad I didn't have it. Reading it in California would have been excruciating. It was hard enough that first year without a detailed reminder of all that I'd lost.

But now? It feels a bit like an old movie, the kind that people's grandparents project onto their living room wall, flashes of compelling images from another lifetime.

I flip open to a page stuffed with notes, the ones that were once folded in elaborate shapes, and pull one out with a satisfying crinkle, edges rough from being torn from a spiral notebook.

At the top of the page is Wilder's handwriting and the sight of his familiar script sends off warning bells in my mind. Warning bells I do not listen to.

W: Go WITH ME TO THE APPLE ORCHARD THIS WEEKEND?

I smile stupidly (aware that I'll regret this later, much like the temptation of a second piece of cheesecake that is sure to sit like a rock of doom in your stomach) remembering when I got this in Mrs. Lemon's math class in the fall of sophomore year—she was a notorious note shark, famous for catching them and reading them aloud, making it all the more fun to slip one past her. And on this particular day, we tossed this thing back and forth until we literally ran out of space, deeply impressed with our stealth.

M: You wasted a whole note on a question you know the answer to? On a day when Mrs. Lemon is clearly under-caffeinated???

W: Does PASSING NOTES WITH ME MAKE YOU NERVOUS?

M: Are you flirting with me right now? Cause you can save that shit for your admirers.

W: ARE YOU TRYING TO TELL ME YOU'RE NOT ONE OF THEM? OUCH.

M: Pride goeth before a dick becometh, or whatever that expression is.

W: *Pride? Nah. It's actually super important I know where you stand on my admiration. Critical really. Can't proceed without that info.*

M: Nice baiting.

W: *No worries. Silence is golden and all that. I guess I just won't ask you what I wanted to ask you.*

M: I will hurt you in all the ways.

W: *It's probably for the best anyway. Lets me off the hook from that big speech I was going to give.*

M: I'm this close to kicking you from across the aisle.

W: *Temper temper*

M: It's hard not to have one when your best friend is a sly fuck.

W: *You heard I was sly in bed? Which of my admirers have you been talking to exactly?*

M: Don't get too worked up over there. We all know you haven't made it past first base.

Or at least I do. My God I hope Mrs. Lemon
finds this note.

W: Go AHEAD. THROW IT IN HER PATH. I'm NOT
EVEN A LITTLE EMBARRASSED. I'LL HOOK UP
WITH SOMEONE WHEN IT MEANS SOMETHING,
NOT BEFORE.

M: Okay now you're just setting yourself up as
the romantic. Can you feel me rolling my eyes
right now? Cause I really really am.

W: YOU THINK I'm NOT?

M: Romantic? I don't know. Maybe??? Should I
ask one of the girls you took to the movies
this summer?

W: THAT OR YOU COULD JUST COME TO THE
MOVIES WITH ME AND FIND OUT.

I remember hesitating then, a thrill shooting up my spine. A
lot of our conversations had skirted up against this type of thing,
something safe enough that it could be dismissed as friendly
banter, but charged in a way that felt more like flirting. I could
feel him watching me, noting the extra time I was taking to
respond.

In a flash decision, I decided to push the envelope.

M: Okay, Wilder, I'm calling your bluff. Woo me.

He silently chuckled when he saw the paper.

W: *With pleasure, Madeline DeLuca.*

And he did take pleasure in it. He was always the type to hold doors open and offer to carry your bag, but all of a sudden it was like I came first in everything. He was aware of me wherever I was in the room, always anticipating me. He knew when I was cranky and when I really needed an ice cream pick-me-up. He brought me small presents—not showy things like flowers, but smaller and infinitely sweeter things like my favorite lip balm on a cold day, or a pen that had a secret compartment he could fit a note in. And my God, did it work. By the time he kissed me three weeks later, I was helplessly in love with him.

I fold the note up and place it back in my journal with a heavy sigh, promising myself that this was a one-time indulgence. I do not want to think about Wilder Buenaventura. Unless it's to imagine kicking him in the shin. But I don't have time to dwell because my door opens.

"I told Spencer I would make him up a bed on the couch," my mother says, coming into the room, and I shove the diary back in the drawer. She eyes me as I take a fast step away from the vanity like *Who me? Reading love letters? That's just bananas.* My lack of subtlety earns me a raised eyebrow. "But he said he wanted to stay in here with you."

Spencer squeezes around her and plops his bag on the floor. He's afraid of the dark, and while we have a routine at home that makes him feel comfortable in his own room, he always stays with me when we travel.

I grab him around the waist and pull him onto the fluffy comforter, blowing a raspberry against his cheek. "Gotta get the kid snuggles while I still can."

He laughs and wipes his cheek. "Gross. You totally slimed me."

My mother watches us, seemingly unsure if she's horrified or oddly fascinated by our caveman behavior. She opens her mouth to comment just as a wet finger pokes into my ear. I yelp, which causes Spence to double over in laughter and my mother's eyes to double in size.

"I'm headed to bed myself," she says, fluffing the ruffles on her white blouse. "We'll talk about the matter concerning your father's will on Sunday."

And just like that, I stop laughing. I know that's what instigated this trip in the first place, but her sudden declaration feels off-putting. "Is it a good matter or a bad matter?" I ask before I can stop myself.

She was cryptic on the phone, leaving me to draw my own conclusions. As far as I ever knew there were only three major things in my father's will—this house, his collection of antique leather-bound books, and the bakery. She mentioned it only once right after he passed, and I got the impression that it pained her to delineate the summation of their thirty years together in such plain terms. My mother came from old money and has always acted like it, even though she lives in no such luxury and hasn't since the day she married my father and her parents cut her off. Which leads me to conclude that this will issue most likely concerns the bakery. Part of me wonders if she's ready to sell, a thought that makes my pulse unsteady and my stomach sour with guilt.

"We'll discuss it on Sunday," is all she says. "10:00 a.m."

It's official. I'm back in Eleanor-Land, a totalitarian kingdom where you plan a meeting time for personal conversations.

CHAPTER 3

## SPEAK OF THE DEVIL'S
## FOOD CAKE—

*extra potent chocolate for rich color
and a heaviness that's sure to sit in
your stomach like an anvil*

The promise of coffee propels me down the stairs, dressed and already braced for the comment from my mother about how I slept late. I head for the kitchen, and before I reach the doorway, I hear the clink of a cup on a stone counter. As I step through, she's pulling a tea bag from a tin.

"Good morning," she says without looking up, "or should I say good afternoon."

I smile at the predictability of it. "Oh, come now," I say, amused. "It's only 11:15. I've been known to sleep till two." Humor is the only way I survived our relationship as a teen. Of course, my jokes were largely underappreciated, but you can't have everything.

I pull a bag of coffee beans out of the cupboard and switch on the coffee maker.

She glances up at me, her steaming kettle poised to pour. "I wasn't trying to be funny," she announces and I stifle a smile. "I just don't know how you can get anything done when you miss half your day." Her tone is perfunctory, not like it's an insult but a matter of fact.

"I manage," I say. It's difficult to resist the urge to defend myself—to explain how I usually average only six hours a night between picking up freelance catering work, hunting for a job in a patisserie or upscale restaurant, and taking business classes at the community center to one day start my own café. Not to mention that I spent what tiny savings I had to get us here and now I have *jetlag*. But I know that if I say those things we'll be back to my least favorite conversation, the one that involves all my squandered potential.

"I guess you do," she replies, dunking her tea bag in her porcelain cup.

We're silent for a long minute, her tidying the counter and me waiting for her fancy coffee machine to spit out my frothy single cup. Normally I would brew a double, but all her coffee cups are small 8 oz things. She doesn't possess a shelf of mismatched mugs of varied sizes with cartoon cats, bad wine jokes, and keepsakes from Yellowstone like the rest of the world. Hers are a matching set, too small to support coffee fiends and too delicate to give to children for hot cocoa; they're basically useless.

Mom seats herself at the small breakfast table in front of the large window overlooking her backyard. "Do you have any plans for the rest of the day?" she asks.

"Uh, yeah," I say, opening the refrigerator to survey my milk options. "Jake is coming to get Spence in a few minutes to take him to lunch, which means I'll probably spend the afternoon job hunting."

"Jake?" my mother says, her eyebrow lifted in objection. "That's a surprise."

I close the refrigerator door, opting to drink my coffee

black over using the 2 percent. At home, I make my own creamer, a decadent mixture of coconut milk, cinnamon, vanilla extract, and dates, and while I didn't expect her to have anything like that, I was hoping for the farm-fresh heavy cream Dad always kept.

"Yeah," is all I say. "He seems to have grown up a bit."

My mother harrumphs into her cup, and while I agree with her that Jake isn't winning any prizes in the responsibility department (given the nonexistent child support that he always promises to pay, but doesn't), I also don't want to have that conversation with the possibility of Spence overhearing. He doesn't need my mom's take on how Jake screwed up my life and then didn't have the decency to marry me. Not that I wanted to marry him.

As if we spoke him into existence, the doorbell rings and my mother frowns. I swipe my coffee off the counter, unwilling to let it get cold, and make my way toward the front door.

"I'll get it!" Spence yells from the stairs as he barrels down them. He flies past me and yanks open the front door. "Dad!" he exclaims, diving in for a hug.

Jake's dirty blond hair is relatively short and very neat in comparison to his younger surfer days, perfectly highlighting his gold-hued skin. His smile is big and warm—probably his best feature—and he eagerly embraces Spence. "Hey there, kid."

"Come in," I offer.

He steps into the foyer, which is really just a slightly wider section of the hallway that houses the staircase, closing the door behind him. Jake looks from Spence to me, his grin widening. "Hey, Maddi." He has a way of saying my name, emphasizing it, that is so charming that I have a flashback of him as a teen, tanned and glistening in the waves at our town beach.

"Would you like some coffee?" I offer, raising my cup.

But it's my son who answers. "No time, Mom. Too much to do."

Jake and I both laugh, which feels odd. We don't have a strained relationship the way many separated parents do, most likely because we didn't have much of a relationship to begin with, but we don't have a congenial one, either. While I never expected Jake to step up given the circumstances, I also didn't realize how much his lack of involvement would affect my kid, or me for that matter. Because that's the thing about being a parent—someone hurting your kid's feelings is so much worse than that person hurting yours. And for reasons unknown to me, Spence idolizes Jake, making the situation feel all the more precarious.

"You heard him, Jake. No coffee for you," I say with an ease I don't feel.

Jake rubs Spence's head, a gesture he probably picked up from dads in movies. "Why don't you come with us, Maddi? After pancakes, we're going to the holiday market."

I shake my head. I know Spence was hoping for some alone time with his dad. Not to mention there's no way I'm going to the packed holiday market on a Saturday afternoon, no matter how much I enjoyed it as a kid. I know my presence there will only inspire gossip.

But again, it's my son who answers, "Mom has this benefit thing," quickly dismissing my possible intrusion on father-son time.

I hear my mother's steps falter behind me and I wince. I didn't get around to telling her about the benefit, and I'd really rather she didn't know about me hitting Liv's car.

"Jake," my mother says coolly.

"Mrs. DeLuca," he replies. "You're looking lovely as always."

Leave it to Jake to try to sweet-talk my mother of all people.

"Enjoy your afternoon," Mom replies, not responding to his compliment.

Jake's eyes find mine. "Maybe you'll join us next time?" he says and there seems to be some unspoken question there, besides the obvious one, that is.

But I don't find out what because Spence is already bundled up. He gives me a fast hug, agreeing to call me in a few hours with an update, before flying outside with his dad.

The second the door closes, I feel my mother's eyes on me. "Benefit?" she says, her interest piqued. "The *Buenaventura* Benefit?"

I give her a wary smile. "That's the one."

"I wasn't aware you were in touch with—"

"I'm not," I say, cutting her off before she can say Wilder's name. While in my mother's estimation Jake is a reprehensible scoundrel of the highest regard, Wilder Buenaventura is a god among men. Cue the mental eye roll. "I ran into Liv on my way into town." For a brief second, I consider telling her the double meaning of my sentence, but it would involve admitting exactly how broke I am, so I decide against it.

"Well! Isn't that something," she exclaims. "Do you know what you're going to wear?"

I head for the stairs, coffee in hand. The anxiety I had efficiently buried about going to the benefit rises to the surface. "Nope."

"Maybe we should go shopping," she says, and I sigh. This is what gets her excited—me going to a party she approves of. Not that I'm surprised; she's prided herself on her friendship with the Buenaventuras since forever. They're the ultra-wealthy socialites she has been trying to reclaim her status among since she found herself tossed in with the commoners thirty years ago—the first and only time my mother ever broke the "rules." And while she always loved my father and I never got the sense she regretted her decision to marry him, she didn't hide the fact that she resented her parents for stripping her of her inheritance. She hasn't talked to them since and likely never will.

I stop at the bottom of the stairs, turning to face her. "I'm sure I have something in my suitcase."

"It's black tie, Madeline," she says more insistently, as though I just rode in on my horse and spit tobacco onto her clean floor.

"I know, Mom." I refrain from telling her that I knew better than to show up here without formal clothes.

"And the Buenaventuras are my closest friends." But what she really means is that their name is practically carved into the bedrock of this Massachusetts harbor town—and that she doesn't want me to embarrass her.

*Too effing late on that one.*

"I'm going upstairs to do some work on my computer," I say, cutting the conversation short.

She gives me a perfunctory nod and walks away. I stare after her for a long second, wishing one or both of us were better at this. I can't help but wonder if things might have been easier if my mother had another child like she wanted. If my parents might have stopped trying to mold me into the perfect daughter, or if simply having someone else to talk to would have changed things when I inevitably let them down.

*ee ee*

Liv trills her horn in my driveway and I grab my black peacoat from the closet, briefly assessing myself in the hall mirror and hoping my favorite red dress gives me the confidence I need to make it through this evening. "I'll be back soon, Mom!" I holler.

Two seconds later my mother appears in the living room doorway (Eleanor does not yell from adjoining rooms like an uncouth bar patron, or so she's told me many times). She gives my dress a once over. It's floor length and has a slit up one thigh, but is otherwise pretty plain. What it lacks in frills, it makes up for in fit, hugging my body in all the right ways.

She raises an eyebrow, refraining from comment, which if I've learned anything from my seventeen years in this house, is approval sprinkled with a dash of disapproval just to stay on brand. "Have fun," she says. "And tell the Buenaventuras I send my regards." As she finishes her sentence, I realize that she's not coming. I mean, I knew she wasn't coming, but it hadn't occurred to me until just now that it was unusual. I was so caught up in my own worries that I'd forgotten my mother's status as the unofficial social chairwoman of Haverberry. And the only conclusion I can draw is that she isn't going because my dad isn't going, because they always did these things together.

"Mom . . ." I say, now feeling guilty about turning down her shopping offer.

"Be sure to thank Liv for the invitation," she says, steamrolling the sentiment that is probably showing on my face. "The benefit has been sold out for weeks, you know."

I sigh, aware that the divide between us is just too large. "I will." I throw on my coat, giving her a quick smile before I slip out the door.

The air outside is frigid and I pull my wool collar tight around my neck.

Liv leans over the console and pushes open the car door for me. "Get in, beauty! We're late," she says as I slide into the heated passenger seat.

Her dark hair is pinned into an elegant French twist with an antique studded hair comb as an accent. And her dress, which is angled and high fashion, is midnight velvet blue. She's breathtaking.

I glance at her car clock that reads 6:15 p.m., exactly what she told me in her text. "I thought you said—"

She cuts me off with a mischievous grin as she reverses out of my driveway so fast that I fear whiplash. "I did. We're intentionally late. I figured we'd show up just before dinner, eat, and then hit the bar while everyone drones on? But apparently there's been some mishap with the sound system and Mama Buenaventura is all revved up." Liv says their last name with a touch of an accent, a nod to the Spanish and Italian her family speaks fluently.

"Oh," I say, worry working its way onto my forehead. I haven't seen her family in nearly ten years and unlike mine, they aren't ones to hide their disapproval in puritanical silence. The thought of seeing them now with Mrs. Buenaventura in a bad mood, makes me wonder if I should jump out of this moving vehicle with a tuck and roll.

Liv grins at me as she races down the street at an ungodly speed. She drives like the bad boy of parental legend. And the nostalgia of her, the way she moves and speaks, hits me so hard that I momentarily feel fifteen again. I remember her first car—a sleek red BMW whose gas pedal she also abused. Liv wasn't the handholding older sister who was determined to ease Wilder and me through our awkward phase by taking us under her wing, she was more of the *you learn from your mistakes* type. But more often than not, she offered us a ride to school. And those days—parking in the front of the lot with the older kids, walking into school with Liv and her popular friends—I felt invincible.

"So," she says without pause. "Are you dating anyone?"

"Uh," I say, gripping the car door as she takes a sharp turn. "Not recently. I don't tend to date in front of Spence. Plus, I haven't had much time these days."

"What's it like?" she asks. "Having a nine-year-old at twenty-six . . . seven?"

I've been asked this question many times, and it's usually less about the question and more about the subtext. But her approach is direct and there's no judgment lingering in her tone.

"Twenty-seven," I say, and decide to answer her honestly. "I'm not going to say it's easy. I mean I worry more about him than I ever thought possible, and I often wonder if I'm getting it right. But Spence's also the single brightest thing in my life. He's my best friend and I swear I learn more from him than the other way around. The other day I told him the word he used was made up and he just shrugged and said: 'Yeah, but all words are made up.'"

She smiles. "Kids are funnier than adults."

"They really are," I agree. I'm about to ask her about her life, but she's too quick.

"How'd you do it, Mads?" she says, not looking at the road as much as I think she should. "How'd you move to LA pregnant and make it work at seventeen?" While her tone is as direct as before, I swear I catch a little bit of something else, almost like awe.

I sigh. "I think I'm in for this question a lot tonight."

A small laugh escapes her matte red lips. "Damn. You're right. The gossip hounds will be out in full force. Consider my question officially stricken from the record."

"Nah," I say. "It's fine. You're Liv—you get a pass."

"I really am her. And yes, I deserve all the passes. Please and thank you."

I take a moment to consider it. "Honestly? I don't know how I did it. I was deeply stubborn and pretty pissed off that everyone was either telling me what to do or telling me what I'd done wrong. I had my college fund, the one my parents saved for me since I was born—"

"Vassar?" she says, and hearing it out loud makes my chest tighten.

Choosing to use that money to set up a new life instead of going to school was the single hardest decision I've ever made. Not moving to LA pregnant, not going to culinary school on the nights and weekends while simultaneously working behind the counter in a bagel shop. Letting go of Vassar *hurt*. I even deferred for a year, convinced that once I got on my feet that I'd find a way to make it work. But by the end of that year, I couldn't manage the expense, my work, and an infant all at once. My parents did show up briefly when Spence was eight months old. But their trip took the form of an ultimatum—either I moved home or my life would inevitably descend into ruins. To which I told them I had proudly taken up the DeLuca torch of resentment and preferred to suffer in silence the way only a true New Englander could. They didn't think it was funny.

I sigh again, big and heavy.

"Okay, that's it. We're changing the subject," she says. "I know this sounds unbelievably stupid, but I hadn't thought my question through properly or the serious territory it might lead to. I half expected you to say, 'I'm a goddamn mommy superhero, so suck it.' And while I'm all for serious conversations, they should be had over expensive whiskey and not when we're beholden to the extra depressing obligation of sitting through a long dinner with my family."

I smile at her, happy for the out. "Okay, then, what about you?" I say, following her lead. "Are you dating anyone?"

"There you go. That's the kind of fluff I'm here for," she says with a sparkling smile. "As it so happens, I'm dating a model from New York. But I mostly just see her on weekends and it's not that serious."

I smile. Of course she's dating a model. "It's Saturday. You didn't want to bring her with you?"

She chuckles. "Not if I want to keep seeing her. You know

as well as I do that my parents' idea of small talk consists of alma maters and real estate fluctuations." She rolls her eyes. "Be honest, would you have come if you didn't feel obligated?"

Her straightforwardness catches me by surprise and I half-laugh half-choke. And once again I have the urge to tell her the truth: that I'm nervous about seeing her family after all these years, and slightly ill over the possibility of seeing Wilder. I desperately want to ask her if he'll be there, but before I work up the nerve, her car jerks to a stop in front of The Black-Eyed Susan, a sprawling historic inn on the edge of town.

She's immediately out of the car and headed around the side of the inn instead of up the front porch. I follow as she speeds along the stone path, her long dress in hand, and through a side door. She walks the way she drives, fast and with enviable confidence. We step into a large kitchen and the scent of cherry pie in browned buttered crust wafts my way. Maybe she didn't want to get slowed down by having to say a million hellos at the front door?

Liv stops and turns to me, shrugging her coat off. "Would you mind terribly hanging this up for me? I need to find Mom before she hyperventilates."

For a second, I hesitate. She's leaving me already? No regret or bolstering words about how I'll do great out there on my own (I won't). But there's no way to refuse, and if I'm honest, she's always been like this—full steam ahead. As a teen, she once told me she could never do what Wilder and I did. How we were never apart, how even when we were together, we went out of our way to check in with one another. She vastly preferred when people did their own thing and let her run free.

"Yeah, of course. No problem," I say.

With a quick thanks and a promise of a forthcoming drink, she speeds off through the kitchen and out the far door that leads to the party. For a split second, I consider spending the rest of the night right here, offering up my baking skills in exchange for refuge. It's with great reluctance that I weave my way around racks of hors d'oeuvres and push through the same door Liv did, trading the delicious scents of the kitchen for a warm elegant dining room full of small-town sharks.

A stage is set up to my right and a crackling fireplace lights the far wall, whose mantel is draped with pine garlands interspersed with festive candles. The guests mill about with their glasses of wine, many of whom I recognize from school, from my mom's clubs, or as business owners in town. Whatever courage I gleaned from Liv's vivaciousness, fizzles out. It's not that I'm a wuss; I'm categorically not. In LA I'm outspoken and outgoing, equally happy to jump on a field trip bus and wrangle elementary school kids as I am designing a catering menu for a posh event. But right now, I feel like I'm back on that baking show, fingers crossed and heart pounding, hoping everything will work out for once.

*"It's been an exhilarating couple of months,"* the Ultimate Bake Off *host says in his perky camera-ready voice. "Twelve contestants, jumping through impossible baking hoops, with lots of sugar and more than a few tears."*

*I glance into the wings of the stage as a crew member repositions a light. Spence gives me a thumbs-up, but despite his enthusiasm, he looks just as nervous as I feel. I pull a face in response, grabbing my mouth and pretending to gag to erase the concerned wrinkle between his eyebrows. Spence rolls his eyes like I'm super embarrassing but laughs all the same. The director calls for action and I straighten my posture and readjust my eyes forward.*

*"Here we are with our three amazing finalists . . ." the host continues, "who have made everything from patisserie to four-tiered cakes. And, now, the moment you've all been waiting for."*

*He pauses dramatically, my stomach growling as I swallow down stomach acid. "The winner . . ." The table of judges stares at the three of us with frozen smiles, the cameras panning across their faces and ours. "Of* Ultimate Bake Off *is . . ."*

*My chest squeezes. I cross my fingers behind my back.* Please, please, please.

*"Cindy!" the host exclaims, and my heart constricts as the woman to my right lights up. My stomach flips aggressively, and the room blurs, people moving around me and possibly talking to me, not that I hear them.*

*I don't know if Cindy yells in victory or cries from overwhelm. Or even if the director calls cut. All I know is that in short order I'm seated on a pink plush armchair in the "commenting room" for a one-on-one.*

*"Tell us, Maddi," the host says, "how do you feel now that it's all over?"*

*I swallow. "I don't know," I reply, my voice unfamiliar and quiet.*

*"Are you disappointed with how things ended?" he asks and despite his understanding tone, I bristle.*

*My discomfort must be obvious because he tries again, "You told us on week three that if you had won you wanted to use the money to start your own dessert truck in LA?"*

*My eyes find his, not really in the best control of myself, worry seeping through my frayed edges over the mistakes I made on my final piece, upset by the hope I allowed this show to represent, and just plain frustrated that I'm finding it impossible to plaster a smile on my face and say something like, "Yes, but I'll get there one way or another. This show has been a ride and I learned a lot. Onward and upward."*

*Instead, I stare at the host, my chest tight, searching for words. The host sighs, dropping some of his stage voice. "You were a great contestant, Maddi. Take it from someone who's been part of seven seasons. And you're driven. That's obvious to anyone who saw you bake."*

*But instead of comforting me, the praise stings. I find myself shaking my head. "It's not that."*

*"Then what is it?"*

*I know I shouldn't answer, that he doesn't need anything more than a sound bite, but some part of me feels reckless—emotions jumbled and stretched after a long day of filming. And my mouth opens, the truth sneaking out past my defenses, "I was recently let go from my job," I admit. "And, this money? It meant rent. So there's that." I take a breath. "It was also a way for me and my son to get a leg up; it meant independence, not shifting from restaurant to restaurant as the LA market and tourist season forever changes. And it proved that . . ." I trail off, my throat taut with the words I never say aloud. "My father was an award-winning baker . . . back home, on the East Coast, I mean. He had a bakery my entire life." My voice has gone quiet again. "And well, he recently died."*

*"I'm sorry to hear that," the host says, but I don't register his words. I'm too ensnared in my emotions.*

*And then I feel my chin wobble. I try desperately to stop it, to rein in the messy sadness I've spent a lot of time burying, but as if to spite me, a tingle works its way up my throat and into the bridge of my nose, dampening my eyes and making it hard to breathe. Maybe it's the exhaustion, or that this is just one in a long line of disappointments, but my chest tightens, my ribs pressing in on me like an unforgiving weight.*

*A tear falls. I bat at it with my fingers, disbelieving. But another follows. "I'm not a crier. I never cry." My words are not only wholly unconvincing but interrupted by a tight inhale that rattles them. "I swear," I continue, tears now falling more readily down my cheeks, my control all but gone. Then I hear myself say the words*

I swore I wouldn't: "I just really wanted to make my dad proud. And once again, I've failed."

That's the moment I lose it. Big heavy sobs and makeup streak down my face. And a snot bubble. A goddamn snot bubble that, as it so happens, the network did not edit out later.

A few heads turn my way followed by looks of surprise and gasped comments. I'm not sure if it's my mortifying breakdown on *Bake Off* that's got them going or if it's my messy teen years a decade earlier. And while I know I shouldn't feel shame, that if it were my friend going through this, I would be adamant that there was nothing to shrink from, I suddenly feel like I lost a few inches just the same. I avert my eyes and make my way along the wall of the dining area to the front room, where a tasteful Christmas tree decked in blue ribbons and white lights stands next to a wrought iron menorah on an elegant stand. Guests peruse silent auction tables and I circle the crowd, heading straight for the coat check.

I slip off my peacoat and hand it along with Liv's to the man behind the table. "Two tickets, please," I say and he obliges.

*Wine*, I think. *I need lots of wine.* But as I tuck the tickets into my clutch, a familiar voice trills behind me.

"Maddi DeLuca? You're *here*?"

I glance at the front door, an easy five steps away. But my coat has already disappeared into the coatroom, and I have no desire to end up like a frozen Jack Nicholson in *The Shining*.

I turn around, my body resisting the motion. "Kate," I say with a tight smile. Kate Van Doran was a year ahead of me in school and a force to be reckoned with—a dancer's body, perfect hair, and an ability to make you feel uncool just by looking at you.

"I'm just so shocked," she says, one hand touching her chest. "That I'm in the town I grew up in, or that I was invited to this benefit?" I ask and immediately regret my defensiveness, guilt springing up before I finish my sentence.

She sizes me up, her lips pulling up at the corners. "I just had no idea you still knew the Buenaventuras," she says. "You and Wilder were friends as kids; am I right?" I know full well she remembers. Everyone who knew Wilder and me (and many who didn't) knew that we were inseparable. And when we started dating at fifteen, no one was surprised; the town gossip mill was practically planning our wedding.

But with happy thoughts of Wilder, also comes the bitter—a flash of the last fight we ever had—Wilder and I standing in Tony's Pizza, both of us fired up and irascibly stubborn, the bond we once shared ground down until it was no longer recognizable.

I weigh my options, wanting to respond, but aware it'll only extend this unpleasantness. "I was just about to go grab a drink, do you need—" I glance at her full glass of red.

"All good here," she says, tapping a French manicured nail on the glass, and I move around her with a strained smile. I can feel her eyes on my back as I leave.

It's fine, I tell myself as I beeline it to the drinks table, I'll just avoid Kate and pretend the silent auction is super interesting until Liv comes back.

"A glass of white, please," I say to the bartender, who obligingly pours.

A bell rings and I glance over my shoulder. "If you'll all kindly make your way to your tables, we'll begin dinner service," a butler says in baritone.

I sigh in relief. Liv wasn't kidding about our well-timed arrival. I accept the wine from the bartender with thanks and take a couple of sips while the guests head for the dining room.

When the front room is three-quarters empty, I follow suit, lingering in the doorway and scanning the crowd for Liv and her velvet blue dress. While I don't see her, I do see Mr. and Mrs. Buenaventura claiming seats at a rectangular table that tees off with the center stage. All the other tables are round, marking this one as special, like the bride and groom's table at a wedding.

The idea of being on display like that with the Buenaventuras makes me itchy. But then another thought strikes me, specifically what might happen if Liv doesn't show up for another ten minutes or so? Am I supposed to walk to that table by myself and slide in with a nonchalant "Hey guys, remember me? I'm the one who screamed in public that the only people more shitty than Wilder were his parents? So lovely to see you all again." No fucking way.

My only consolation is that Wilder is nowhere to be seen. Still, I find myself backstepping just as a hand touches my shoulder.

"There you are," Liv says, and I'm so jumpy that I slosh a bit of wine on the floor.

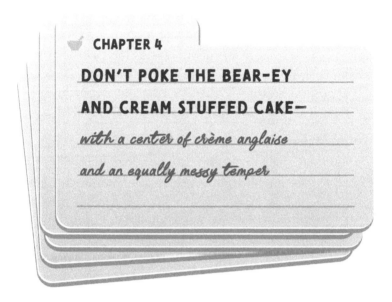

## CHAPTER 4

### DON'T POKE THE BEAR-EY

### AND CREAM STUFFED CAKE—

*with a center of crème anglaise*

*and an equally messy temper*

"Let's get this over with, shall we?" Liv says, gently pulling my elbow forward, otherwise, I probably wouldn't move.

While it makes me feel ever so slightly better to have solidarity in wanting to escape the benefit, it doesn't make walking into the dining room any more appealing. But like in all things, Liv takes charge, flashing me a decisive smile.

I train my eyes forward, once again avoiding eye contact. I hear my name whispered as I follow Liv, but I don't investigate. Eat dinner. Have a drink. Make an excuse and leave before the socializing starts. That's the plan, folks.

When we reach the table there's already a middle-aged couple sitting with Liv's parents, an elderly woman who must be the woman's mother, and a teenaged boy who looks like he might die of boredom.

Liv and I take two empty seats next to each other, and her parents are so engrossed in their conversation that Mrs.

Buenaventura barely registers our presence from the other end of the table. I exhale audibly and take a sip of my wine as the butler from the front room announces that food will be served. A string quartet plays classical music next to the fireplace and the guests drink and chat happily at their tables. So far so good. But my relief is short-lived because there, entering the dining room, is Wilder.

Wavy dark hair swoops across one side of his forehead as though it were intentionally tousled, lazily framing his large brown eyes and aristocratic features. His clothes are impeccable—a perfectly tailored black suit and shiny black shoes. His mouth is curved in his signature smirk, an expression that makes him look like he's privately enjoying a joke. He's devastatingly good-looking, more so than I remember, his shoulders have filled out nicely and his facial structure is more defined since the last time I saw him at seventeen.

For a split second, my heart stumbles over itself. I'm taken aback by how familiar he is. How the kid part of me that fell in love with him feels bolstered, like he's not just a person, but *my* person, my other half.

*"Smile, you crazy love birds," Liv says, lifting her camera.*

*We turn, grinning at her as she snaps a picture, our skin tanned from endless hours outside and our hair salty from the wave that crashed over us one minute prior.*

*Liv takes a long look at us, shaking her head. "I have to say, this whole dating deal suits you two. You're kinda perfect in a stupid way."*

*Wilder fakes shock. "Liv? You feeling okay? That sounded like admitting that romance is a good thing."*

*She rolls her eyes. "Romance is for idiots. But, I'll admit, you two make it seem not so awful." Her friends call her name, and she saunters off with a grin before we can reply.*

*Wilder's attention shifts back to me. His dark wavy hair drips onto his warm bronze skin and he rubs his hands over his face, shaking out the errant drops. He's a perfect mixture of his British mother and his Argentinian father, with strikingly elegant bone structure, an infectious laugh, and magnetic eyes.*

*I smile. "Are you sure you two are related? Liv's like a rockstar with a studded leather jacket and a lady-killer smile. And you?" I say, reaching out to touch the bare skin on his chest.*

*"Go on," Wilder says, winding his hands around my lower back and pulling me into him. "And me, what?"*

*"You're like Jane Austen–level period romance. Complete opposites," I say, as he pushes back my wet hair and plants a kiss on my forehead, basically proving my point.*

*"So, what you're saying is that I'm marriage material?" he replies with a smirk, his fingers working their way down my neck, his lips following.*

*I laugh as shivers radiate from where his warm mouth grazes my skin. "The good news for you is I've always found old-timey picnicking men in straw hats impossibly sexy."*

*He pulls back, smiling at me, his fingers tracing my collarbone like it were a fascinating discovery. "That is good news because I've always found Italian girls with magical baking abilities impossibly irresistible."*

*His words move through me like the sun heating me from the inside out. "Is that so?" I muse, our faces now inches apart.*

*"It really, really is," he says, his breath on my lips, scented with the Capri Sun we shared not ten minutes earlier. As he presses his mouth to mine, my stomach dips and my heart surges and I wonder how I'll ever get enough of his touch.*

I forcefully shake the memory away, scowling at myself for having thought it in the first place, blaming my lapse in judgment on my unease. And like a calculated assault on my nerves,

Kate steps through the door behind Wilder, taking her place by his side. She leans in to tell him something privately and when she places her hand on his arm, he smiles down at her.

They walk toward us, chatting, but as they near the table, Wilder looks up, seeing me for the first time, the simple act of eye contact enough to make my pulse pound in my ears.

He stops dead in his tracks a couple of feet from the table. "Maddi?" he says, shocked.

"Hey, baby brother," Liv says, thankfully saving me from having to reply.

Wilder frowns at the diminutive greeting but doesn't take his eyes off me. Which of course makes Kate frown in turn. And there's something about his look, something weighted and meaningful that makes it all the more uncomfortable.

I swallow, and even though it feels impossible, like I'm attempting to tear space-time itself, I look away. I do not care about Wilder Buenaventura, I repeat like a mantra—in fact, I actively dislike him.

They take their seats, Wilder across from me and Kate across from Liv. Kate keeps her gaze trained on Wilder, and by the way her eyes tighten at the corners and her jaw tenses ever so slightly, I can tell she's more than aware of the way Wilder's looking at me. There is nothing I would like more right now than to slide directly off my chair and under this table, followed by an army crawl out of the inn, Haverberry, and the state of Massachusetts.

My heart beats roughly in my chest and I take a big gulp of wine. I glance up at the podium, but there's nothing to see. I've been a pastry chef in a friggin' Michelin-starred restaurant, I remind myself. I supported myself as a new mom at *seventeen*, for God's sake. I can handle one simple dinner with Wilder. *Buck the fuck up, Maddi, you're better than this.*

Wilder looks from me to Liv, his frown turning into an accusation.

But Liv only smiles and places her hand on my shoulder. "Look who I bumped into on her way into town. Or maybe she bumped into me?" Liv laughs lightly and glances in my direction. "Maddi's home for the holidays for the first time in ten years; can you believe it? And I thought we should give her the old Buenaventura welcome—you know, stodgy banquet with droning speeches and mediocre wine."

Wilder stares at his sister and I find myself reading his expression the way I used to—the dent between his eyebrows representing his frustration, and his jaw tensed the way it always is when he's holding himself back from saying something. But the more I register his emotions, the more I simmer in embarrassment. He has no right to be mad that I'm here; I have dibs on all the pissed-off-ness from here to eternity.

I raise my almost empty glass, now emboldened by my indignity. "You might want to snag yourself some of that mediocre wine, Wilder, it might help you look less horrified." I know it's not a way to start. *I know.* But I refuse to feel small and unwanted again.

Wilder meets my eyes and Liv chuckles.

But it's Kate who speaks. "How nice you decided to come home after all these years," she says, drawing out her words as though our previous conversation near the coat check never happened.

I blink at her.

Kate nods thoughtfully. "Tell us, what have you been up to? And don't leave out *Ultimate Bake Off.* I swear I don't know anyone who didn't watch it. You've been *quite* the gossip here. I do hope you sorted everything out with your job . . . and your rent?"

And perfect. Now I'm on Kate's kill list, the girl who has a talent for finding peoples' insecurities the same way those nose strips magically pull out the tiniest of blackheads. My cheeks warm, my unease increasing tenfold.

"Kate's right, you were a total boss on that show," Liv says, shifting Kate's intended slight to a compliment. "I can't believe you didn't win. Highway robbery."

Wilder and Liv look at each other, and I swear there is something more to their gaze. Wilder leans back in his chair, shaking his head ever so slightly at his sister.

Which is when Mrs. Buenaventura pulls away from her conversation to look up at us. I can tell, she too, is shocked to see me, although she hides it much better than Wilder did. "You all know the Floreses," she says in her British accent, faded through many years of living in the states. "Except maybe Madeline." She says my name in an underwhelming tone that tells me everything I need to know. And while I don't expect her to jump for joy that I'm here, the disapproval sucks. She's known me since I was born.

She moves through introductions smoothly, while Mr. Buenaventura sips his drink and says hello in his slight Argentinian accent. And for a brief moment, I think this might be the answer to all the tension—a long conversation with them about their recent trip abroad or the new apartment building they bought. The Buenaventuras have a chatty and engaging quality to them, placing their hand on your arm as they talk, making it easy to just listen and blend into the background. But unfortunately, we only say polite hellos and they continue their previous conversation without us, leaving Liv, Wilder, Kate, and me to fend for ourselves.

I adjust my gaze back across the table and find Wilder staring at me.

When his eyeline doesn't shift, I reach for my wine, only to discover it's empty. And in my peripheral vision, I see Mrs. Buenaventura steal another look at me, one that is followed by a frown.

Liv grabs a carafe from her parents' portion of the table. She refills my glass and pours one for Wilder. "I think Maddi was right about that drink."

Wilder's eyes flash from me to Liv. "My problem isn't lack of alcohol," he says and even though his tone is perfectly pleasant, my stomach drops.

Liv sighs. "Think, baby brother. Do you really want to do this? Have a not-so-veiled conversation that's going to make this night a million times more uncomfortable than it needs to be?"

"If you didn't want the night to be uncomfortable, Liv," he says smoothly, but his tensed jaw gives him away, "then you shouldn't have orchestrated it that way."

Liv frowns, but before she can respond, my defenses flare. The only thing worse than realizing Wilder is disappointed to see me (while it occurs to me this is a double standard, I do not have the bandwidth to analyze it right now) is that he's vocalizing it. "You know I can hear you, right? That I'm sitting right here?"

Kate spears her salad in uniform bites, a small smile of satisfaction on her lips.

But Liv remains focused on her brother. "First of all, I invited Maddi because I wanted to spend time with her." An opinion it's clear Wilder doesn't share, not that I want to spend time with him, but still. There's something primitively satisfying about your ex seeing you and feeling remorse for his crappy actions like you won some small life prize. Today is not that day.

Blood rushes to my cheeks in a prickly flush and I have a deep desire to shut the whole conversation down. "It's like Liv said, she ran into me in town," I interject, attempting to imbue my voice with nonchalance. "Everything isn't about you, Wilder."

"No, it's not. But you can ask Liv yourself," he says so confidently that I now regret chiming in. "Ask my sister why she brought you here without warning me or our parents?"

And that's it. That's the very last straw. My already fanned embarrassment explodes like a firework finale, my heart trying to make a speedy getaway in my chest. I sit there for what feels like ten years but is probably only four seconds, trapped in the amber of unease. And for just a hair of a moment, I think I see regret on Wilder's face. Only I don't care. It's as though every fear I had tonight is being actualized in this moment, heightened by the fact that it's with Liv and Wilder, people I once considered family. I don't even realize I'm speaking until I feel my voice like the base of a too-loud stereo, vibrating in my chest.

"*Warning?*" I breathe the word back at him, now full-on warrior-porcupine. "I was unaware that my mere presence came with a warning. But you want one? Fine, you're getting one. *Warning*, Wilder, I'm back in town for two weeks. *Warning*, you should stay out of my way. *Warning*, if you do try to talk to me again, I'll only tell you that you're a self-righteous jerk who can take his attitude and shove it *right up his pampered asshole.*"

As I finish my sentence, I realize my mistake—the room must have fallen silent just as my voice raised in volume. A woman stands at the podium and clears her throat into the mic. "Good evening," she says to the audience, looking away from me in a deliberate way that tells me she heard everything I said.

I glance at the crowd, only to find I'm right—people lean into each other whispering and shooting glances our way. And in a desperate attempt to flee, I push my chair back. But instead of sliding smoothly, it collides hard with something and I stop short, catching sight of the food stand the waiter behind me must have just set up. I don't upend it, thank God, but the change in motion has me falter and I grab the table to steady myself, managing to knock over my now full glass of wine.

Humiliation rages inside me as I search for my napkin, which appears to have vanished. My chest tightens and I know if I don't get out of here that I'm in serious danger of crying, the type that comes from feeling trapped in misunderstanding. And to make matters a million times worse, Wilder gets up, fast as lightning, and starts helping me clean up the mess.

*As though the universe were aware that I was having a terrible day and decided to pile on, the paper plate I was using as a palette crashes to the art room floor, sending splatters of color across the tile, in what is arguably a much prettier piece of art than the portrait on my canvas. But the mess isn't contained to the floor, it's also on the legs of the art easel, my new sneakers, my bare calves, and my backpack that sits propped against my stool.*

*My eyes flit to Wilder, who's perched next to me in this godforsaken elective that I mistakenly thought would be so romantic. The instant our eyes meet, I know he knows, that this isn't one of those moments I can laugh off, not after my Murphy's Law morning, and in about one point five seconds, tears are about to happen. The thought only winds me tighter. I hate crying in public. Maybe it's stodgy New England's influence or maybe I just wasn't blessed with that emotionally-in-touch-and-accepting gene, but either way, it feels like humiliation.*

*Only before I get the chance, Wilder is off his stool, bending down to pick up the plate and getting it on himself in the process.*

*"Don't," I say, my churning emotions seeping into my voice. "You'll get paint all over yourself. I'll only feel worse if I drag you into my shit day."*

*For a split second his eyebrows push together like he's considering it. Then slowly a grin spreads across his face. "Maddi," he*

*says, now placing his hand directly into the globs of paint on the
tile. "Whatever day you're having, I'd like to have it, too." Then
he wipes his hand right across his pristine white T-shirt.*

*I'm so taken aback that I have trouble forming a response.
"Wilder," I say slowly, disbelievingly. The only thing about him that
is ever out of place is his hair, but in a way that makes him look re-
latable and sexy, not messy like the rest of us. "What are you doing?"*

*But he only shrugs. "I'm painting," he says and pulls his finger
across his forehead, giving himself a rainbow unibrow.*

*And somehow the ridiculousness of Wilder Buenaventura
painting his own face does it, a true kindness, which lifts the weight
that was grinding me into the ground. I laugh. Bright and loud, my
upset evaporated like a puddle in direct sunlight. I dip my hands in
the paint, too. And I lean in to kiss him, right there in the middle
of class, me getting paint on his cheek, him getting it on my neck as
he pulls me into him, smiling against my mouth. Of course, Mrs.
Mehta gives us both detention and mumbles something about this
being fine art class, not Burning Man. But it doesn't matter, because at that moment I have everything I need.*

I stare at Wilder, who's patting the table dry, horrified that he's
the one helping me after I just cursed him out publicly. I search
around me, locating my napkin on the floor next to my chair.

"I don't need your help," I breathe, wishing he would sit
down.

"It's fine, guys," Liv assures us as I furiously pat the tablecloth. "Don't worry about it."

But it's not fine, it feels like a marker for all that has gone
wrong, both this night and in the past. When the pool of wine
on the table is sopped up, I mumble something that resembles
an apology and I flee, a handful of guests following me with
their eyes as I go. I don't dare look at Mrs. Buenaventura, not
wanting to know what she must think.

My hand shakes as I dig through my purse for my coat check ticket, speeding through the front room as fast as my heels allow.

"Maddi, wait," Liv says, jogging to catch up with me just as I hand my ticket to the man.

I can barely make eye contact with her. I've eclipsed humiliated and moved into uncharted territory, where my mouth is no longer working in partnership with my brain. "Just tell me, Liv," I say, hoping her brother was wrong. "Was Wilder right? Did you invite me here to get at him in some way?"

She closes her eyes for a brief second. "It's not that simple," she admits.

I wait.

She sighs. "Look, I want to explain, I really do, but—"

"Right," I say, cutting her off, willing my chin to remain steady, not wanting to believe that the person I looked up to for so long would use me in a sibling rivalry tit for tat. I lower my eyes to my purse, pulling out her coat check ticket and handing it to her.

"Listen—" she says, taking it reluctantly.

"Don't," I reply, unable to mask the hurt in my voice.

"Shit, Maddi," she says, "I didn't realize it would play out like this . . . I'm sorry. Can I at least give you a ride—"

I shake my head.

She opens her mouth, but I don't wait to hear her objection. I take my coat and walk out the door into the cold. She doesn't follow and I don't look back. On top of everything else, I realize I just lost my ride home and I don't have money for a taxi. And it's not like I can call my mom; she'll hear about this soon enough as it is. In fact, there's only one person I can call. I curse under my breath, feeling seventeen all over again.

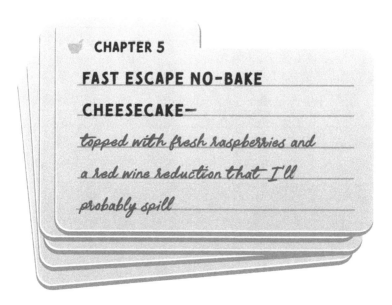

## CHAPTER 5

## FAST ESCAPE NO-BAKE
## CHEESECAKE—

*topped with fresh raspberries and a red wine reduction that I'll probably spill*

The icy wind billows the slitted skirt of my red dress and pulls strands of my hair across my face. I yank my coat tighter, ducking my chin into the collar, anxious to get away from this benefit. So when Jake's headlights finally move across the steps of the inn, I fly down them, grabbing the door to his pickup truck as it rolls to a stop.

Jake gives me a knowing look. "Making a fast escape?" he says cheerfully as I jump into the passenger seat, closing the door behind me.

"Something like that, yeah," I admit, yanking my seatbelt harder than necessary. But the air is warm and toasty in the cab, relaxing my muscles. I reach my hands toward the vent and a little of the tension thaws out of me.

"Better or worse than that time you brandished a keg hose as a weapon?" Jake says with a chuckle, referring to the period where I did a bit of spiraling while Jake and I dated. As he finishes speaking, Wilder exits the inn, alone and seemingly pissed off. He makes eye contact with me through the truck window and stops so fast you'd think he walked into a screen door. I guess he didn't expect me to still be here, which I suppose I wouldn't be if I could have justified spending money on a cab.

For a flash of a second, I think he's going to come right up to Jake's truck, and so I avert my gaze, putting a kibosh on whatever Wilder's thinking. Jake takes note of my reaction and then of Wilder staring at us. And just like that, his grin fades. He hits the gas.

"So, Wilder . . ." Jake starts as we pull onto the sleepy street, and I hear the disdain in his tone. I know their friendship fell apart around the time we started dating, but I didn't realize they still had friction all these years later.

"Is it okay if we don't talk about it?" I ask a little embarrassed, shifting in my seat. "I'm hoping to forget this cringeworthy episode of Maddi interacting with the locals ever happened."

"No problem," he says, unclenching his hands on the steering wheel. "I'm just happy you called."

"Are you?" I say like I can't quite believe it, turning to look at him. His grin has returned and he leans his elbow on the console between us.

He laughs. "Yeah, yes I am. It's been too long since I've seen you, Maddi." And now he's turned on his charming voice, the one that once made teen girls faint up and down the coast.

I raise an eyebrow. "You know you're always welcome to visit California. Spence would be excited to see you," I say, reestablishing the boundary between us.

"I'd like that," he replies. "Maybe I can come in the spring."

I nod, even though I doubt that will ever happen.

Jake turns down the road, heading for my house, and as we get closer, I sense the inevitability of my mother grilling me about my early exit, demanding to know what I did and how embarrassed she should be by my behavior. As if she knows I'm thinking about her, my phone rings and lights up with her name. I shove it back into my purse.

"Uh, Jake?" I say, not sure I want to prolong our time together, but also certain it's the lesser of two evils. "Are you hungry?"

His eyebrows shoot up. "Are you asking me out on a date?"

"Yeah, not so much," I say with a chuckle. "I am, however, trying to avoid my mother. And well, I didn't actually get to eat before I ran out of that benefit."

"I'm starving," he says, his enthusiasm infectious, something our son definitely inherited from him. "How does *Bella Luna* sound?"

My stomach growls at the suggestion of handmade ravioli, but my wallet protests louder. "I was kinda thinking we could drive over to Middleton and grab burritos?" It's cheap, it's delicious, and between the drive and the eating, I'll hopefully get home after Mom goes to sleep.

"Absolutely," Jake agrees without hesitation.

I exhale in relief and pull out my phone to text Spence.

Me: You okay, little dude?

It only takes a second for him to reply.

Spence: Reading

Me: Be home in an hour or so.
Text if you need me.

Spence: Obvi

I smile at the text, at my funny kid, and at the relief I feel
that I won't have to face my mother tonight.

"Thanks, Jake," I say with all sincerity.

His eyes twinkle. "Anytime, Maddi. Any. Time."

In a way, this is what Jake has always been good at—mel-
lowing the serious. Which is needed when you're seventeen and
hurt or likewise when you're twenty-seven and toppling wine
at fancy dinner parties, but not so great when you're dealing
with the everyday practicalities of raising another human. That's
fine, though, because I don't need him to do the heavy lifting
tonight. I simply want an hour and a half of burritos and nonsense, and that's Jake's specialty.

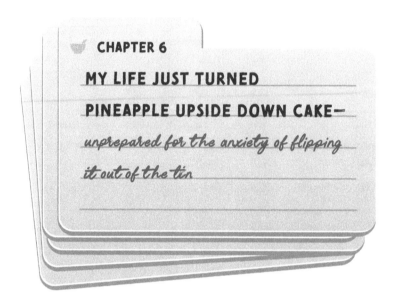

## CHAPTER 6

## MY LIFE JUST TURNED

## PINEAPPLE UPSIDE DOWN CAKE—

*unprepared for the anxiety of flipping*
*it out of the tin*

I squint at my phone, trying to understand why in the heck it's yelling at me. Slowly I register my childhood bedroom and my son's knee digging into my back, remembering setting my phone alarm for the 10:00 a.m. "meeting time" my mother insisted on. After a couple of seconds of resistant grumbling, I accept that there's no possibility of going back to sleep, which is also the moment the events from last night spill into my consciousness. I bolt upright, the awkward motion jostling one leg onto the floor. It doesn't help that the bed is full-sized and my nine-year-old is occupying ninety-three percent of it.

The motion does nothing to wake Spence, who continues to sleep soundly, mouth open and splayed out like a starfish. We're both night owls, which I'm eternally grateful for. I've told him several times that if he was one of those kids who got up at 5:00 a.m. with a bounce in his step I'd trade him in for a goldfish.

I squint at my disheveled self in my vanity mirror and decide

I look exactly how I feel. For a split second, I consider changing out of my Grinch onesie before going downstairs, knowing my mother will frown about it, but I don't want to risk waking Spence. Kids have spookily accurate radar for sleep defiance. When you need them to get up, you could blast music and jump on the bed with no result. But when you really want them to stay asleep, all you have to do is breathe too loudly and they spring up spouting fun facts you don't understand about YouTube videos. And right now, I'd rather he didn't overhear what is bound to be a difficult conversation. So instead, I quickly run a hairbrush through my hair and tiptoe out of the room, easing the door shut behind me.

The smell of fried potatoes drifts past me and quickens my step on the stairs.

"Mmmm." At least there's food.

I follow the yummy scent into the dining room, hoping like hell my mother hasn't heard about the benefit yet. "That smells delicious . . ." I say, stepping through the doorway, figuring my cheery mood will make it easier to break the news to her. But instead of finishing my compliment, my voice trails off and I stop dead in my tracks.

There, sitting at my dining room table like he has any right, is Wilder Buenaventura.

My mother freezes, too, possibly stunned by her dawning horror at my attire.

I whip my eyes to her, instantly remembering her missed call last night, and curse myself for not checking to see if she left a message. Did she invite him here to make me apologize like I'm five years old? Because I won't.

The only person who does not look completely put out is Wilder, who sips his coffee and leans back in his chair, his over-whelmed look from last night noticeably absent. "Maddi," he says by way of hello, a small smile appearing on his lips.

And seeing it stings—a smile I once searched for, one that made me feel grounded and whole before it didn't. Before he changed everything in one fifteen-minute conversation. One day he's enthusiastically planning a romantic outing to a bakery in Salem and the next he just wants to be friends, giving no viable explanation. The problem was we were never just friends; we were something infinitely more entangled and confusing, attached to each other for our entire lives, spending every waking hour together as kids and then sharing more intimate parts of ourselves as teens. Wilder was my first everything, and I was his. And I could have forgiven him for all of that. In fact, I did, many times. But it didn't matter because when I needed him most he wasn't there.

I feel the pang of my old naiveté like a slap in the face.

"What is *he* doing here?" I say, pointing at him like I'm accusing them both of some nefarious conspiracy.

"As you can see, he's eating breakfast," Mom says matter-of-factly. "Now if you'll just go upstairs and get dressed—"

"No," I say stubbornly. Not a chance.

"Well, really Madeline, do you think it's appropriate?" Mom says, her frown deepening and her ever-present ruffled shirt seeming to deflate in an effort to match her dismay.

And then Wilder has the nerve to add, "I don't mind, really," like I give a flying rat's ass if he's bothered by my pajamas!

I glare at him. "It doesn't matter, because I'm sure he was just about to leave." He couldn't have thought coming here was a good idea. Is he trying to get back at me for yelling at him last night?

His eyebrows rise behind his coffee cup. "Am I?"

My mother clutches her chest, like my impropriety is causing her heart palpitations. "No, Wilder, you're not. For heaven's sake, Madeline, he's here for the same reason you are—to discuss your father's will."

Even though I'm standing still, I lose my footing.

*My father's will?* But that's . . . That's not . . . *WHAT*?! My thoughts tumble over one another in a jumbled mess with no plausible explanation within reach.

"Sit," my mother says in a tone that leaves no room for argument, gesturing at the spot across from Wilder.

I'm so taken aback that I comply, my racing pulse unsteady.

She places food in front of me and I stare at it in confusion, looking anywhere but at Wilder. But in my peripheral vision, I can't help but notice he's dressed in a black, long sleeve T-shirt with a chunky gray cardigan over it—one with large wooden buttons that looks like it was designed for the explicit purpose of making people look elegant and casual all at the same time, probably hand-knit by grandmas in Ireland from the virgin wool of cashmere sheep butts. I scowl and pour a cup of coffee from the carafe on the table, deciding that whatever is happening cannot be endured without caffeine.

I want to say that Mom could have warned me that he'd be here, but that would only be admitting to him that I might have acted differently had I known, which I would not have. I would have worn this Grinch onesie proudly either way . . . I think.

My mom takes her seat between us at the head of the table, stirring cream into her tea. "Right," she says, concluding a thought she hasn't shared, "might as well get started."

Wilder nods, but I don't say a word. Having him here is so outrageous that I can't muster a response that doesn't involve profanity.

"I was contacted a few weeks ago by our lawyer, Mr. Horowitz," she begins. "It seems Charles had an addendum to his will that I was unaware of."

The sound of my dad's name makes it suddenly hard to breathe. I look at Mom, expecting to find frustration in her expression. As private as my parents were, they never withheld information from one another. But she doesn't seem put out the way I'd expect.

"When was the addendum written?" I ask quietly, wondering why the lawyer only just revealed it.

"A couple of months before your father passed," she replies, and the last word seems to take a physical toll on her, inflicting a heaviness that now reverberates in my own chest. But Dad passed of a heart attack, so this timing doesn't explain anything.

Mom unfolds the piece of paper next to her plate, taking her glasses from the breast pocket of her blazer. She sighs, opening her mouth to read, but hesitates.

"If it's easier," Wilder says with genuine concern, "I'll happily offer to read it for you."

My eyes flick to his face, my annoyance surging at his continued intrusion into this deeply personal moment. But I don't say anything, my voice lost in my tight throat.

"No, that's quite all right. But thank you," Mom says and concentrates on the paper once more. "I, Charles DeLuca, declare this to be a codicil of my will, to take effect one year after my death." She begins slowly. "All allocations are to remain the same, with the exception of There's Nothing Batter Bakery, which I previously bequeathed to my wife, Eleanor DeLuca, should she survive me."

My heart thunders in my chest and my stomach twists, guilt grabbing ahold of me like a fierce undertow.

*Dad sits on the couch across from me, placing his glass on the table between us. "You've been here for less than forty-eight hours and you're already leaving," he says like an accusation.*

*I shift uncomfortably. "My job——" I start.*

*"Your job at that restaurant," he says like it's a fast-food place.*

*I frown. "Yes, my job at that* Michelin-starred *restaurant."*

"Where you're working for free," he continues.

My chest tightens as he diminishes my accomplishment. "I'm in training, which is how things are when you start."

"Madeline, don't snip at your father," my mother says, stirring her teacup and taking a seat next to my dad. Always in league, these two, so much so that I often feel like I'm on the opposing team.

I open my mouth and close it again, shaking my head instead of voicing the obvious. There's no winning here.

My mother looks from my dad to me. "I think what your father's trying to say is that you have a perfectly good job here in Haverberry Cove, yet you prostrate yourself to these flashy Hollywood types for no reason."

I exhale, trying to rein in my reaction. I worked nights for years so I could put myself through culinary school. I worked my way up from bad to mediocre restaurants, proving my skill in each one, finally landing a job working for one of the best pastry chefs in LA, and they dismiss it like it was nothing. "Besides the fact that I don't want to live here," I say, hurt and frustrated. "Working at the bakery in Haverberry is your dream, Dad, not mine. I prefer to make my own way in LA."

My mother's eyes widen. "That's your father's life's work you're talking about. A little respect."

Why did I come back here? Why did I think it would be any different? "But it's okay to dismiss everything I've done for the past five years?"

"This Los Angeles life isn't you, all these nouveau riche people trying to step on each other to get ahead," Mom says with a wave of her hand like I'm too young to see myself clearly. You'd think she was the queen instead of a housewife to a modest baker. "If things had gone the way they were supposed to you'd have gone to Vassar and you'd be here working with your father."

My eyes flit to Dad, but he stares at the fireplace, his eyebrows *pushed forcefully together. From the time I was little, I talked end-lessly about growing the bakery. Mom wanted me to go to school first, Vassar, she suggested, just like she and her mother had, so I could learn everything there was to know about business and then bring that knowledge home with me. And I loved the idea, clung to it, maybe because I was on a mission to gain her impossible ap-proval or maybe the reason was softer and more fragile than that, my way of claiming both my parents, binding us together like the unit I so desperately wanted us to be. But things are different now—they're broken—and there's no way to put the pieces back together.*

*I press my lips into a hard line. It always comes back to this.* "By things going the way they were supposed to, you mean if I hadn't gotten pregnant?"

*Dad sighs and shakes his head.* "You get so worked up, Made-line. You're so busy being angry with me and your mother that you miss what's right in front of you."

My mother looks up at me for a split second and my eyes search hers. "Ownership of There's Nothing Batter Bakery shall heretofore be transferred to my daughter, Madeline DeLuca."

Guilt thumps along with my pulse, thundering in my tem-ples and making me contract.

Mom pauses. "And to Wilder Buenaventura in equal parts."

My heart stutters and I choke on my coffee, wiping it from my mouth with the back of my hand. My mind does som-ersaults, trying to make sense of her words—her nonsensical impossible words.

*Wilder Buenaventura? WILDER BUENAVENTURA?!*

My mother reads a couple more sentences, but they don't compute. I'm frozen in place, my spine rigidly straight.

"Did you just say . . ." I start, my voice strangled by shock.

"Yes, I did," my mother replies, her expression unreadable.

I look from her to Wilder, who's solely focused on me, not

giving away whether or not he knew anything about this. She begins to read once more, but I cut her off.

"Wait, hold on . . ." I press my palms into my temples. "I don't understand. Dad left me the bakery . . . and he also left it *to Wilder?*"

"He did," my mother reaffirms. How can she be so calm? How can she sit there like a giant emotional bomb didn't just blow us to smithereens?

I shake my head in staunch denial. "This has to be a joke." Except my father wasn't the joking type, especially not about something so important, which only leads me to believe he truly wanted Wilder to have it. And that thought hurts more than any other.

Wilder puts down his coffee cup.

"You may have a look yourself if you'd like," my mother says. She offers me the paper, but I don't take it.

"Wilder doesn't . . ." I start. "He isn't family." It was one thing when my dad left the bakery to my mom. I knew I was a disappointment to him, that we never became the father-daughter baking duo he dreamed of. But this is a stab to the heart, a confirmation that he thought so little of me that he gave half my inheritance to Wilder effing Buenaventura.

Wilder shifts his weight in his chair, his smile gone.

"There's more if you'll let me cont—" my mother starts.

"This is not okay," I blast. "This is just Dad pun—" I stop before I say *punishing me for not being the daughter he wanted*. I shake my head, now looking at Wilder. "You don't need it. Your family practically owns the entire town. You DO NOT NEED my father's bakery."

He sighs like he expected my reaction. "No, I don't *need* it," he says, his voice muted as though he were concentrating hard on a new recipe rather than discussing my future happiness. "But I do want it. Which, I assume, is the point."

I suck in a sharp breath, his words cutting deep. "And I *don't*? Is that what you're saying?"

He breaks eye contact with me, shaking his head, like he knew I'd take it here and he doesn't want to follow.

"Wilder?" I say his name like a warning, wanting to yell that the problem isn't my reaction, it's the big fucking curveball of this inheritance.

Wilder frowns, a small sigh escaping his lips. "Let me ask you, how many times have you visited the bakery in the past year? Or the years before that?" His voice is carefully calm and I hate him for it.

"How dare you," I breathe.

"Madeline," my mother intercedes in a tone that attempts to diffuse the ratcheting tension. "I know this comes as a—"

But I'm laser-focused on Wilder, hurt humming inside me. "You don't know anything about me," I fire back.

"Maybe not," he says, still far too composed. "But I do know that your father wanted it this way, and I have every intention of respecting that."

I see red. "And how's that going to work, Wilder? You're telling me you're actually going to take time from your busy life of screwing French models to grace the bakery with your presence? How long before you get bored and run back to Europe?"

He flinches like I slapped him, and in truth, I feel bad for saying it, but I'm currently in the smashing-everything-phase of wounded and too upset to temper it. My mother's face goes pale. She and my father told me two years ago that he was briefly engaged to a French model. Both Wilder and my mother open their mouths to respond, but a sleepy voice cuts them off.

"Mom?" Spencer says behind me, worry tinting his tone.

I forcibly take a breath and unclench my hands, the mom in me overriding everything else. I stand up, turning away from the table and focusing on my son, who's wearing a matching Grinch onesie.

"Hey, little man," I say in an attempt to normalize my voice. "Want me to get you some breakfast? You hungry?"

He looks from me to his grandmother and then to Wilder, sleepy confusion knitting his eyebrows together. "I could eat," he agrees, his cowlick bouncing with his nod.

"How about this," I continue, purposefully moving away from the table. "You head into the living room and pick out a holiday movie for us to watch, and I'll make you a batch of waffles."

His eyes meet mine. "With ice cream?"

"Is there another way?"

He pulls his arm down in victory. But before he exits the room, he looks at Wilder. "I like your sweater," he says, nodding thoughtfully. "But I get the sense my mom doesn't like you, and like she says, 'clothes don't make the man.'" Then he leaves without another word.

I don't bother explaining his recent honesty obsession or try to make the situation more comfortable for anyone. I just turn on my heel and head for the kitchen. I'm certain my mother is staring daggers at my back, but I also know she's not going to stop me—Eleanor does *not* make scenes. And while I get that I'm leaving before the conversation is over, I'm also physically unable to spend one more minute in a room with Wilder without murdering him.

## CHAPTER 7

## ALL ROADS LEAD TO
## ROMAN APPLE CAKE—
*apples folded into vanilla goodness and topped with a trip down memory lane that feels inevitable*

In typical DeLuca form, my mother pointedly ignores me for the rest of the day, giving me a wide berth and directing all dinner conversation to Spence. It's obvious she's mad by the way the skin around her eyes tightens whenever she accidentally looks in my direction, which is fine by me because I'm upset, too. I finally listened to the message she left me last night, and while it did in fact warn me that Wilder would be joining us for breakfast in the morning, I don't forgive her. She knew what was in that codicil and instead of telling me privately, she dropped it like a bag of flaming shit on my doorstep. And then there's the bit where she somehow didn't find it outrageous that my father freely gave away half of our family's bakery, the bakery he designed and built with his own hands through countless years of hard work, to *Wilder*?!

My parents' love for Wilder isn't in dispute. I'm half surprised there isn't a framed picture of him hanging on their wall. Even when he broke my heart the summer before senior year, they treated him with grace. But this is something else entirely.

I grumble under my breath as I poke the remnants of my pecan pie, willing the last moments of this meal to disappear so that I may hide in my bedroom like all repressed adults are wont to do. Part of me is itching to get my hands on the will, so I might scour it in private and try to understand the how and why of Dad's decision. But there is no "private" when you have a nine-year-old and I'm not ready to discuss it with Spence until I can approach it calmly. I've barely been in control of my stress levels all day and going over it again will only get my blood pressure up. I already lost my temper once and I'm feeling a smidge guilty about that. No, I'll sleep on it and ask my mother for the will in the morning when I'm hopefully less frazzled.

"Would you like more pie, Spencer?" my mother offers.

He leans back in his chair and pats his belly. "That's a big fat yes," he says with enthusiasm, his cheeks lifting at the prospect. "It's sooo good, like next level. It might even be better than yours, Mom. You should totally get this recipe."

My head flies up, my pride stung. But I manage a smile—you can't teach your kid to be generous while being stingy yourself. "Maybe I will."

My mother smiles, too, only hers has a certain knowing that reeks of gloat. "It's from your grandfather's bakery, dear. You should have your mom take you there tomorrow. It's filled with all sorts of amazing treats."

Her words hit me right in my gut. I stare at my mother and her formidable posture, knowing she's booby-trapped me.

"Yeeesss," Spence agrees, perking from his slouched pie-laden position. "Mom?"

I press my lips together, biting back my thoughts on the matter. "Yeah," I say. "We'll visit the bakery tomorrow."

*eeee*

Because it's Monday morning, there are parking spots aplenty in the square and I snag one a couple of doors down from the bakery. I zip my coat, pulling up my hood. Spence is already bouncing out of the car, all vim and vigor as I reluctantly slink onto the sidewalk.

I throw Spence's scarf around his neck.

"*Mom*," he objects, but his face is plastered with a huge grin as he sets off toward the bakery, the one place I've been adamantly trying to forget these past ten years.

*I pull into the square, my thumbs tapping anxiously against the steering wheel. I slide my used-like-new Prius quietly into a parking spot right next to Dad's bakery. I frown at the gentleness of the motion, as though it were an affront to the tumult I currently feel. It's been one month since Wilder and I broke up, two weeks since I decided we could try to be friends, and three days since he started dating some girl named Alice—a rich prep from Boston with a khaki personality. The worst part is, he asked my permission. Told me that our friendship was more important. And worse still, I said he should go for it. Then I spent the rest of the night eviscerating the ice cream supply in our freezer (which is both horrific and a record of some kind) telling myself I didn't care. I've avoided him for the past couple of days. But if I cancel our Sunday bake-off, he'll track me down and try to have an even-tempered conversation about things I do not feel even-tempered about at all.*

*I kick open my car door like it personally offended me and step out into the humid salt-scented air. It's always been one of the things I love about Haverberry, the way you can smell the ocean from anywhere in the town, a hint of brine from seaweed and glistening shells drying in the bright sun. But not today. Today I would burn the whole town down if I had a match.*

*I grumble my way into my dad's bakery, the chimes on the door giving a shocked jingle. Mrs. Varma stands behind the counter, her black hair braided down her back, hints of gray framing her face, her warm brown skin creased deep with laugh lines, and an eye patch over her right eye, which she lost some years back.*

*She lifts her eyebrows as I enter, and smiles when I kiss her on the cheek.*

*I slip through the door leading to the bakery kitchen and find Wilder is already there, pulling ingredients from the shelves and lining up bowls. His hair is messy like a handsome scholar who fell asleep with his books and rushed to class thereafter. While his face is all well-cut angles, his brown eyes are soft and gentle. And as he turns them on me, my stomach fluttering and pulling toward him like he was my center, I hate the way I feel.*

*I yank my blue and white striped apron off the hook by the door.*

*"Battle of the chocolate tarts," he announces, the corners of his mouth turning up. "I hope you brought your A-game, DeLuca, because I have a recipe that is going to make you want to propose—"* *He stops abruptly, realizing his mistake and looking slightly horrified. In a way, his remorse makes it worse, because it indicates that he has no idea how to be normal with me, either, that our default is set improperly to something much more intimate than we now share.*

*"Sorry, I didn't mean . . ."* *He lets his voice trail off, clearly unsure how to finish that sentence without embarrassing us both further. He scratches his eyebrow even though I'm positive it doesn't itch.*

*For my part, I stare at the ingredients like they're fascinating as I remove them from my dad's supply shelves, plunking them down* at my usual spot on the counter. For years now, Dad has reserved a bit of his counter for us, personalized with ceramic jars filled with our favorite spoons and a rack of measuring cups and piping tools. He claims he did it because otherwise we'd run roughshod over his entire kitchen, but I know the truth is a bit more fuzzy and warm than that.

I set to measuring and pouring, all the while not looking at Wilder.

He sighs next to me and I can feel him stealing glances in my direction. "I hope you don't mind, I mean—" Wilder pushes his hair back, like he's just realizing whatever he's about to say is a bad idea, but he's in it now for better or worse. "I sorta told Alice she could stop by when we're ready to judge these things."

My skin prickles and my eyes whip to Wilder. "You invited her here?"

"Yeah," he admits like he already regrets it. He puts down his spoon. "I just thought it would be better if we could all be friends. I did ask you straight out if you minded about me dating her. You told me you didn't. I'm not trying to upset you, Mads," he says in his mature voice that I used to find magnetic.

I lose some of my heat at the unarguable truth of it. "I know."

"But you're angry with me?"

I purse my lips, holding my reaction at bay. I don't tell him that up until a few days ago. I thought this was all a passing trial, something we would go through and come out the other side stronger and more in love. But the truth is he's moved on. Wilder is not in love with me the way I am with him. And now my anger turns inward, forcefully vowing not to care about him that way anymore, desperately trying to snap the invisible tethers that have bound us so tightly all these years. I feel a strange sense of recklessness, an unwanted freedom that's a bit like a speeding car on an icy street. "You know what, Wilder? You're right. Have Alice come."

*He stares at me, not quite sure if I've come to my senses or if I'm disarming him so that I can take a swing. "You sure?"*

*"Yeah, I am," I say, and in that moment, I mean it. I pull out my phone and type a text to Jake.*

Before we enter the bakery, we stop at the window to admire the cozy winter scene elaborately crafted from chocolate.

"No way! That is insanely cool," Spence breathes.

"It really is," I agree, once again wondering where my mother procured this display. It's a perfect replica of Haverberry Town Square, I realize, right down to the ornate lampposts.

"Come on," Spence says, pulling me away from the window and through the bakery door.

The bells give their telltale jingle and the warm pastry-scented air wafts toward me. The familiarity is so overwhelming that I gasp. The heavy wooden tables with their antique chairs and the arched wooden shelves displaying birch bark birdhouses and old lace gloves (a design choice made by my mother when they were first married) are the same as they always were. Despite the cute name and the small-town location, it looks more like an elegant teahouse plucked from a cobblestone alleyway in Italy, something hidden and intimate that only the locals know exists.

I register the elderly man behind the counter who is *not* Mrs. Varma, feeling further disoriented.

"Let me know if I can help you with anything," the gentleman says, giving me an inquisitive glance no doubt because I'm staring at him like a spooked cat. His hair is mostly gone, save a thin line of white curls that loops over his ears. His smooth umber skin is clean-shaven, and he wears a pair of round spectacles that elevate his grandfatherly energy to expert level. But the fact that he doesn't know me, that I'm a stranger in my own family bakery, causes such acute pain that I can't think how to respond.

Spence, of course, skips up to the counter with his hand

extended. "I'm Spencer DeLuca and that's my mom," he says happily, leaving out my actual name as he gestures in my direction. "My grandpa used to own this place. I came here once when I was five. He was making cookies in the kitchen, and he let me taste the batter."

My breath catches at the memory, nostalgia sending a right hook to my already wounded heart.

The old man's eyes brighten with recognition as he shifts his gaze to me. "So that would make you—"

"Madeline DeLuca—the one and only," a voice announces as the door to the kitchen opens behind the counter. My shoulders tense and my hands twitch. I don't need a visual to know who's speaking. "Maddi, this is Albert. He's been here since Mrs. Varma retired," Wilder continues, walking up to the counter and smiling at Albert like they are the best of friends, only further exacerbating the feeling that I don't belong.

Guilt snakes through me that I didn't know Mrs. Varma had left.

"Pleased to meet you," Albert says, standing a little straighter, his suspenders pulling tight against his belly.

I return his greeting. But my eyes flit to Wilder, who's wearing an apron spotted with flour from baking in the kitchen. The indignity I felt yesterday spikes at the sight of him invading my dad's bakery. It's been twenty-four hours since my mother delivered the news of our inheritance and he's already here laying claim?

"Spence, you okay if I pop in the back for a minute?" I say, my voice strained, giving Wilder a brief look that indicates I need to speak to him privately.

Spence absently nods, currently too taken with the display case to notice my stiff posture. Albert joins my son as he oohs and aahs over the deep-fried bomboloni donuts stuffed

MOM COM                    71

with Nutella and cream and the custard-filled zeppole topped
with sour cherries, everything labeled with handwritten plaques
showcasing cute names like Take My Heart Chocolate Tart that
I made up when I was a just a girl. The sight of them sends me
reeling, tightening my throat.

While Spence doesn't verbalize a response, too busy spouting fast and furious questions about the pastries, Albert tells me
he'll keep an eye out. And so I walk around the counter, not
meeting Wilder's gaze, not wanting him to see how difficult it
is for me to be here.

I push through the kitchen door, and Wilder follows me
without hesitation. The moment it closes behind us, I turn to
face him, crossing my arms like a shield. His dark wavy hair falls
lazily onto his forehead, and when he makes eye contact with
me, he smiles ever so slightly. There's something in his eyes, like
he's trying to puzzle through a complicated equation.

*"What's that look for?" I say, balancing plates of chocolate tart
in my hands.*

*Wilder holds the door open for me, and I step from the kitchen
into the bakery behind the counter.*

*"Nothing," he says, his eyes flicking to Jake and Alice chatting at
a window table in the bakery. "I just didn't realize you invited Jake."*

*"Yup," I say. "Is that a problem?" I want to add that Jake is
sitting with Wilder's new girlfriend and that any objection he has
is one thousand percent moot, but I hold back for the sake of avoiding a scrimmage, which I think is rather big of me.*

*"No," he says, but his voice says otherwise. Only I don't feel
satisfaction at his jealousy, the exact opposite.*

*"Look," I say, "the last thing either of us needs is more tension.
You asked me to be mature about this, and now I'm asking you the
same." He doesn't get to pick and choose as he pleases.*

*"And as your friend," he says, trying to sound casual, but I*

can clearly see this is bothering him. "I'm just saying that Jake is a player."

I shake my head, losing patience with the conversation. "He's actually the opposite. There's no game there. He just likes girls, probably too many of them too enthusiastically, but he's not slick about it. Also, I'm a big girl. I don't need you to warn me."

Wilder's frown deepens. "So what then? You plan on dating him?" He sounds hurt about it and it sends me right over the edge.

"All I did was invite him to judge our tarts, just like you invited Alice."

"Right," Wilder says with the distinct tone that implies he doesn't believe me.

"And what's that supposed to mean?" I say, feeling my thin hold on my emotions growing weaker by the second. He doesn't get to move on and then be hurt that I'm trying to do the same.

"Come on, Mads," he says, letting his composure slip a little. "You and I both know you invited him because he's my friend and you knew it would bother me."

"Our friend, you cocky asshole."

Wilder bristles. "Good to know we've already arrived at the point in the conversation where you just fling insults at me. I guess there must be more truth to what I said than I realized."

I slam the plates I'm carrying down on the front counter, causing a few of the customers to turn in our direction, including Mrs. Varma, who fixes us in a glare that I imagine translates to "If you take this fight one step further and disturb my peaceful bakery, you better believe there'll be hell to pay." I mumble a guilty apology to Mrs. Varma, refusing to look at Wilder.

Instead, I take off my apron, throw it in the dirty rag bin, and push back my hair.

I move around the counter with determination. "You coming?" I say to Jake. And to his credit, he doesn't hesitate. He gets up with *a grin and tips his nonexistent hat at a scowling Wilder on the way out. And that is the last time Wilder and I ever attempt a bake-off.*

"It's really great to see you here," Wilder says, and even though it sounds like it's meant to be friendly, it gets my back up, remembering his remark yesterday about my lack of visits.

"What are you doing here, Wilder?" I ask calmly, eyeing his apron with the distinct feeling he's intruding yet again.

"I thought I might get a jump start on working in our bakery," he says like it's a good thing.

His use of *our* makes my stomach flip unpleasantly. And the enthusiasm that had him coming here so quickly, before the paperwork is even settled, shines an unwelcome light on my own reluctance. But all I do is grunt, determined not to let him get the better of me today.

I watch as he pushes his tousled hair from his forehead and glances at the place on the counter where he was obviously just working, my dad's recipe book splayed out next to bowls and ingredients. The red fabric cover is worn thin at the edges and is so stuffed with handwritten recipes, notes, and pictures that it bows triangular. To deepen the sting, sitting right next to it is a tray of freshly baked ladyfingers, and from where I'm standing, I can smell the coffee and rum in the mixing bowl. Wilder's not just enthusiastically jumping into his duties at the bakery, he's making tiramisu—my dad's favorite dessert, his prized recipe passed down from his great-grandparents in Italy. My breath hitches and my eyes tingle before I can stop them.

Wilder looks from the counter to me, his expression apologetic like he gets that this must be difficult for me, making me feel even more foolish. And it's all too much—this bakery, Wilder, my dad's tiramisu, the memory of the young girl I used to be, the one who cared so deeply about this place that the wound inflicted in parting with it hasn't healed after ten years.

The need to run is so strong that it takes everything I have not to bolt out of the kitchen. "So, this is what I'm thinking," I say, doing my best to even my tone. "You said yesterday that you wanted this place, right?"

He pauses like I've caught him off guard. "I do."

"Good," I reply like a conclusion, emboldened by his agreement. "Then what I propose is . . . you buy me out." As the words leave my mouth, I immediately feel guilty about them.

For a long moment he just stares at me, his smile gone, no hint of what he's thinking in his eyes. Finally, he just says, "No."

"No?" I repeat, a bright spark of frustration nipping at my calm, trying to justify my proposal to both him and myself. "Think about it. You want to be here. I want to be in California. It's not a financial strain on you by any means. It's the only thing that makes sense."

"No, I'm sorry," he says again, no explanation or rebuttal, just that one stupid word followed by an apology that makes me think he's experiencing the one emotion I will not stand for—pity.

I press my lips tight, my eyebrows pushing together. I want to mention how much nerve he has to even accept this place, *my* family's bakery, *my* dad's beloved business. But instead, I say, "I'm gonna need more than that."

"Maddi," he says with weight, like I'm putting him in an untenable position. "Your father wanted us both to have it. You *and* me. Those were his dying wishes. And whether or not you want to respect that, I'm going to."

Gut fucking punch.

"This isn't about my father," I say, barely above a whisper.

"You're wrong, Maddi," he says gently. "That's exactly what this is about." His voice is clear where mine is garbled.

"I'm not moving back here, Wilder. Not in a million years,"

I say, intending my tone to be firm, but it comes out tinted with panic. I take a breath, collecting myself. "If you refuse to buy it, I guess you'll just have to send my share of the profits to California."

"Sorry, but I can't do that," he says, his eyebrows momentarily pinching like something I said was off.

Death by pastry knife is now looking like a decent solution. "You'd actually refuse—"

"Not me," he says, and opens his mouth. But there's a lag before his words follow like he doesn't know how to deliver this next part. "I think . . ." he starts reluctantly, "that you might want to read the rest of your father's will."

My frustration instantly turns to sweat-laden anxiety. I almost ask him to explain but can't seem to get past my own pride and admit that he's right that I didn't read it.

Eyes locked, we stand there for a long moment at an impasse, neither of us sure what to say. And the longer the silence stretches, the more embarrassed I become.

*"Did you know it was my grandmother who taught me to bake, Madeline?" my father says, turning the pages of recipes encased in plastic sleeves.*

*I push a wooden stool to the counter and step onto it so I don't have to stand on my toes to see the ladyfingers he's soaking in rum and coffee.*

*"She used to watch me while Mom was out. And while I wasn't a loud child, I was sensationally curious. Gram used to say she couldn't leave me alone for ten minutes without me tangling all her yarn into a giant ball. So, in an act of self-preservation, she brought me into the kitchen one day. She said, 'Charlie, today we're going to create an entirely new flavor of scone for your grandfather's bakery, one the world has never heard of. And I need you to help design it.'"*

*I stare up at my dad. "What did you make?"*

*He smiles. "Orange and chocolate—not a new invention by any means, but new for me, which I suppose was the point. And once she got me measuring and mixing, I got the baking bug." He points to the recipe book, to one of the pages written in neat loopy cursive. "See here, this is the recipe we made up that day."*

*I run my fingertips over the numbered instructions, thrilled by the idea of creating new recipes that might also be in this book one day.*

I break eye contact with Wilder. "I have to go check on Spence," I say.

He starts to say something, but I'm already pushing through the door into the front of the bakery, putting on my mom mask, and building a big fucking wall between me and everything that just happened in that kitchen.

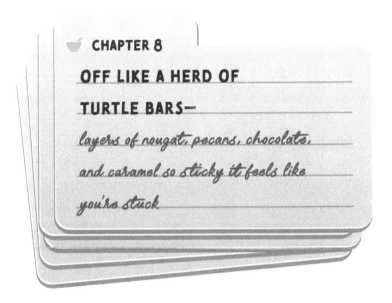

## CHAPTER 8

### OFF LIKE A HERD OF TURTLE BARS—

*layers of nougat, pecans, chocolate, and caramel so sticky it feels like you're stuck*

In direct contrast to my frustration with Wilder and my hellish anxiety over Dad's will, Haverberry Square is serene—frosted shrubberies surrounding a stone gazebo strewn with twinkle lights and red velvet ribbons twirling up its columns. On the south side of the lawn is a giant tree decked in matching reds and whites. Likewise, the whimsical menorah sculpture is topped with bulbs that imitate flickering candles. The only thing that mars the bay-windowed shops with Victorian arches is the ubiquitous Buenaventura family logo—a calligraphy-inspired B that I used to think was fancy but now reminds me of boobs with ungodly large nipples. And while every raw nerve in my body is telling me to jump into my car and race home to find out what that addendum says, Spence is lit up like the neon singing Santa on the roof of Christmas Barn, and I simply cannot drag him away. He shoves the last bite of his maritozzo into his mouth—a sweet brioche bun stuffed with whipped cream and drizzled with salted caramel, an addition I made to my dad's recipe when I was ten, convinced I was onto something special.

"No way," Spence says, pointing at the toy store with giant stuffed animals and an impossibly elaborate Lego sculpture. "Do you even see that castle? It must have like five thousand pieces."

I hold his hand as he drags me across the square toward the toy store, guiding us both inside with enthusiasm. As we enter, I sneak a peek at the Lego castle price, and it reads a whopping $389 *on sale*. My heart constricts, struck once again by the knowledge that I don't have the money to buy it. It's not that he needs it. No one needs an expensive toy; it's my lack of freedom surrounding money, the constant voice in the back of my mind that tells me something is wrong and that I'm the only one who can fix it.

I glance out the window and across the square at the bakery, jaw clenched, when I feel a tap on my elbow and spin so fast, I nearly take down the display.

"Maddi!" Kate says with a bright voice, and my stomach plummets. "You remember Lyndsay, right?" Kate gestures to a woman with a very pregnant belly and freckles on her pale cheeks.

My first thought is, I wish I didn't. It's not that there's anything wrong with her, it's that no matter how old or young Haverberry residents are—if they were here while I was growing up then *yes* I know them, their parents, and the goddamn color of the trim on their houses. Haverberry is an earworm of the highest regard.

"Of course," I reply, trying my best not to look like I want to run. I gesture at Lyndsay's belly. "And congrats."

Lyndsay touches her stomach lovingly. "My first," she says. "I'm so excited. And well, a little nervous about birth."

Kate, whose makeup is both precise and tasteful and whose clothes are the hallmark of wealthy preps everywhere, turns in my direction. "How was it for you, Maddi?" she asks. "It must have been difficult being in California all by yourself."

My eyes flit to Spence, who's enthralled with a worktable filled with the sand version of slime.

I manage a smile. "Truthfully, I think it's challenging no matter where you are or who you're with. But also, I don't think I've ever had an experience that proved my own strength in such a dramatic way. I kinda felt like a superhero . . . if superheroes have hemorrhoids and wear mesh underwear over diaper pads, that is."

The toy store owner (and mother of four) chuckles behind the counter.

"That's what I've heard," Lyndsay says with the non-frightened dreaminess of someone who has never pushed a large human through a small hole.

Kate, however, is far too focused on my face for my liking. I know I caused a scene the other night, and no one regrets that more than me, but honestly, it's starting to feel like this is personal, like she sees me as a threat. I wish I could tell her just how absurd that notion is without it being ten kinds of awkward.

"I'm not sure I would be brave enough to do it all alone," Kate says with a sigh.

"How far along are you?" I ask Lyndsay, redirecting the conversation before it turns into one about my past.

"About seven and a half months. We're actually here shopping for my baby shower." She indicates the sizable shopping bags on Kate's arm. "Kate's the one planning it. I was just going to do something simple, but you know Kate . . . always so elegant."

Kate perks up in response to the praise. "Oh, it's nothing," she says and with a small laugh adds, "you've been a lifesaver helping me come up with ideas for my one-year anniversary."

My heart slams into my ribs, the ferocity of my reaction taking me by surprise. I don't know why, but I assumed her relationship with Wilder was short-term, six weeks tops. "One year? Wow." I hear the hitch in my voice (and I'm certain she does, too), which annoys me. This is categorically not something I care about.

"It's funny because it doesn't feel that long," Kate says with an easy shrug. "But then again, if our mothers had anything to do with it, Wilder and I would already be picking out our china patterns."

And once again, my nervous system takes a blow, my heart doing calisthenics. The notion that Wilder's mother wants him to marry Kate rings true. She's exactly the sort of person Mrs. Buenaventura gushes over—wealthy family, outwardly perfect. But why, oh why is my body betraying me and acting like this is a big deal? They deserve each other; go forth and get married, spawn beautiful, horrible babies together for all I care.

"See, my mom's old-fashioned," Kate continues. "She swears that a woman's biggest nightmare is ending up alone."

Here we go again. Maybe she's not trying to instigate an argument, but fuck if I'm going to let her insinuate that my life is a nightmare in hearing range of my kid. "Funny, my worst nightmare is sitting on the toilet and having a hidden spider attack my vagina, but to each their own."

Lyndsay bursts into embarrassed laughter, which she quickly squashes.

Kate appears a little horrified, which I have to say is satisfying. "Anyway, we were just headed over to Nothing Batter," Kate says, clearing her throat, "if you'd like to join?"

The mention of my father's bakery brings my anxiety back front and center. "I've just come from there," I manage.

"Oh, well, in that case, we really must run," Kate trills. But as they exit, Kate says to Lyndsay, "I think it's so sweet Wilder has an interest in that little bakery. It will be such a fun pet project for the both of us."

And there it is, a dagger on the way out, leaving me with no doubt that she sees me as a threat—a problem I don't need and certainly don't want.

I'm about to tell Spence that we have to go, my desire to get home to find that addendum transforming into a visceral need. But as I turn around, he's already there.

"Really?" he says with raised eyebrows.

"Really what?" I say, unsure what he heard or what he made of it, my mom-fixer-sense activating in case he picked up on Kate's subtext.

"I mean, you know I'm proud of you for being an independent woman," he says, lowering his voice and looking around him, "but if you could just not yell about your vagina in here, that'd be awesome. I'd really like to come back."

As always, he manages to say the one thing that takes me out of my head.

I nod, and this time when I smile, it's real. "You're right. I'll definitely work on that."

He gives me an evaluating look like he's not totally convinced, but he's hopeful.

I make it back to Mom's ready and raring to ask her for the will. But as it turns out, her car isn't in the driveway—like the final fuck you of this never-ending afternoon. No matter, I think, I'll simply find the thing myself.

"Christmas movie?" Spence offers as we step through the door.

"Sure thing," I reply, pulling off my coat and haphazardly

tossing it onto a hanger, trying to mentally suss out where my mother might have stashed the addendum. "You go pick one out and start it. I'll be there in a few minutes with snacks."

The instant he disappears into the living room, I make a dash for the antique mail table in the foyer. I pull open the drawer, but a couple of minutes of shuffling through envelopes indicates it's not there. So, I head for the dining room, yanking open the top drawer of her sideboard where she keeps her passport and such. Only I don't have to search this time, because Dad's addendum is right on top, unfolded, making me feel even more foolish for not seeking it out last night. But the convenience of it strikes me as ominous, indicating whatever I'm missing is so important that my mother laid it out for me to find.

I snatch up the paper and scan through the part I remember her reading, wincing at the line: *Ownership of There's Nothing Batter Bakery shall heretofore be transferred to my daughter, Madeline DeLuca, and to Wilder Buenaventura in equal parts.* But two paragraphs down is where I find what I'm looking for:

*For the duration and entirety of the first year of ownership, both parties must not only be present but involved in the day-to-day activities of There's Nothing Batter Bakery. If one party does not comply, said party forfeits their share to the other.*

Hang on. *WHAT*???

I speed ahead, hoping I read it wrong, skimming where it frameworks day-to-day activities, desperately searching for a loophole. But it goes on to say that each party must spend a minimum of forty hours per week in the bakery and that the only exceptions are a medical or family emergency.

"Holy fuck!" I breathe, grabbing the sideboard for support, my thoughts in ruin.

A year?! A year in Haverberry? No. That's not . . . I *cannot* do that. *I won't.* But the idea of allowing the bakery to pass solely to Wilder is unthinkable. Somewhere in the house, I hear a door shut, but I'm too overwhelmed to give it significance. My mind is pinging between the utter horror of being trapped here and the image of Wilder casually usurping the bakery this afternoon.

*"So if you refuse to buy it, I guess you'll just have to send my share of the profits to California."*

*"Sorry, but I can't do that,"* Wilder says, his eyebrows momentarily pinching like something I said was off.

Blind fury rises in my throat and I'm certain I'm going to be sick.

I shove the document back in the drawer, slamming it shut with a dull and unsatisfying thud. The vase on top of the sideboard rattles in response.

"Do you plan on fighting with any other furniture this afternoon, because if you do, I would like a warning so that I may safeguard the breakables," my mother says, appearing in the doorway, her purse in her hand and an edge of warning in her tone.

I spin to face her, my upset vibrating through me like an impending earthquake. The door, I think. That was her coming home. I want to take a minute, to think through my reaction, but one thought is screaming inside my head and it seeps past my lips before I can collect myself. "You knew," I say, feeling betrayed. "You knew when you invited me here for the holidays that I was supposed to be here *for a year*, and you said nothing. Then you sent me to that bakery today, fully aware that Wilder would be there and that he knew what I didn't."

Her expression turns steely. "First, do not suppose you know my mind. And second, if you hadn't run from this room while I was reading the addendum, you'd have already known yourself."

Embarrassment spears me. But this is also quintessential Eleanor, twisting my objection into a personal shortcoming.

"I just don't understand, Mom. How could Dad do this? How could you let him do this?" I no longer imagine that she was completely ignorant of this plan—it has the workings of my mother written all over it.

She purses her lips, telling me she's just as frustrated as I am. "Are you asking me how your father could be so generous as to leave you half of the bakery, a bakery you could not even be bothered to step foot in more than once in ten years? In this moment, I'm actually not sure."

I wince, the truth of her words flaring my indignation. "This has nothing to do with gratitude and you know that. I never asked for the bakery. In fact, I've never once in all the years asked you for anything—"

She holds up her hand. "Enough, Madeline," she says in an authoritative tone. "I do not care if you like or dislike your father's will. It was his bakery and his choice to make. Be happy he left you anything at all."

My eyes flick to the ceiling and I inhale. She's using my love for the bakery and my remorse over Dad's passing to force me back into a position where I'm beholden to her. "Mom," I start in the most civilized tone I can muster, "you know this—"

Only this time she cuts me off, indicating she's much angrier than I originally presumed. "If you are bent on discussing what people know and do not, why don't we discuss the benefit that you were graciously invited to two days ago?"

Shit.

"The one where you yelled profanity at the hosts for the whole dining room to hear?"

Double shit.

"Because I was taken completely unawares at my lunch today with Mrs. Templeton, who is not only the prestigious head of my ladies' club but is the godmother of Kate Van Doran, whom I hear had a front-row seat to your blow up?" she says, arching one furious eyebrow.

"Mom—" I start but stop, realizing that I've backed myself into a corner. There are very few things my mother takes as personally as public embarrassment. And Mrs. Templeton, like Mrs. Buenaventura, is a premiere Haverberry socialite, whose good opinion is essential in my mother's view.

"Do you know what else Mrs. Templeton told me?" she asks, her tone far too reasonable.

I shake my head, but I have a few guesses. The game of telephone is beloved in this town.

She straightens the cuffs on her blazer. "Mrs. Buenaventura's thoroughly put out I have yet to contact her about the whole thing."

My stomach twists into a knot of despair. I hadn't considered the fallout from that angle, but now that I do, it seems stupidly obvious. Only before I can think of how to apologize for it, she's speaking again.

"So, now I have the unpleasant job of explaining, and hopefully making amends before our dinner with them this weekend."

"Them?" I blurt out, taken aback.

"Yes, dinner with the Buenaventuras. At their house."

*I stare at the ice cream freezer in the supermarket, looking for a pick-me-up. Wilder and I have been in a nonstop verbal boxing match this past month since he started dating Alice and I started dating Jake. I can feel the tension building between us into something unruly that I fear, unchecked, will mangle even the most steadfast parts of our friendship. But I also don't know how to stop it. It seems to have taken on a life of its own. Him buying Alice stupid thoughtful presents and always rushing from school to meet her. Me talking about Jake's gorgeous body with my lab partner loud enough for Wilder to hear.*

*What sucks the most, though, is that it feels like there's still something unspoken between us, some deeply woven connection that shows up in the still moments, when we accidentally make eye contact from across the room, or when we bump into each other in the hall and we both hesitate before moving on. Maybe I'm overanalyzing it, but my gut tells me that some part of him continues to care about me, not just as his childhood best friend, but as something more. And as much as I try to squash it, the pull toward him—the warmth in my center that makes my pulse race and my stomach jittery—just will not die. I hate us both for it.*

*As though my brain manifested it, I hear someone say Wilder's name. Not just someone, but his mother in her unmistakable British accent, and my heart leaps squarely into my throat. I whip toward her voice just in time to catch her long silk cardigan flowing behind her at the other side of the store. And before I can decide it's a terrible idea, I follow, peeking around the end of the aisle.*

*"I'm just glad it's over," Mrs. Buenaventura says to her husband, a handful of feet away with their backs to me as they pick out yogurt. I'm not certain I'm relieved or disappointed that Wilder isn't with them.*

*I'm about to retreat when Mrs. Buenaventura continues: "In the first place, it was far too serious a relationship for seventeen-year-olds."*

*I freeze, realizing she's talking about me and Wilder.*

*Mr. Buenaventura only shrugs. "They're teenagers. Of course they're passionate."*

*Mrs. Buenaventura drops Greek yogurts into their basket. "As long as she doesn't drag Wilder to some culinary school in the middle of nowhere because of that passion, then fine."*

*My heart slams so hard against my ribs that I take a step back. Drag Wilder to some culinary school? You mean the Culinary Institute of America that, yes, happens to be only half an hour from*

*Vassar but is also a world-class facility? The accusation is infuriating, and just plain wrong—that choice was his, not mine. Is this how they see me? Like I'm a bad influence on their son?*

*Mr. Buenaventura sighs like he doesn't believe it's a crisis, but also isn't going to argue with his wife.*

*"Let me tell you, Francesco," she continues. "I could not be more grateful that he listened to reason and ended things."*

"You don't really think I'm—" I start, but as my mother's eyes meet mine, I clamp my mouth shut, realizing I'm trapped. If I refuse to go to the Buenaventura's, I'm practically ensuring maximum tension. But if I agree, then I have to spend an entire dreaded evening not only with Wilder but also with his parents.

I glance over Mom's shoulder in the direction of the living room where I can hear the TV playing *Elf,* and begrudgingly, for the sake of my son, decide that to continue would be unwise. My shoulders slump a little in resignation.

Check effing mate.

"Now if you'll excuse me, I have a phone call to make," she says.

And before I can formulate a response, she's gone, her shoes clicking rhythmically on the hardwood floor. I clench my hands and close my eyes, silently screaming at no one. She finally did it. She got me back here in some wild ruse that once again gives her control over my life. Well, I'm not going to roll over, I decide. I'm leaving after Christmas just like I planned. That gives me a week and a half to figure out how to sidestep the rules in my father's will. And starting tomorrow morning, I'll log those required hours, because no matter what, the last thing I'll ever do is let Wilder take over my dad's bakery.

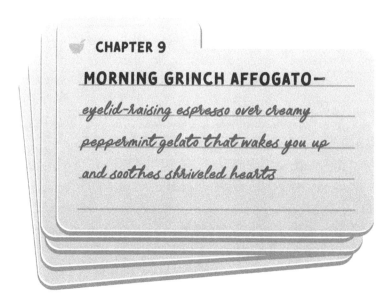

## CHAPTER 9

## MORNING GRINCH AFFOGATO—

*eyelid-raising espresso over creamy peppermint gelato that wakes you up and soothes shriveled hearts*

Frost dusts the grass in the square and outlines the edges of the store windows illuminated by strands of white lights. In the dark wee morning hours, the stillness is almost complete, no noises of people bustling or families chatting, not even a stray car passing by. The decorated tree and the menorah glow, giving the space an almost magical feel, but it does nothing to take the edge off my nerves about working in the bakery.

I wind my scarf around my neck, the cold tingling my cheeks and erasing the remnants of sleep. I dig in my purse for my father's bakery key that Mom gave me last night with a knowing (or was it gloating?) smile, telling me Albert starts at 4:00 a.m. At which point I mildly panicked about what she might say to Spence and asked her to please not mention the addendum because I haven't had a chance to talk to him about it yet. She replied with: *Haven't had time or haven't wanted to?* Which it turns out is a damn good question, but not one I was prepared to answer.

As I shut my purse, I catch a glimpse of my phone, which reads 4:01 a.m. While I'm not a morning person by a long shot, I enjoy baking when no one is awake, kneading dough and stirring cream; there is something relaxing and meditative about it. Plus, it'll give me time to think about how to maintain ownership of the bakery while returning to California. I only hope that Albert doesn't mind the intrusion as I reacquaint myself with the baking schedule. I figure if I come here in the early mornings, I can be out by eleven or so, giving me the whole day with Spence and avoiding Wilder all in one go.

I step onto the sidewalk but stop in front of the window to admire the display once again. The portrait of Haverberry is exquisite, more art than skill really. And the longer I look, the more details pop out at me: the inclusion of the bench where I always sat to watch the Christmas tree, the car parked in front of the bakery that looks an awful lot like my Prius, the words *molten chocolate cake*—my favorite dessert—written on the replica of the bakery window.

I straighten so fast you'd think I'd been pinched because I know with certainty who made this display—Wilder—and suddenly the world is spinning off its axis.

I walk away, trying to convince myself it's meaningless, and instead concentrate on slipping the key into the lock. The bells give a bright jingle as I push open the door and step into the dark café. Only it's not pitch-black; a faint glow illuminates the round window in the door leading to the kitchen, where I can already smell dough baking to a buttery flake.

For a moment I hesitate, heart hammering at the sight of the familiar bakery, the cover of dark allowing my mind to drift to memories of my father—the way pride made him stand a little taller behind the counter, the careful way he used to tie his apron, tucking and pulling it until it was pristine, and the way he used to hum to himself when he was measuring or cleaning the counters like a joyful dance.

My breath leaves my lungs in a whoosh, and I blink away the images before I lose my nerve. I stride across the room, taking off my coat and scarf as I go. *Sink into the work and forget everything else*, I tell myself. *This is temporary. Only temp*—

But my thoughts are cut short as I push open the kitchen door, the chocolate-scented air warming my chilled skin, because there—standing at the mixing bowls where Albert should be—is Wilder.

"Shit," I say before I can consider it. "You're not supposed to be here." My bravado from yesterday is distinctly absent.

He looks up from where he shaves a block of baking chocolate. "I'm usually not," he admits. "But I decided to give Albert the morning off."

"Did my mother tell you—" I stop short, realizing how ridiculous that sounds, like she specifically called him up to alert him of my movements.

He waits for me to finish, his shirtsleeves rolled up to combat the warmth from the ovens, but when I don't speak, he says what I can't. And after all those years he lived in Europe, the words wind up sounding more British than American. "I take it you're displeased."

I don't reply directly because this is awkward enough as it is. Instead, I place my things on a hook and reach for an apron, only to discover that the one I used as a girl is still hanging where it always did, its baby blue and white stripes faded from too many washes. For a moment I'm frozen in place, eyes locked on the apron that has been waiting for me to return for ten years. A lump forms in my throat, and my chest rises a little too fast.

After an extended pause, I yank a plain white one down,

feeling exposed, my upset turning to fluster. "And tomorrow? I mean, tomorrow you'll be here in the afternoon?"

He pauses filling his mixing bowl, which from the smell of it is filled with something of the gingerbread variety. "Actually, no," he says slowly. "I'd really like to be present for the bakery's most important tasks, and the morning baking is the top priority in my opinion. So, I'll be shifting to an earlier schedule from here on out."

Panic grips my chest. I press my lips together, holding back my flood of objections. Of course this would happen; it's as if Wilder and I were destined to find ourselves in impossible scenarios. If this were any other situation, I'd just take the afternoon shift, but there's no way I'm missing holiday time with Spence because Wilder sucks.

"Then I guess that means we'll be here together," I say.

*The beach parking lot is packed with cars, but since it's after hours, Jake just makes his own spot by the cattails that enclose the adjacent marshland, pulling the front wheels of his truck into the soft grass.*

*Barefoot, I plod onto the pavement that has cooled in the night air, yanking my sweatshirt down over my head. Jake takes my hand in his warm calloused palm as we step onto the sand. And as we make our way through the groups of partyers, I find myself instinctually searching for Wilder even though I promised myself I wouldn't. I haven't spoken to Wilder since I saw his parents in the grocery store last week. I didn't tell him what I heard his mom say or that I'm done with him in general. He texted me a couple of times, but when I didn't respond, all went silent.*

*"Drink?" Jake offers.*

*"For sure," I reply, distracted by my thoughts.*

*He heads for a cooler surrounded by a group of his football buddies, and I wander around the bonfire, my bare feet plodding through the cool sand.*

*And that's when I hear it—the most frustrating sound in the world—Wilder laughing. My head whips toward his voice only to find him holding court with a group of girls from our school. His eyes are lit up and his gestures are big. Is Wilder tipsy?*

*"So, we're waiting for the book signing to start, only the event before it was running late—some kid storybook thing—and the library is swarmed with toddlers. And as their big finale, they bring out a live duck. The kids are out of their minds with excitement. Maddi? Not so much. Terrified, squirming like a giant spider just landed on her head."*

*The girls laugh and I suddenly feel all the blood in my body rush to my cheeks. Wilder loves this story and used to tease me about it in private all the time. But telling it now after everything that's happened?*

*"And to make matters worse, as Maddi's trying to get away from the duck, it escapes and flies right toward us," the idiot continues as I march toward him and his admirers. "Maddi loses it. Starts screaming. And the toddlers don't know why, but they figure something terrible must be happening, so they start screaming—"*

*"What exactly do you think you're doing?" I demand, approaching the group.*

*Wilder shifts his gaze to me, his smile deepening when he sees me. He moves aside, making room for me to stand next to him, and then looks back at the girls. "So, the librarian manages to scoop up the duck, but it's too late to calm the toddlers," he continues like I wasn't threatening to kill him with my eyes. "And no joke, there's what can only be described as a mini stampede. Maddi straight up jumped on my head. I had to carry her out of there through ruins of Goldfish and smashed juice boxes. That was the day—"*

*My blush deepens. I yank him by the arm, pulling him toward the ocean before he can continue.*

*"Hey now," he says with a chuckle.*

I stare at him incredulously. "Seriously? You're telling that story to random girls?"

"They're not random. They're—"

"I don't care if they're your new best friends and you're about to have a foursome! I'm not your cheap pickup line, Wilder."

He stares at me for a long moment. "You think I'd use that story to hit on girls?" He shakes his head. "I wasn't going to tell them about our first kiss, Mads. You should know me better than that."

His smile falters and so does my confidence. Embarrassment rushes in, not because I was wrong about his intentions, but because I admitted that story was still important to me.

"What I was going to say to them," Wilder continues, "is that was the day I discovered that you, Madeline DeLuca, the girl who isn't afraid of anything, who punched a bully in the face in third grade, who entered a baking contest for adults when she was barely thirteen, is terrified beyond belief of ducks. And it only made me fall harder. I'm pretty sure it was the cutest thing I've ever seen."

I stare at Wilder, frustration warring with the part of me that is reflexively softening at his words. I can smell the alcohol on his breath, but I can also smell him—the lingering scent of fireplace that he lights all year round, even in the middle of summer.

"So, you're drunk?" I say, needing to explain away the humming sensation and dismiss it as something meaningless.

"Maybe," he says with a shrug. "But that doesn't change that it's also the truth."

I level him in my gaze, needing to squash whatever is happening. "Truth?" I repeat. "The last time I checked, we could barely make it through a simple hello without fighting."

He sighs, looking briefly at the ocean. "Yeah, I know. I hate it."

And for reasons I can't fathom, I respond. "I do, too."

I turn away from Wilder, resolving to just focus on the task at hand for the rest of the morning. And for the most part, besides a quick conversation here and there about who's making what and the schedule going forward, we're silent. I catch him looking in my direction every once in a while, like he's trying to sort something out, but it only makes me focus harder on my work, letting the scents and motions guide me, and trying not to think too hard about where I am or whom I'm with.

CHAPTER 10

## HALF-BAKED IDEA COOKIE—

*a comforting gooey center that I'll probably regret later*

The fireplace in my mom's living room is freshly lit and I stare at the flames, tucking a throw blanket around my legs.

"You cool?" Spence asks, munching on one of the decorated Christmas cookies we made this afternoon and looking up from the game he's playing on his laptop. "'Cause you've been holding that book for like twenty minutes without turning a page."

I shift my gaze to him with a reassuring smile. "Just thinking."

"About baking?"

"Something like that," I say.

"About Grandpa's bakery?" he continues, and I exhale.

"Actually, yeah," I say, wondering if he overheard something or is just being his usual observant self.

He lowers the screen on his laptop. "It must have been weird to go there this morning . . . I mean without Grandpa there." Only nine and yet he always seems to get to the core of things.

"It was," I say slowly. "It's been a long time since I've baked at that bakery. I used to do it all the time as a girl, and there were a lot of memories."

"Good ones?"

"A whole variety, but yes, definitely good ones among them."

Spence nods and when he doesn't immediately go back to his game, I realize that even though I haven't made up my mind about what to do, he's sensing my discomfort and I owe him an explanation.

I close my book and put it on the coffee table next to my phone. "So, you know how your grandmother and I were talking the other day about your Grandpa's—"

But I don't get my sentence out before our phones ding simultaneously.

His face instantly brightens. "Dad!" he exclaims, and one glance at my screen tells me he's right.

> Jake: Up for some root beer floats?

"Can I?" Spence asks, his voice elevated with excitement.

"Definitely," I confirm. It's a relief that Jake's taking the initiative and I don't have to hunt him down and coerce him—it's the one thing about this trip that's actually easier than expected.

Spence rapid-fires a response to our group text telling Jake he's getting ready, and then jumps up from the couch.

> Jake: Maddi, you joining?

"What do you think?" I ask Spence, not opposed.

"Uh, yeah, I mean, you can come," he says, but his tone tells me everything I need to know. He's been waiting for this dude bonding time for weeks and I'm not going to intrude on it unless he really wants me there.

"You know what?" I say, "Would it be okay if I skipped this one? Maybe went on the next one?"

He looks a little too happy about it. "For sure!" And then he bounces out of the room to get ready.

I lean back on the pillows while Spence runs around the house gelling his hair and putting on his camo earmuffs. He gives me a fast peck on the cheek and barrels outside the instant Jake's truck enters the driveway. I watch from the living room window to make sure he gets in safely.

Then everything returns to quiet once more, and my thoughts return to the memory of the party that had occupied my mind this morning with Wilder.

*The light of the bonfire doesn't reach me and Wilder down by the break, and between the dim reflective glow and the rhythmic crashing of the waves, it suddenly feels far too intimate. I glance back at the party and at Jake who's doubled over laughing with his buddy Benny. But when I look at Wilder, he's entirely focused on me.*

*"I hate that I can't tell you things," he says, so serious that my breath hitches.*

*"What things?" I ask even though I know I'm pushing where I shouldn't.*

*He pauses a second like he's debating his answer. "For one, I miss calling you at night, talking to you before I go to bed."*

*I know I should end the conversation here, trample it into the sand, but my idiotic feet aren't moving. Instead, I'm just staring up at him not saying a word.*

*"And I know this sounds stupid," Wilder continues, hooking one hand behind his neck, "but sometimes at night I let myself imagine you snuck into my house like you used to, and that you're lying next to me, with my arm curled around your waist."*

*My heart catapults itself against my ribs like a spooked horse. I'm* terrified he's going to continue and also terrified he's not. Wilder isn't an open book, far from it. I don't know whether it's the aloof Brit in his DNA or simply that he just overthinks everything into oblivion, but when he says something emotional, it's specific and he means it.

And he's not done. "Some days I even succeed in fooling myself that I never screwed things up between us."

"You don't mean that," I breathe, because I need to believe what he's saying is nothing more than drunken ramblings. "You're just—"

"You're right that I'm drunk," he says, anticipating me the way he always has. "But—" He pushes his hair off his forehead. "Shit," he says under his breath more to himself than to me, a rare lapse in his always-polite speech. "But that doesn't change the fact that I still want to be near you so damn bad."

I try to break eye contact, to shift in some way that might break the force that holds us in place, but it's no use. The more intensely he looks at me, the more intensely I look at him.

Wilder steps closer, reaching up and pushing a stray piece of hair from my ponytail off my face; his touch is so gentle that my stomach dips and my heart thrums. At this proximity, I know that if I lean forward even a millimeter, he'll pull me into his arms; I can feel him wanting to, emotion radiating off him like a heat lamp. And that goddamn pull kicks into high throttle. For a split second, I almost forget myself and move closer.

But then I remember. I remember the months of heartache trying to work past my feelings for him. "You're dating Alice and I'm dating Jake," I say, plain and simple. Only I can't keep myself from quietly adding, "You were the one who wanted it this way." And while I realize I'm revealing it isn't my first choice, some part of me hopes he'll admit that it isn't his, either. But I can already see the conflict forming in his expression. And I can feel my cheeks flushing hot from embarrassment, angry at us both that some part of me actually believed him.

*"Maddi, I . . ." he says, opening and then closing his mouth, suddenly at a loss for words.*

*I take a step back, hurt rising in my chest like a tsunami, furious he put me in this position in the first place.*

My frustration spikes that I've once again been put in an untenable position with Wilder. What on earth was my dad thinking? And just like when I was a teen, there is no easy solution that doesn't involve loss—either Spence and I give up our LA life/school/friends/apartment (and most importantly) independence from my mother, or I give up my dad's bakery to the one person who doesn't deserve it. But as I start down that rabbit hole, my phone dings.

> Liv: Hey gorgeous . . . I know I'm not your fav Buenaventura right now (which is to say I'm so far in the doghouse that I might as well start forwarding my mail) but I was hoping you were around for a drink?

> Liv: A delicious drink of the whiskey persuasion? On me, of course.

> Liv: And not just one, as many as it takes before you're so drunk that you forget what I did.

> Liv: Not that I'm diminishing it!

> Liv: I'm also not above groveling. In public.

I laugh despite my murky mood and type a response.

> Me: Appreciate the offer, but not
> sure I'm into the idea of going to
> Tony's, no offense.

Tony's—pizza joint by day and bar by night, also the place most likely to be filled with people I went to school with, especially around the holidays when everyone is off work or embracing their give-no-fucks celebratory attitudes.

> Liv: NEVER. You think I want to watch
> our classmates dance off beat and
> paw each other? I mean . . . kinda.
> The situation is always rife with
> cringe. But not tonight! Tonight is all
> about classy lady cocktails.

> Me: In that case . . . I feel like
> maaaybe I could be convinced.

> Liv: Hand to heart, Mads, I didn't
> know it would go down like that the
> other night. I mean I know Wilder can
> be obtuse, but that was something
> else. And I feel just awful for putting
> you in that position. Not that I'm
> gonna lie and say I didn't enjoy
> watching you tell him off. Plus there
> was my mother's face, which was
> goddamn priceless. But for real, I'm
> sorry. VERY VERY SORRY.

I sigh. Yes, she put me in a bad spot, but I also had no intention of digging my heels in. I was just too embarrassed and hurt at the benefit to deal with it.

> Me: All is forgiven. Besides . . .
> you had me at classy lady cocktail.

> Liv: Fuck yeah! I'm calling you a car.
> And don't bother resisting. I owe you
> for not driving you home the other
> night.

I'm off the couch in a second, freshening up and telling Mom I'm headed out, weirdly enthused to be doing something that isn't bakery related or an uncomfortable Haverberry social event.

My mother of course looks a little too pleased when she hears my plans are with Liv, but doesn't say anything except that she'll put Spence to bed if he gets home before me. For just a second, a bit of the heaviness lifts, like someone opened a window to let in the fresh air. And while I'm not deluded enough to think it'll last, I also plan on enjoying the lack of conflict for this brief moment.

*eeee*

I pull the heavy wooden door open to The Corner Bar—an old-school bistro filled with dark wood and a single chandelier located on the periphery of the square. It was always a popular spot for the forty-plus crowd to grab a glass of wine and an overly expensive burger. Loud enough to not have people listening in on your conversation, but quiet enough that you don't have to raise your voice to have a conversation.

Liv sits at the bar, shiny dark hair in a high ponytail, wearing a black blazer with a hot pink blouse underneath, black skintight jeans, and high heels that give me vertigo just looking at them.

She slides off her barstool to kiss me on the cheek. "Damn it's good to see you. You had me sweating there for a second. I thought you were going to tell me to go fuck myself, not that you would have been out of line for holding a grudge," she says with a smile.

I slide onto the empty barstool next to her with a shrug, my feet lifting off the ground and balancing on the rung. I smile, too. "Don't flatter yourself; that wasn't nearly grudge-worthy."

"Wow, tell it like it is Mads," she says and laughs. "You wound me."

"Like I believe that for a second. Aren't you the one who told me you had a heart made of ice?"

"Fuck, you're right. That is me. But like, way to blow my cover."

She waves down the bartender, ordering two fig-infused whiskey drinks. And as I watch him prepare them in his shaker, I realize the ingredients are just alcohol upon alcohol—basically the elegant adult version of a Long Island Iced Tea.

The bartender sets them down in front of us and despite my skepticism, I actually say *Mmmm* as I sip it. "Okay, you were right. These things are dangerously good."

"Let it be known that I always deliver on my promises." Liv takes a generous sip herself. "Now, apologies . . . but since I screwed myself the other night by not being forthcoming, I'm just going to bring up the behemoth in the room and ask you what the hell is going on with this inheritance rumor I keep hearing about?"

My good mood deflates, and I lean into my cocktail for support. It's only been a handful of days and already everyone knows—not that Liv is everyone, but still. "Honestly? I wish I knew."

"So this thing is real? Your dad actually left the bakery to you and *my brother*? Did you know anything about this or—"

The look I give her stops her short.

"Got it. Blindsided. Wow," she says, knocking her glass against mine like even she needs a drink from the stress of it. "So, you just show up here and bam, your mom tells you that you have to share your inheritance? You must have shit yourself."

"Yup," I say, taking a swig. "And you know my mom. She says exactly what she wants and nothing more. I've basically gotten no information out of her besides a heavy guilt trip about gratitude. Plus, we've been fighting, which doesn't help with the question asking."

"Ooph. Any idea why your dad set it up that way?"

"None whatsoever," I admit. "But that addendum was like a bear trap. Apparently, if Wilder and I don't work at the bakery full-time for the next year, we lose our stake."

"No shit."

I nod and the motion feels a little like being underwater. I look at my half-drained glass accusingly. "You wanna hear shitty? I got caught off guard in my Grinch onesie the morning after I yelled at Wilder at the banquet."

Liv chuckles. "Sorry, that's not funny, but it is kind of amazing. And I want to bet that in comparison, my brother looked like he just came from visiting the queen." She laughs again, and despite my horror over the whole thing, I find myself laughing, too.

"You should have seen my mom's face when she realized I wasn't going to change out of my neon green."

Liv touches my arm. "Please promise me you'll wear it to my parents' Christmas Eve party this year. I feel like I missed out on something really special."

We both grin like idiots.

"You know, Liv, you're really easy to talk to. I forgot that about you," I say, mildly aware that it isn't something I would normally say out loud.

"And you, my friend, are the breath of fresh air Haverberry desperately needed. *I* forgot how much this town sucks without you. No wonder my brother is all in a twist."

I shoot her a look like she can't be serious. "Wilder is never in a twist. Wilder would be the single human calmly drinking his morning coffee during an alien invasion."

Liv snorts and waves over the bartender. "Chris, please continue to make love to my cold heart by serving us two more of these drinks." She fiddles with the tiny charm on her necklace that features a Buenaventura "B," a beloved symbol they all sport with pride, and the nostalgia of it hits me hard, remembering how as a teen I always wished my family had a similar kind of solidarity.

"I really shouldn't—" I start, but Liv is having none of it.

"You really actually should. You just found out your life is upside down and you have an ultimatum to move back to Haverberry. I think a barrel full might not be enough."

Well, I can't argue with that. "I just don't drink much these days. I mean I have a glass of wine here and there, but being a single mom, it's not something I normally do. Makes me a lightweight among other things."

"And where is my favorite child tonight?" she asks.

"With his dad and then headed back to my mom's."

She raises a mischievous eyebrow. "So, what you're saying is that there are not one, but two adults caring for him and this is a rare opportunity to live a little?"

The bartender trades out our empties for a second round, the glasses looking suspiciously fuller than the last.

"Well, when you put it that way . . ."

Liv slaps a sizable tip on the bar. "So, what's the deal with Jake anyway?"

"Jake?" I repeat as I sip my drink.

"Still pretty hot if you ask me," she says, and I choke on my whiskey.

"Uh, yeah, I guess. But honestly, his wishy-washy parenting is a turnoff." And then I find myself saying something I absolutely do not mean to say. "What did you mean when you said Wilder was all twisty, by the way?"

Liv smirks, thoroughly amused, an expression she shares with her brother. "What I mean is that every time I've seen him since you've arrived, he's acted like he's late to a meeting, all edgy and flustered. You'd think he never saw a gorgeous woman before."

I frown. "I really don't think that's the reason."

"So, you believe your showing up here had no effect on him?"

I shrug. "Not no effect, just more one of annoyance that I invaded his beloved Haverberry."

Liv clucks her tongue off the top of her mouth. "While I enjoy the image of Wilder as a grumpy dog defending his chew toy, I think you know that's not true. Why on earth would he be working at your father's bakery if you annoyed him?"

I hesitate. "To get me back for beaning him with that Cherry Coke ten years ago?"

She smiles into her glass. "You two should just bone and get it over with. You know you want to."

And for reasons unknown to me, a laugh bursts out of me that is so violent that I start coughing. "You did not just say that," I manage, trying to regain my composure. "That is not . . . you're way off."

"Am I though?"

"First of all, there's Kate," I say, not sure why I'm even jus-tifying this with a response.

"Ugh, don't remind me," she says. "Actually, if you could somehow scare her off, that would be amazing. Thanks."

"Uh . . . no," I say, shaking my head like I could unhear this whole thing. "But I get it, she sucks."

"Like a viper in Chanel," she agrees. "But don't think I didn't notice that your reason was Kate and not that you didn't secretly want to."

I try to glare at her, but I'm halfway through my second cocktail and I wind up looking more like I have something in my eye. "I'm not sure if it escaped your notice, but Wilder and I hate each other."

"Wilder does not hate you," she says, so sure of herself that for the briefest of seconds, I waver. "If you ask me, my brother never got over you."

I grunt. "Bullshit."

"You wanna bet?" she says.

"If you like losing," I say with a too-big grin.

Liv laughs. "You're on. Loser buys dinner."

"I mean, sure, that's not even really a consequence, but okay."

"My God, you're a reckless bitch and I love it. Okay, scratch dinner, the winner gets a prize of their choice. Open-ended."

"That is . . . oh man. Okay," I say, knowing I should be much more worried about this than I currently am.

Liv swishes the last of her drink and downs it. "Then I'm sorry to inform you, Mads, but if we're going to resolve this bet, we need to venture down the road to Tony's."

I stare at her, my brain not forming the connections it needs in order to understand.

"It's pool night," she explains, handing her credit card to

the bartender. "Otherwise known as Haverberry bros drinking together. And while that isn't usually Wilder's jam, it's Matt Mazzeo's birthday."

"So, your plan is that we go to Tony's and do what exactly?"

I should be nervous about the grin that appears on her face, but my defense grid is currently short-circuited by whiskey. Instead, I find myself sliding off my stool, my body made of sloshy warm liquid and false confidence, flicking my hair over my shoulder and saying, "Fuck it, lead the way."

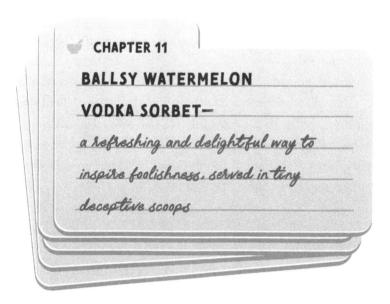

## CHAPTER 11

## BALLSY WATERMELON
## VODKA SORBET—

*a refreshing and delightful way to inspire foolishness, served in tiny deceptive scoops*

You'd think the cold air would sober me up, but it turns out those drinks Liv ordered were made of rocket fuel and stupidity.

"I cannot believe you convinced me to do this," I say, my breath a white cloud in front of my face, waving my hand at the town before me. My recent TV debut flashes through my thoughts like overly bright headlights.

Liv somehow maneuvers like a lioness in stilettos even though I know she's at least one drink ahead of me. "Think of it as a good thing. Going to Tony's tonight is like reclaiming this place by pissing in the town square to mark your territory. You can't give these people the upper hand or your life here is going to be total shit."

"One of the many reasons I want to go back to LA," I declare and frown at the words I've said so many times recently that they're losing their desired effect of comfort. "Liv, you went to law school . . . you know about things like wills, right?"

"Not my expertise," she says, "but I understand the language if that's what you're asking."

"I know it's a lot to ask, but would you mind looking at my dad's?" I say, clearly having blown past the point where I care about appropriate social norms. "See if there's a loophole or something that could get me out of this arrangement?"

She stops abruptly.

I stop, too, a motion that causes me to stumble. "What?"

"No . . . nothing. I just . . . is that something you really want to do, Mads? Try to find a way out?" What she doesn't say, but what is evident in her tone is *find a way out of your father's last wishes.* "Shit, sorry. I'm not judging, I'm just wondering."

For a couple of seconds, I'm silent, the chilly breeze kicking up a few stray leaves that smell like wet earth and frost. "Maybe? Yes? Does that make me a bad person?"

She shakes her head. "Not in my opinion. But I'm not everyone." I'm guessing what she means is that she's not my mom—who will very obviously have a humungous problem with it. "But if you want me to have a look at it for you, I definitely will."

"Thanks," I say, surprised she's willing to help even though I know it'll put her in a weird position with Wilder.

She loops her arm through mine. "Okay, now let's get to Tony's before you think too hard and decide not to let me embarrass my brother." She wags her eyebrows at me.

At any other moment, I would assert that it doesn't matter to me what Wilder thinks one way or the other. But I don't really *want* reality right now, I just want a bit of stupid fun with an old friend that doesn't feel like drowning. And if I'm being truthful, my curiosity is piqued. Could there possibly be some buried part of Wilder that still thinks about me that way? And the moment I have the thought, I know it's dangerous, but kind of deliciously so. Oh God, I really must be drunk. Maybe I—

Liv flings the door open to Tony's like she's walking into a board meeting to announce she just took over the company. And instead of hiding behind her, nervous about what I got myself into, I play along, hyped up on her energy and my own lack of inhibitions, my gaze sweeping over the crowd of twenty- and thirtysomethings like *That's right bitches, I'm back and I'm doused in whiskey. Come at me at your own peril.*

Tony's smells like pizza and beer, and has a décor reminiscent of a Western saloon, with rustic wooden beams running along the ceiling and barrels as the support structure for the bar. There are dartboards along one wall and a worn pool table, where Matt's birthday crew congregates in a sea of empty beer bottles.

The response of the crowd is a little thrilling—people taking note of me and Liv with their wide-eyed expressions and Wilder completely missing the ball on his pool shot. I hesitate a moment as we stop at the bar, wondering if this was the right decision, but the concern doesn't linger the way it normally would.

Liv orders us two glasses of wine, claiming a switch to beer would be perilous. And while I'm faintly aware that more alcohol is unnecessary, I'm also staring down the barrel of my youth and I need all the bravado I can muster.

Liv clinks my glass and I take a big sip.

"So, what are the parameters of this bet?" I ask, trying not to look in Wilder's direction and failing. "I mean, what decides who won?"

"Hmmm," Liv says, scanning the crowd. "How about this, leave the convincing to me. If I don't get Wilder to say or reveal something that indicates he still cares about you, then you win. Pressure to perform is squarely on my shoulders, just where I like it."

"Um, can I get a loan on some of that confidence? Because I could really use it for the next week or so."

She grins at me mischievously. "Oh, I don't think you're lacking in the confidence department. I very clearly remember the time you climbed onto the bed of Jake's truck at school and told off an entire parking lot of people for gossiping about you."

I laugh, even though normally that memory would make me cringe. "You weren't even there when I did that."

"See what I mean?" she says, raising her glass. "News of your badassery reached all the way to Yale."

I open my mouth to respond but Matt has made his way over to us, grinning from ear to ear. "Fuck me, this is a surprise. I'd heard you were back in town, Maddi, but having you show up to my birthday celebration makes me feel all kinds of special."

Liv cocks an eyebrow and a smile. "Actually, we're here for the basic drinks and the juvenile atmosphere."

Matt nearly breaks into song. "Perfection. I'm an ambassador of juvenile atmosphere. Search no further, ladies, I'm at your service."

I catch Wilder stealing looks at us from the pool table and frowning.

Raff, Matt's best friend, claps him on the shoulder, joining our small group. "Why do I get the impression that I should already be apologizing for you?"

"Because you haven't drank enough beer?" Matt suggests. "Or because those ginger curls on your head are actually pubes and you're really a giant limp dick?"

It's so stupid that I laugh despite myself.

Matt nods at me approvingly. "See, even Maddi thinks you're lame."

Raff doesn't miss a beat. "That's not what your sister said last night."

"Man, what did I tell you about sister jokes? Not fucking funny," Matt says with a warning glare.

Liv swirls her glass, the ice cubes clanking against the sides, and cuts them off before they melt our brains with bro-y posturing. "Mads and I are after a game of pool. Anyone call winners on this game?"

My eyes flick to Liv. While I'm not bad at pool, per se, I also didn't think she was going to throw us into the lion's den of Matt's crew.

Matt, of course, lights up like the string of rainbow lights above the bar. He turns around, waving his hand for us to follow. "Yo Wilder, Maddi, and Liv call winners!" he bellows. It occurs to me that Matt must be Wilder's teammate. "Don't mess this shit up."

There are hoots and hollers as we approach, but Wilder's eyebrows are still pushed together like he's concentrating too hard.

Liv winks at her brother, which does nothing to soften his expression.

"It's your go," Wilder says to Matt.

I get a look at the pool table, which only has a few remaining balls. It takes Matt about two minutes of calculating and one fast shot to sink the last of the striped set and then pocket the eight ball, which is surprising because I would have wagered he was too drunk to identify the cue ball much less hit anything at an angle. And while Wilder resets the table like he's in a bad mood, Liv and I shrug out of our coats, piling them on a stool next to the wall.

"I hope you're comfortable with losing," I say in a whisper, gesturing in Wilder's direction. "*That* is not the face of someone who's happy about my presence. He looks like he's going to pick an argument with the pool table."

She shakes her head like I've got it all wrong. "Nope. That's just Wilder's resting face when his sense of antiquated decorum is disturbed by the improprieties of rabble-rousers." She adds a

British accent and makes a bit of theater out of it with an exaggerated bow.

I can't help but giggle.

"I'll break," Liv announces loudly, pulling away from our huddle, and giving me a wink.

My stomach does a fast flip like it's trying to warn me about impending danger, but the sensation is immediately dulled with another sip of my drink. And by the time Liv hands me a chalked pool cue, my hesitation and common sense are a distant memory.

Of course, Liv smashes the balls apart artfully, followed by the approving jeers of Matt's buddies. She sinks two solid balls and one striped. Then proceeds to sink two more solids before yielding the table to Wilder, who returns by pocketing three striped balls himself.

"Damn. Could you two please leave something on the table for the rest of us?" Matt says, then leans toward me to add, "Couple of pool sharks, am I right?"

I give a friendly shrug, my muscles loose and buzzing, stepping up to the table. "Meh. They've been like that since always. They once played a game of miniature golf that was so competitive that they got us banned for a year."

Matt laughs.

And to my surprise, Wilder chimes in. "We were kicked out because Liv was yelling such colorful profanity at me that the family behind us actually left to go pray."

Liv barks out a laugh. "Mom always said I was gifted."

"That's one way to put it," Wilder agrees. Then he gives her a look written in subtle sibling speak that I would struggle to translate even if I wasn't three sheets assways in a whiskey barrel, but I'm guessing it equates to something in the realm of *WTF are you two doing here?*

I line up my shot, albeit swaying slightly, and sink a solid ball.

"That's my girl. Hole in one," Liv says, thoroughly enjoying herself.

Matt chuckles. "Hole in one—that's actually not a bad nickname for you, Maddi."

It's as though someone flipped a switch on the fun. The laughs stop and the energy flatlines. Wilder turns on his friend like he might deck him.

Matt seems to realize his mistake, but before he can get out the words *I was joking, guys. It was a joke,* I cut him off.

"I'll take it," I declare, not shrinking from the insult. "Hell of a lot better than hole-in-none, right Matty? I seem to remember a certain story in the girls' locker room senior year about how you lost your virginity on Jenna's thigh before she could even get her pants undone?"

Raff laughs so hard and so suddenly that beer sprays out of his mouth and mists the air in front of him. The guys descend into a chorus of taunts. Liv looks my way with a proud nod, but Wilder still appears thoroughly unamused.

"Uh . . . that did not happen. All lies," Matt attempts as they chant *hole-in-none* at him.

In that moment something changes for me. I knew there was no way I was going to get through this night without some jabs about high school, but I also don't feel angry and uncomfortable the way I thought I would.

"You're up, hole-in-none," Liv says, but before Matt can respond, his friends start howling with laughter. And then I see why—Jenna just walked through the door. Her black leggings are shiny, her sweater is cut in a deep V, showcasing her girls, and her hair is teased in a way that would make Madonna proud.

Matt shakes his head. "Joke's on you guys. I'm the one that

gets to marry that woman. I'm a card-carrying stud." The idea that they're engaged makes me smile, and for unknown reasons, I glance momentarily at Wilder.

To my surprise, Wilder not only returns my look, but approaches us, bringing with him his telltale smoky scent that's so nostalgic I get a flash of us sitting together on his couch in his family's home library as teens, fire crackling, my legs draped over his lap, and his thumb drawing lazy circles across my palm. Involuntarily, my temperature raises a notch.

"Can I get you each a bottle of water?" he asks, and I find myself blushing at my memory of him.

"No, you cannot. Can I get you a whiskey?" Liv offers.

Wilder laughs. "Some of us have to work at four in the morning." He glances in my direction.

"I'm actually glad you brought that up, Wilder," Liv says. "You see, Maddi here told me that you're planning on working at the bakery full-time for a year . . . is that right?"

Wilder focuses on his sister, like he's certain this conversation just took a turn. I, too, stare at Liv, afraid that if I look directly at Wilder, he might pluck knowledge of our ridiculous bet from my thoughts.

"That's right," he says calmly, and I'm struck by the déjà vu-ness of it all—him calm and composed, her bold and brazen, exact opposites.

Over Wilder's shoulder, I see Matt in the process of taking his fiancée up to the bar, pausing our game for the time being.

"But that's not why you came back to Haverberry, little brother," Liv says, and I stop fidgeting with my pool cue, snapping to attention.

"No, it's not," he replies, his tone questioning like he knows she's pushing against something she shouldn't.

My pulse quickens and I find myself searching his face,

trying to figure out what mysterious thing Wilder is doing in Haverberry.

"So then how will you manage full-time at the bakery and, well, everything else?"

"*Liv*," Wilder says, drawing her name out like a warning, his eyes momentarily flicking to me.

"What?" she says innocently. "All I'm saying is that I want a heads-up if—"

My heart thumps and I lean forward, waiting for her to name the thing he clearly doesn't want to talk about.

But Wilder cuts her off before she continues. "Yes, well, as long as we're making requests," he says, a hint of a smile appearing on his lips. "I'd like a warning the next time you two are up to something that involves me."

Oh shit.

Wilder looks from his sister to me and back again, his amusement increasing as he realizes he's correct. "I'm guessing it has to be quite interesting to get Maddi to agree to come here because I doubt she'd volunteer to go to Matt's birthday on her own accord. And then there's all the whispering and unsubtle plotting you two have been doing. Was it some sort of bet, Liv? And now I'm wondering, what's the prize?"

All the heat I felt a moment ago rushes to my cheeks.

Liv laughs, only whatever she was going to say in response gets lost as her gaze draws toward the bar. "Well, now if this didn't just get more interesting," she says almost to herself.

As I follow her eyeline, my pulse quickens. There, shrugging off his coat and giving Jenna a quick embrace, is Jake.

*The waves crash rhythmically into the sand, sending white sprays of foam into the night sky. I pull my knees up and wrap my arms around them, yanking my coat a little tighter and handing my now empty beer bottle to Jake.*

"Cold?" he asks, stuffing our empties inside his bag.

I shrug. "Maybe a little," I admit. "But I'll be better after another beer."

Jake laughs. "Would if I could, but two was all I could swipe without my parents noticing." And even though I'm certain he knows I'm a bit off, he doesn't question me about what's wrong the way Wilder would. "Here, why don't we go to my truck and warm up."

"I'm not ready to go home yet," I say, a phrase I've repeated a lot these past few months ever since the bonfire where Wilder got tipsy.

"Who said anything about home?" Jake replies with a grin. "We'll swing by Tony's and grab a couple of slices."

I laugh. "Are you ever not hungry?"

He considers it. "When I'm sleeping . . . maybe?"

For a second, I hesitate, recognizing that Jake didn't suggest Matt's party, even though that's where he probably wants to go, because I said I didn't want to. But that thought only makes me angry, because we both know the reason I don't want to go isn't so much a reason as avoidance. But why the hell am I the one hiding from Wilder? He's the one who screwed everything up.

"Actually," I say, emboldened by the injustice of it all, "why don't we go to Matt's?"

His eyes flash with surprise. "Yeah? I mean, I thought you—"

"Changed my mind," I say, standing up and dusting off my jeans.

"Then yeah, definitely," he agrees enthusiastically, pushing himself up from the sand. He swipes his messenger bag, throwing it over his shoulder.

We plod along the path through the dunes and onto the pavement. The parking lot is empty—besides the fact that it's early November, I'm willing to bet the entire school is at Matt's. His parents are away for the weekend, and it's supposed to be something of a rager.

Jake stops by the passenger side door and opens it for me, tossing

*his bag into the back, the beer bottles clinking together as they land.
I step up onto the running board and into the gray upholstered seat.
But instead of closing my door, Jake grins at me.*

*"You're really beautiful, Maddi," he says, and I turn to face
him, legs dangling out of the truck instead of neatly tucked forward.*

*I laugh. "Look, you don't have to convince me to go to Matt's,
I was the one who suggested it."*

*He laughs, too. "So, that's what you think of me, huh? Brutal."*

*"Tell me you're not secretly stoked."*

*He grins, easing my knees apart and stepping between them.
"Oh, I'm stoked. But mainly because it means I'm going to be
hanging out with you all night."*

*I grin back. "Oh, shut it. What's next, flowers and a poem?"
I tease, knowing he thinks all that stuff is ridiculous.*

*He grabs me by the hips and pulls me forward, wrapping my
legs around his waist. "There once was a girl from Haverberry."*

*A laugh bursts out of me. He leans forward, finding my lips
with his, his warm breath heating me from the inside out. I wrap
my arms around his neck, pressing my chest against his, enjoying
the feel of his strong back under my hands.*

*He pulls away for a brief second, just long enough to breathe,
"Whose beauty was so intense it was scary." His hands slip inside
my open coat and under the rim of my shirt, rough fingertips sending a thrill up my spine. "The boy tried hard to be good." He kisses
my collarbone, his mouth leaving moisture that tingles in the cool
air. "Always heart before wood."*

*He moves his right hand to my stomach, his fingers drawing a
tentative circle around my belly button. "But fuck me, she smelled
just like strawberries."*

*"I take it back," I manage as I recline the seat and pull him onto
it with me. "You should enter that thing in the town newspaper."*

*He lies on his side, with me on my back, our bodies pressed in such a way that I feel him wanting me through his jeans. He traces a line along the band of my underwear, sending a wave of warmth to my core. "I think maybe you're right. That's exactly what this town needs," he says, his eyes searching my face. "But right now, all I care about is what you need."*

*His hand slips below the fabric, slowly, like he's not in a rush. "Tell me what you need, Maddi."*

*Heat bursts through me and suddenly I know what it is that I need. I need to move on, not just tell myself I'm going to, but actually do it.*

*"Do you have a condom?" I ask, my voice soft and breathy.*

*His eyes widen. "I thought you said—"*

*"Yeah, I know. But I'm ready."*

*"You sure? I mean—"*

*But instead of answering him in words, I kiss him, his muscled body pressing down on mine with comforting weight. And for a moment I forget Wilder, I forget my anger, I just let go.*

Jake's here? No, he can't be. That makes no sense; didn't he just go out with Spence? I head for the stool near the wall where I left my things, leaving Liv and Wilder to their non-argument argument, and pull my purse from under the pile, nearly knocking my and Liv's coats to the floor as I try to simultaneously maintain control over my purse and the pool cue. Apparently, I'm not the walk-and-chew-gum type I thought I was. And annoyingly, I catch Wilder noting my fumble.

I scowl at the latch on my purse that's refusing to give. After some jabbing and pulling, I get my phone out, which informs me that somehow two hours have passed since I met up with Liv. And also that I have a new message from Spence.

> Spence: Home. Had soooo much
> fun! But now Gma is telling me to

> take a shower before bed? Ugh!
> I'm gonna do it I guess . . . because
> for some reason my bathing seems
> super important to her. You two are
> weirdos.

I snort, silently thanking my mom for winning that battle.

> Me: Love you, my dude. Still out,
> but heading back soon. Text if you
> need me.

I nod to myself. That's exactly what I'll do; I'll simply go home. Yes, yes. A perfect solution. I tuck my phone back in my purse and rest my pool cue against the wall (it takes two tries to get it to balance), determined to walk over to Liv and tell her I'm out of here. But then I hear my name.

I turn too quickly, almost colliding with Jake.

"Well, this is a surprise," Jake says and picks me up in a giant bear hug, my feet lifting a couple of inches off the ground.

"Uh, um, yeah," I say as he puts me back down. I straighten my rumpled shirt and tuck my hair behind my ear. "Here I am."

He chuckles. "Let me guess, you suddenly missed Matt Mazzeo and you just couldn't let another hour go by without seeing him on his birthday?" Then he adds, "Which is why you turned down my offer of root beer floats?"

I laugh. "First off, I don't like root beer," I say good-naturedly. "Well, I kind of do, but I would pick literally a thousand desserts before that one."

"Ouch," he says, touching his chest like I slugged him, but still grinning. "Looks like I'm going to have to up my game in the future."

"And second," I continue with a pause. Is he flirting with me? "I actually had no intention of coming here, but Liv and I were drinking at The Corner Bar and we made this stupid—" Wait, that's not what I meant to say; what I meant to say was that I didn't go out with him because his son was after some guy bonding time and I didn't want to intrude.

"Yes?" Jake says since I stopped directly in the middle of my sentence.

My eyes involuntarily flick to Wilder and Jake notices. "Oh," he says, his grin fading.

"Anyway," I say, "I was just about to leave."

"Have a beer with me first? I mean if I'm being honest, the motivation behind that text might have been to get you to come out for the night," he says with a smile I remember well from my teenage years. I think that smile might have gotten me pregnant. But the idea that his ask was about me and not a deep desire to get to know his son is a big fat turnoff.

And I still have just enough sense to know that hanging out drinking beers with Jake is a bad idea. "Thanks, I'd love to, but I actually have to get up at three thirty in the morning, so . . ."

He whistles. "Serious sunrise hike?"

"Ha! The day I get up to willingly exercise before the sun's up, please stage some sort of intervention because things are really, really wrong."

"Then?" he asks, and I realize this is the longest conversation we've had in years. And while it's easy, it always is with Jake right up until things get serious and he mysteriously disappears.

"The bakery," I say. "Wilder and I have the early shift."

"Wilder?" he says, his tone losing its humor. "Why's Wilder working at your dad's bakery at four in the morning?"

Crap. So maybe there is someone in town who hasn't heard the gossip yet. But that's really the last conversation I want to have at Tony's while surrounded by a bunch of drunk guys who would pounce on it and start making jokes.

I scratch my eyebrow, hesitating.

At which point Wilder walks up, plucking his coat from the stool next to us. "I'm on my way out. I'd be happy to give you a ride, Maddi," Wilder offers and Jake stiffens. "Liv mentioned you might need one."

For a moment I'm stunned, and I scan the room for Liv so I can accuse her of being a traitor, but she's immersed in a conversation and isn't looking my way.

"Uh . . ." I say, not sure what else Liv might have told him.

And then to make things a million times more awkward, Jake chimes in with, "Or I could take you."

I look from one to the other, about to laugh, but neither of them appears to be joking.

"No need, since I'm on my way out," Wilder says, his tone decisive.

Jake shrugs, but it's not an easy motion. "Just giving Maddi an alternative."

"That seems to be your specialty," Wilder remarks, and I look at him in shock.

"It is, isn't it?" Jake agrees, and I know in my gut that his next comment is going to be about how I usually accept his offers. What in the holy hell is happening right now?

"Don't worry about it, Jake," I interject in an attempt to break up the uncomfortable and ridiculous battle over a five-minute drive. Besides, even if Wilder isn't my first choice for a ride home, I also don't want Jake to think I'm returning his (probably meaningless) flirting. "You just got here. Enjoy your beer."

"It's really not a problem," Jake says, as I slip my coat on and pull my hair from under my collar. "It's a quick drive."

But it's Wilder who answers. "I believe she declined you, Jake." He says Jake's name like a warning.

The fuck is going on here? Am I so drunk that I've started hallucinating? Neither of them is interested in me—Wilder is dating Kate and Jake can barely be bothered to call when I'm in California. Lord help me if I don't kill them both.

I consider walking away but decide the fastest course of action is just to go with Wilder. "I'll see you soon, okay, Jake?" I say with a smile.

"Anytime you want," Jake replies and gives me a hug that lasts a second too long, causing Wilder to frown.

I say a quick goodbye to Matt and Jenna and hug Liv. She grins at me with such delight when she sees Wilder by my side that I roll my eyes. I hope she doesn't think she won this bet because a ride proves exactly nothing.

"I'm texting you tomorrow, when I've regained my senses," I say to Liv as Wilder and I head for the door. "I have many, many things to say to you."

"I'd be hurt if you didn't!" she calls after me.

But as the door closes and it's just me and Wilder on the chilly street, a canopy of lights above our heads, I wonder what I've gotten myself into. I hope he doesn't think we're friendly now because this doesn't change our decade-long standoff.

"My car's just over there," Wilder says, his expression relaxing now that we're alone. He points across the street and holds out his palm for me to go first. It all feels so very strange and so very normal to be doing such an ordinary thing with him that I find myself giving him an assessing look.

"What?" he says with a pinch of curiosity.

"You know what," I say, as our shoes click on the quiet empty street.

Wilder stops at the passenger side to open the car door for

me, which only deepens my frown. "I really don't," he says with a hint of a smile. "But I'd like to."

I slide into the seat with a perfunctory thanks. Am I imagining things, or does he think this situation is funny? It's not funny.

I plow forward with the conversation the moment he gets in, too loose to edit it the way I normally would. "You didn't have to be rude," I say. "To Jake, I mean."

He turns on the engine and pushes a couple of buttons on his dashboard, one of which controls the heat to our seats. "Believe me, that wasn't me being rude."

"That wasn't you being nice, either."

"True," he concedes as he pulls out onto the road.

"What's the thing with you two anyway?" I ask, my brain clearly not possessing an off switch.

Wilder shrugs. "I don't like him."

"But why?"

"I have my reasons."

I stare at his profile, feeling like I need to make a point. "Please tell me we're not reliving some teenage rivalry thing." And then my last brain cell withers and dies as I repeat my thoughts from earlier. "Because I'm pretty sure you have zero interest in me."

Oh, fuck me.

The corners of his mouth pull up at that, and my embarrassment rages bright and hot.

He steals a look in my direction, his smile fully present. "I'm simply ensuring that my baking partner doesn't confuse the sugar with the salt tomorrow morning."

"I know what you're thinking right now . . . about what I just said, and you're wrong. If I was implying anything, it's that I'm considering murdering you, like in ugly ways," I say, not doing anything to help my case.

"Really?" he continues with a light laugh. "I didn't know that my being interested in you was this important."

"Oh. My. God. Stop this car; I'm walking."

"And miss this fascinating conversation? Not a chance."

I turn to face him. "Actually, you know what, Wilder? I do have a question." (Not that he asked me if I did.) "What's this thing you're supposed to be doing in Haverberry instead of my dad's bakery?"

He raises an eyebrow. "Technically, I made an agreement."

"What kind of agreement?"

"It's . . ." He hesitates, shaking his head in a way that makes me think he was almost going to tell me, and decided against it. "It's just the kind that's going to be difficult to get out of."

"Then why bother?" I ask.

"Because it's worth it," he says, making eye contact with me.

For a split second, my emotional safety system fails, and I find myself hoping Liv's right that Wilder is somehow choosing to be near me, the thought pooling in my chest like warm liquid.

Drunk Maddi is definitely a hazard.

"That doesn't make any sense," I reply.

"If you say so."

"I do," I say emphatically, trying to reacclimate myself with logic.

His car stops then, and I realize we've made it to my house. He keeps his foot on the brake, but never shifts into park. "Goodnight, Maddi," he says, his smirk still present. "Tell your mother I say hello."

I want to shake my fists in the air. How can one person give you so much and yet so little in one tiny conversation? But instead, I glare at him and get out of his car. At the very least, Liv didn't win that bet.

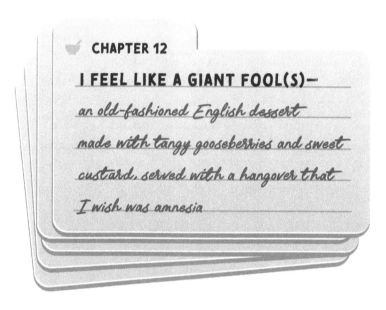

## CHAPTER 12

### I FEEL LIKE A GIANT FOOL(S)—

*an old-fashioned English dessert made with tangy gooseberries and sweet custard, served with a hangover that I wish was amnesia*

Ow. Fucking ow.

My head feels like it's one of those tin cans strapped to the back of a wedding car. My body is pulsing with the faint thumping of my dead heart and my torso is made of stomach acid. The extra time I gave myself this morning to beat Wilder to the bakery was pissed away by a sluggishness that can only be matched by a sleeping sloth. And so here I am, sitting in my car outside the bakery wondering if I stand, will I puke? And if I puke, will it be a relief or will I just lie down in it, making an art piece of myself to fulfill the townspeople's expectations? My only solace is that the sun has yet to rise and mock me with its cheery rays of fuck you.

I peer at myself in my rearview mirror, only to discover that I look exactly the way I feel, and then I go about easing myself out of the car like I was nine months pregnant.

I'm never drinking again.

In fact, no one is. I'm burning down the bar. Both of them. Fuck all y'all.

I laugh halfheartedly. But the sudden movement hurts and I immediately return to cursing everyone I know and mostly myself. I make it through the door of the bakery with a distinct lack of elegance. And as I head around the counter and push through to the kitchen, the memory of my last conversation with Wilder hits me with stunning clarity.

"Don't," I say, as he turns around with a knowing look. "I can't."

His eyes smile, but he doesn't breathe a word. He just turns back to his mixing bowl and leaves me to my misery. At my station, or at least the place on the counter where I was baking yesterday, there are two small black capsules and a giant glass of water. My eyes flit to Wilder in surprise, but the motion makes me queasy. I don't bother asking him what it is; I just shove the vitamin-looking things in my face and down the water.

*Jake holds my hand as we walk down the row of cars lining either side of Matt Mazzeo's private dirt road. Matt lives in one of those big old farmhouses (that his dads transformed to have a gorgeous beachy interior) on the edge of town, tucked away behind a mess of trees that act as natural soundproofing for his parties.*

*Jake opens Matt's front door for me, heat and music spilling out into the cool air. I lift my chin, pulling Jake in with me and wrapping my arm around his waist, replicating a shadow of the closeness we shared earlier, pleasantly surprised by how easy it all is. It's not that I expected it to be awkward; it's just that I thought it would be a bigger deal, weighty the way it had been with Wilder. But then again, Wilder and I only had sex twice. We didn't rush, we were careful, and we made it mean something. Only that was absolute bullshit; it meant exactly nothing, as evidenced by him breaking up with me a couple of weeks later.*

"Beer?" Jake asks, smiling down at me with his arm around my shoulders.

"You read my mind."

He heads for the kitchen, and I pick my way through the living room, saying hellos and politely declining when Jenna waves me over to join her group on the dance floor. And for a flash of a moment, I miss Liv immensely. She was barely home this summer. Not that I can blame her for going to Europe with her Yale friends instead of hanging out with me in tiny Haverberry. But still, it feels like she's a million miles away.

I sigh, some of the thrill of the evening dissipating, replaced by a wisp of anxiety. And that's when I spot Wilder leaning up against a window chatting up some girl who will most likely become girl-friend number four this year, each relationship shorter than the last. For a moment, my anxiety blooms into something more, but I stuff it down, telling myself it's fine and that I'm fine. And as though he could sense I was looking at him, he turns, halting whatever he was saying like he lost his train of thought mid-sentence.

Without breaking eye contact with me, he apologizes to the girl and maybe says he'll be back? It's hard to be sure because I can't hear him over the music.

But when he takes a step in my direction, I pivot so fast that Jake doesn't get a chance to announce his return, and I wind up smacking into his chest with a small yelp.

"Whoa there," he says with a chuckle, rebalancing the cans of beer he's carrying.

"Perfect timing," I say, as I grab a beer and immediately chug it. When I don't come up for air, he looks at me questioningly.

"Everything okay?"

I finish the beer before answering. "Of course, why wouldn't it be?"

Jake's eyeline drifts over my shoulder and back again in a way that makes me think he, too, sees Wilder. Only he's not scowling, *which means Wilder must have changed his mind about coming this way.*

*"Because you just crushed a beer in like ten seconds flat?"*

*I shrug. "I was thirsty."*

*"Apparently," he says, but when I don't immediately offer up an explanation, he doesn't pry.*

*"I'm going to get another. You good?" I ask, and when he nods, I stalk toward the kitchen, determined to get rid of this unsettled feeling any way I can.*

I set to baking, gently and methodically pulling down ingredients and measuring them out. The only sound in the room is the clinking of spoons. Wilder and I work at our separate stations with our backs to each other. And slowly, after three glasses of water and about ten bathroom trips, the pain eases. At which point I deem it safe to speak.

"Thank you," I say, turning away from my mixing bowl and the words feel odd. "I think that stuff actually helped."

"Not a problem," he says facing me. "Charcoal. It works wonders on hangovers."

I reply with fake shock. "Am I to understand that Wilder Buenaventura has actually experienced the uncouth state of being hungover?" Besides the fact that he was an anti-teenager for the most part, (I'm pretty sure he popped out a mature thirtysomething?) not one to revel in bad alcohol mixtures or keg stands, he also seemed to just digest the stuff well. Even if he dared to get drunk, he woke up the next morning like it never happened. Deeply unfair.

"Awful things, really," he agrees. "I believe I swore off drinking the last time."

I grunt. "Yeah, that seems to be a thing . . . a thing that happened to me on my way here. I even considered burning down the town as retribution."

"Well, now I'm doubly glad I brought the charcoal. I quite like this place."

"Of course you do."

He seems surprised by that. "And you don't?"

I shrug, quasi-regretting starting this conversation; in a way, it feels too easy, even my attempt at distancing myself from him feels familiar in a way that makes me nervous. "I'm looking forward to leaving, if that answers your question."

He watches me for a long second. "I remember you once told me that there was no place better. That traveling was great, and having experiences was everything, but that you'd always feel compelled to come back."

Now it's my turn at surprise; that was practically verbatim. "A lot has happened since then."

"Maybe," he says like he's not sure he believes it.

"And I'm not convinced you love it as much as you claim," I continue, even though I know I could fall back into silence and he'd do the same. "Haven't you spent most of your adult life in Europe?"

His eyebrow lifts like he's pleasantly intrigued. "Been keeping tabs on me, DeLuca? Seems like an odd thing to do with someone you dislike so much."

"Don't flatter yourself," I say, but it comes out more like a joking dig than a real one. "My parents gave me updates on you whether I wanted them or not."

"Ah, forced updates," he says with a light chuckle. "I'm certain that you told them you didn't want to hear about me, and they just kept forgetting."

My mouth opens because there is no way to refute that without looking foolish. "And what about you? First a ride home and now charcoal? Better be careful, Wilder, or I'll think you're actually trying to be nice to me."

"And what if I am?" Wilder pauses like something just occurred to him. "Does that mean you or my sister won that bet?"

"Oh God," I blurt out, feeling the acute pain of embarrassment all over again. "That's not . . . I was drunk."

He looks much too happy about my reaction. "So it would seem."

I scowl at him. "You know what? I take back my thank you."

"Noted." But his eyes still smile, and despite my better sense, I feel drawn to them, like the mouse that dove greedily into the pudding and perished.

"At least one of us is amused," I say, trying to regain my footing.

"I would venture to say both of us are."

I stare at him, hesitating to continue this conversation that feels far too close to the banter and rapport we once shared as teens. But even sober, part of me is curious. "Okay, that's it. Are you being friendly because you plan on poisoning my coffee later?"

His laugh is so real that we're both caught off guard by it. "We're working together—long hours and early mornings. I'm just trying to ensure you don't stab me with a cookie cutter when I'm not looking."

I raise an eyebrow. "I've considered it."

"See," he replies, holding his hands out. "As I said."

"Hmmph," is all I say, and after a beat, we both silently agree to go back to our work. But every once in a while, I feel him looking at me, and I catch myself looking at him, too.

*I sway from my perch on Matt's kitchen counter, surrounded by alcohol and a group of girls from my calc class.*

*"Preach," I say with a hiccup as one of them makes an offhanded comment about how we need a fresh pool of guys in this town.*

*Noticing my cup is now empty, I attempt to slide off the counter, a motion which is neither smooth nor easy. I knock over a vodka* bottle, just barely catching it before it rolls off the counter, but lose my footing in the process. Thankfully, someone steadies my arm before I do an imitation of a cartoon character on ice.

"I think we should get you some water," Jake says, who I now realize is the one propping me up.

I grin at him. "I hear that stuff is overrated. Gets in the way of getting drunk."

"Oh, I wouldn't worry about that," he says, looking like he might be concerned. "I think you accomplished that like a champ."

"I did, didn't I?" I say, hiccupping again and also sliding again.

Jake scoops me up then, just picks me up like it's nothing.

I stare accusingly at the floor. "You know, it's really not my fault the floor keeps moving like that."

Jake chuckles, carrying me out into the hallway. "Totally the floor's fault."

I nod as we ascend the staircase, my head bobbing in rhythm with the steps, making me dizzier than I was a second ago. I press my forehead into Jake's shoulder, trying to subdue the queasy feeling.

But as we enter the upstairs hallway, a voice cuts through the noise, "What do you think you're doing?"

I lift my head to find Wilder blocking our path. I try to make out what he means, but I'm at a loss. And I'm vaguely annoyed, but I can't remember the details of why.

"That would be exactly none of your business," Jake replies, a hard edge in his tone.

Wilder doesn't move. "You're not taking her into one of those bedrooms, Jake."

I blink. Huh?

"For fuck's sake, Wilder," Jake growls, now pissed off. "You really think I'd—" he stops short. "She needs to lie down and drink some water. She could barely stand in the kitchen."

I look from one to the other.

"Then you won't mind if I come with you," Wilder says, not backing down.

"I do mind," Jake snaps.

"Well then you'll just have to get over it," Wilder replies, opening the door to what looks like a guest bedroom.

Jake's so tense that I can feel his shoulders lift, but he doesn't continue the argument. He just steps through the door and lays me down on a baby blue bed.

"Ohhhh," I say, finally catching up as my head sinks into the fluffy pillow. I turn to get a proper look at Wilder, who's hardcore frowning. "You were worried?" I say like it makes no sense. "That Jake and I . . ." I laugh, but no one laughs with me. "Well, you can rest easy 'cause you're about four hours too late on that one."

It's as though someone pressed the pause button, freezing everyone in place. Wilder's face drains of color, and he looks so upset you'd think I'd smacked him.

I try to sit up, but the motion overwhelms me and the world sloshes back and forth in my vision. "I think—" I start, the queasy feeling returning tenfold. And suddenly I'm moving, tripping my way toward the bathroom. Someone helps me. Two someones? I don't know.

## CHAPTER 13

### CAUGHT RED-HANDED

### VELVET CUPCAKES—

*stuffed with gooey chocolate and topped with cream cheese frosting that is sure to make you feel guilty*

> Liv: Do you admit that I won that
> bet or what?

I smile, plucking my phone off the couch next to me and giving my laptop a rest from job hunting in LA.

> Me: Not even a little.

> Liv: Can you feel me rolling my eyes,
> cause I am. He practically slapped
> Jake in the face with his glove, ready
> to duel over giving you a ride home.

I laugh, causing Spence to look up from his laptop, where he's busy with nine-year-old game things I'll never fully grasp. But when he sees I'm looking at my phone, he loses interest.

Me: He gave me a ride home
because you told him to . . . not
exactly chivalry.

Liv: Hey now. I merely mentioned you
might need one. Complete innocence
on my part.

Me: Besides, giving someone a
ride and caring about them are
two totally different things.

I feel weird the instant I send it. Debating this while sober feels off-putting and a little reckless. So I add . . .

Me: Not that any of this matters
one way or the other.

Liv: Right, DeLuca, right.

I frown at that. But prolonging this topic is only going to make it look like I'm in denial. So I switch gears.

Me: Gonna get you that will by
the way.

Speaking of which, I look around the room, realizing my mother is in the kitchen fixing her after-dinner tea, leaving me a rare moment of opportunity. If I'm fast, I can handle this now. I fold up my laptop where a spreadsheet of my pitiful finances mocks me, making this decision about staying or leaving all the more pressing and difficult. So like a thief in the night, I speed down the hall into the dining room, my socks sliding on the polished wood. It's not that I want to sneak around, but it's just easier if no one sees me.

I gently ease open the drawer, looking up once to confirm that I'm alone, my cell phone poised to take a quick picture of the addendum. Five seconds and I'll be done. Only it's not where I left it. It's no longer conveniently lying on top of the drawer, unfolded and easily accessible.

Mother-effer.

I put my phone down and rifle through the documents, flipping through receipts and peering into envelopes, but come up short. It's simply not here.

"Looking for something?" my mother asks, appearing in the doorway holding a teacup on a saucer like a silent ninja granny.

I startle, my head whipping up. The truth is too obvious for me to pretend away. "Did you move Dad's will by any chance?" The drawer rattles as I push it close.

"I did," she says, glancing at my phone, and before I can think not to, I shove it guiltily in my back pocket.

"Where did you put it?" I ask, the guilt now seeping into my tone like an emergency flare pointing to my ineptitude. What is WRONG with me?

"Our copy is in the lockbox in my bedroom," she says, a lockbox I've never had the code for. Doesn't matter that I'm her closest relative and only child, I'd have to melt the thing open with a blowtorch if there were an emergency.

"Our copy?" I say, and then realize she must mean that the duplicate is with Wilder, which of course makes sense. "Can I see it?"

"Is there something in question?" she asks, putting me on the spot.

"I just wanted to read the rules again, the ownership rules."

She stirs her tea and places the small spoon on the saucer

with a clink. "Forty hours a week of required work and involvement in daily operations," she says, instead of giving me the paper. Liv's warning plays in my thoughts. If I tell my mom the whole truth and Liv winds up declaring the will ironclad, then I'll have caused a rift for jack all nothing. And if Liv does find something, well, that's a whole different problem.

"Was there something else?" my mom asks.

I stare at her, aware that if I push this, she very well might realize what I'm up to. I sigh. "I guess not," I say, resolving myself to an equally shitty plan B.

"Good," my mother says, visibly relaxing. "Oh, and don't forget, we have the Buenaventura dinner tomorrow night."

I shrink a little, not just because it sounds horrific, but because I actually did forget, or maybe chose to block it out. But I know all too well there's no backing out at this point.

*"Madeline DeLuca, it's nearly noon," my mother says aghast as she enters my dark bedroom and steps over the trail of the clothes.*

*"It's Saturday," I croak in response, even though I've been up for hours feeling rotten. I vaguely remember drinking buttloads of water last night, and I woke up with two Advil on my bedside table, which I downed. Even so, I'm pretty sure I'm dying.*

*She moves to my window, pulling back my blackout curtains. "There," she exclaims as I squint. "Now get up."*

*I run my hand over my face. "Would it be okay if—"*

*"No, it would not," my mom replies, preemptively squashing my plans to weasel out of Mrs. Templeton's luncheon. "And for heaven's sake, take a shower. It smells like . . ."*

*She trails off and my eyebrows knit together as she moves toward me. "What are you doing?" I protest lamely as she approaches my bed. Her eyes widen. "My God, you smell like a back-alley distillery!"*

*I pop up into a sitting position, now on high alert. "Whatever you're thinking—"*

"What I'm thinking is that you were with that boy *again*," she says like I did it specifically to upset her.

"You mean Jake . . . my boyfriend?"

"He has been nothing but trouble since the day you met him."

"I met him in kindergarten."

A warning flashes in her eyes and I close my mouth. "I'd suggest you pump the brakes, Madeline. Right now. With all of it," she gestures broadly. "Or you'll find yourself grounded."

I want to point out that neither she nor Dad waited up for me or bothered to check on me when I got back, so she couldn't be that concerned, but I know that'll only make her angrier.

Instead, I just say, "Sorry."

"I expect you downstairs and dressed at exactly one o'clock," she says and smooths her blouse. She takes a good look at me like there's something more she would say but decides against it. Instead, she leaves, closing the door quietly behind her.

I push back my covers, swinging my legs onto the floor and briefly pressing my fingers into my temples. I slowly plod up to my vanity, getting a look at myself in the mirror and wincing. I look like an elderly lapdog that fell asleep against a pillow and has her face fur pushed up on one side. I'm about to drag my sorry self into the bathroom when I spot the picture of me and Wilder on my vanity, which is usually parallel with the one of me and my dad but has moved six or so inches out of its normal position.

Suddenly, the memory of getting home last night hits me so hard that I stagger.

It comes in pieces. Wilder and Jake arguing about Jake's sobriety . . . flashes of driving home in the back of Wilder's Mercedes—me talking a mile a minute, Jake and Wilder doing the exact opposite, and eventually Wilder following Jake and me up to my door.

"Get back in your car, man," Jake growls.

"I'm taking her inside," Wilder replies with so much confidence *that even Jake pauses. "There's no way she's making it up those stairs by herself without waking her parents."*

*Jake laughs, but it's an angry laugh. "You know she's not taking you back, right? That you thoroughly screwed yourself on that front."*

*I nod along. That sounds like something I agree with.*

*"Which is the difference between you and me," Wilder fires back. "Doing something because it's right, not because of what I'll get in return."*

*"You know what, Wilder, you go right ahead and take her in. Let her parents find you dragging their drunk daughter home and see how that goes," Jake says like he hopes Wilder trips down the stairs on his pretty face.*

*I remember being confused then, or annoyed at Jake? Or Wilder? Both of them? I remember Wilder shushing me as we crept through the house and having the good sense to listen to him. And I remember announcing that I wasn't drunk anymore as I proceeded to haphazardly remove pieces of my clothing and carve a zigzag path to my bed.*

*Wilder turned around then, giving me privacy as I undressed and slid under my comforter. He waited by my vanity . . . and what? Picked up this picture?*

*I throw an accusatory glance at my nightstand where I found the two Advil and the glass of water this morning. I don't need him taking care of me! I snatch up the picture frame from my vanity, loosening the back latches. I'm about to yank the picture out and throw it in the trash, the one Liv took of us at the beach when we first started dating, but I hesitate.*

*A small growl escapes my lips, but I can't actually muster the resolve. And so, I relatch the picture and place it face down, like maybe if I just don't look at it then it will cease to exist, which I realize, has been my strategy for everything lately.*

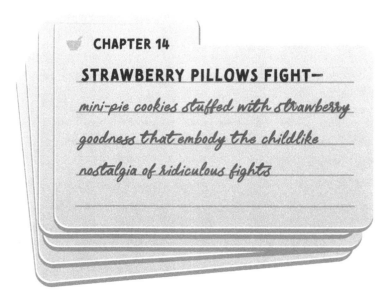

## CHAPTER 14

### STRAWBERRY PILLOWS FIGHT—

*mini-pie cookies stuffed with strawberry goodness that embody the childlike nostalgia of ridiculous fights*

Wilder isn't at the bakery when I show up in the morning. Albert is, which is disappointing because I just spent half an hour figuring out how I was going to breach the conversation about looking at Wilder's copy of the will (plan B as it were). I realize it's no use being frustrated when I can just ask Wilder tomorrow, but I was really hoping to have Liv take a look at it before we all have dinner at their parents' house tonight. Because if there's a way out, then I can just ignore whatever frustrations arise. And if there isn't . . . well then, I don't know what, yank the tablecloth as hard as I can and make a run for it amid the chaos?

The morning passes slowly, as I count down the hours until I can text Liv without waking her up. I repeatedly reprimand myself for not being firmer with Mom yesterday and just insisting on seeing the will. If I had done it then, I realize, it wouldn't have been a disaster, but bringing it up a second time is out of the question. She'll call me out, and I'll fold under her cold scrutinizing glare.

Me: You up?

Two and a half hours later I get a response.

Liv: Sorry. Slammed today with
meetings. Friday before the holidays,
ya know? Trying to be done in time
for dinner.

Me: Speaking of dinner . . .

Liv: You're going to wear your Grinch
onesie and make me the happiest
woman alive?

Me: Lol. I was thinking something
more like hiding under your dining
room table.

But I don't get a response for another hour.

Liv: Ugh. Sorry again! Truth be told,
I'm not looking forward to this, either.

I ask her why, but either she gets caught up at work or she somehow misses it, because by the time Jake arrives (half an hour late) to pick up Spence, I still don't have a response. My mother's miffed, claiming Spence should come with us, but I'm not explaining in front of Spence how I don't want him there for a long dinner with hostiles. I'd just sweat through the whole thing, worrying Wilder's parents might say something about me in front of him that would force me to throw cutlery at them. Or worse yet, bring up the possibility of us staying in Haverberry. I know I should have spoken to Spence about it already, but I'd love a solid-ish plan in place first. Once Liv goes over the will and I've heard from a few of the places I applied to, I'll know what my options are, and it'll make it easier to communicate.

But even though I don't voice my objections, Mom still says, "You always think everything is going to be some big drama. It's just dinner, Madeline."

To which I sigh, and we continue our dance of pretending away the things neither of us wants to look at. But half an hour into socializing in the Buenaventura living room sipping wine, I concede that Mom was right. It's just the Buenaventuras giving a lively rendition of their latest trip to South America interspersed with a discussion of international markets. I can participate by simply nodding my head and saying, "Of course. Yes. And that sounds lovely." Even Mrs. Buenaventura, after a quasi-stiff hello, seems to have lightened up.

Wilder, however, is nowhere to be seen, his parents claiming he had some unexpected obligation, which I'm now really wondering about—he's everywhere I go for a week straight and then I come to his parents' house and he's not here?

Liv joins us an hour late, moments after we sit down at the dinner table.

"Shit, sorry guys," she says, taking the seat across from my mom like she's been moving a hundred miles an hour and just screeched to a stop. "Work was a beast today."

"Really, must you use that language, Olivia?" Mrs. Buenaventura says in her British accent, which is a phrase she has been uttering in repetition since Liv turned eighteen and declared that if she could legally fight in a war, she could damn well motherfucking curse.

"Liv's grown quite the burgeoning company these past few

years, Madeline," Mr. Buenaventura says with pride. "Has she told you about it?"

"It's all very interesting," my mother agrees, dabbing her mouth with her napkin.

Liv winks at me, pouring herself a glass of wine. "I'm very successful and important," she says, which of course is a joke, but has her mom sighing all the same.

"I wouldn't have phrased it quite so bluntly," Mr. Buenaventura says with a light laugh in his Argentinian accent. "But yes, my daughter is a firecracker."

Liv chuckles. "Truth is, it's a lot of work, half of which is absolutely tedious. It's also not expanding quite as fast as I'd like. But I enjoy it, especially the creative aspects."

"I get that," I say. "And even if it's not expanding as fast as you'd like, your reach is great. I constantly see ads for your beauty products in LA."

Liv smiles, but there's something about it that seems conflicted. Only I don't have time to wonder why because the front door closes.

Mrs. Buenaventura leans toward my mom, briefly placing her hand on her arm. "My children enjoy seeing how close they can cut it for dinner. I believe they've made a game out of giving me ulcers."

Wilder walks into the room and gives his mom a fast kiss on the cheek. For a moment the image of him takes me by surprise, the ease with which he moves through a room, the way he's stately but not stuffy, and his smile that somehow makes his jaw more angled and his eyes brighten. Despite the fact that I have no love for Wilder, he really is something to look at.

"Mrs. DeLuca, Maddi," he says nodding his head at us, his smile still present. "It's nice to see you both."

My mother puts down her wine glass. "I'm just glad we were able to arrange this. It's been too long since we were all together."

I glance at her, wondering if the wine is making her fuzzy. She's not remotely the sentimental type.

Wilder takes the seat across from mine. "Apologies if I've delayed your meal."

"Not a problem, darling," Wilder's mother says, her voice like honey. "Anniversaries are important. We all understand. I do wish you would have brought Kate with you, though."

My stomach does a fast drop and I divert my eyes from Wilder. His big pressing obligation was his anniversary with Kate? Not that I care. I don't. I mean, I think I don't.

"I'm glad you didn't bring her," Liv says under her breath, clearly for her brother's benefit.

Wilder's eyebrow shoots up and he gives his sister a knowing look. "So Liv, where's your girlfriend tonight? How come you haven't brought her home for everyone to meet?"

"Yes," Mr. Buenaventura agrees. "Why do you keep her from us?"

Liv scowls at Wilder but answers her father. "I'm heading to the city later tonight, Dad," she explains. "She has a shoot tomorrow or I would have brought her."

Wilder's smirk appears like he's calling bullshit. "Then you'll bring her to our Christmas Eve party?"

"What a good idea," her dad agrees.

I can tell by the look on Liv's face that's never going to happen in a million years. But it's kind of sweet how much her parents want to be involved in her dating life, especially because, despite Liv's super-independent, bad-boy persona, she seems to be in an actual relationship.

"Think of your brother," Mrs. Buenaventura says enthusiastically. "He'll be off to Europe again soon enough. We must soak in this time together."

Wait, he's doing what now?

All eyes turn toward Mrs. Buenaventura.

"Mom," Wilder starts, but my mother interjects.

"I didn't realize you were returning to Europe, Wilder," my mom says with surprise.

"Neither did I," I echo and immediately feel a little embarrassed. Why should I care?

"Oh, yes," Mr. Buenaventura answers for him. "He's going to take over the London branch of my company."

My fork freezes halfway to my mouth. I don't know why I'm shocked; it makes sense Wilder would work for his family. But for some reason, I just never pictured him in real estate development.

"Really? I had no idea," my mom says. "You never mentioned it, Hannah."

Mrs. Buenaventura nods. "I wasn't actually sure we could convince him, but then he came back here a year and a half ago and well . . ."

"I'm here for another year at the very least," Wilder tells my mother, obviously trying to reassure her about the bakery without actually saying the words.

But his mother isn't finished. "A year that is certain to be very busy. He'll be sitting on the board here to train under his father."

Holy shit. So *this* is the agreement Wilder made that he said he'd have a hard time getting out of? I manage to shove my salad in my mouth, not experiencing relief the way I imagined—shouldn't I be beaming with delight that there's no way Wilder will be able to maintain full-time at the bakery? So then why do I have this pit in my stomach?

Mr. Buenaventura looks from his wife to my mom, clearly aware of the tension that has settled over the table. "I hope this doesn't put you out in any way, Eleanor. I know my son has been helping you at the bakery quite a bit. If it does, I can always have my recruiter find you a replacement."

"Thank you, Francesco," my mother says, clearly deflated but too polite to say so. "I'll just need a moment to think about it."

And surprisingly, I find myself worrying about my mom, which makes no sense whatsoever. Shouldn't I be happy that it's Wilder's parents who are pulling the plug on this insanity instead of me? Why aren't I happy?

When I glance across the table, I find Liv looking at me, like she's trying to tell me something telepathically.

"That's a great idea, Francesco," Mrs. Buenaventura says like it's all settled. "And such good luck that Madeline has moved back just in time to fill in."

I open my mouth to say that I haven't moved back but close it again. My mother definitely doesn't need that right now.

Wilder's jaw is tense, and his mouth is set in a hard line. "I intend to stay on full-time at the bakery," he says to his parents, sending a ripple of unease through the dinner table.

"You can always start a bakery later if you wish," his mother says like she's only being reasonable. "Oh, do forgive us, Eleanor, I so didn't intend for this to be a topic at dinner."

Mr. Buenaventura chews his food with his eyebrows pushed together. Meanwhile, Liv's eyes bounce from one person to the next like she's watching a tense Ping-Pong match. She's also the only person still committed to eating her salad.

Wilder sighs. "No, Mom, I asked you not to bring this up at dinner. But you clearly had no intention of respecting that."

Liv chokes on her food and chases it with wine. She nods at me like *see what I mean about our bet?*

I, however, look away, not willing to admit Wilder's words mean what she thinks they mean. Although I'd be lying if I said I wasn't a little impressed by his determination.

His mom appears flustered. And this time it's Mr. Buenaventura who steps in to answer. "Your mother is attempting to clear the air, especially since others are affected by your choices. You should understand this," he says it like it's the family code to air disagreements, which I suppose it is.

"If you try to do both, Wilder," his mother says, "everyone will lose. There simply isn't enough of you to go around."

"You don't want me to choose, Mother; you won't like my answer," he says calmly.

My eyes double. Now *that* I did not expect.

"So, you're just going to betray your father? Are you trying to break his heart?" she says, taking the conversation to a whole new level.

"I fear we've intruded on a personal conversation," my mom says, attempting to dispel the tension, but it has absolutely no effect.

Part of me wants to run for the door, but the other part cannot look away.

"It's hardly a betrayal if I do both," Wilder says, not taking his mother's emotional bait.

"Stubborn," his mom says like an accusation. "Stubborn and willful." Then she turns to my mom. "Eleanor, please tell my son he can no longer work for you."

I bristle, defensive of my mother and annoyed that Mrs. Buenaventura's putting her on the spot. "Mom can't tell him that because Wilder's not working for her. He owns half the bakery, and the decision is his." I don't know why I say it, why I'm getting involved at all.

Wilder looks at me then, clearly shocked. Liv suppresses a laugh into her wine glass. Wilder's mother, however, shoots me a death glare.

My mom opens her mouth, but this time Wilder answers.

"Maddi's correct. As much as Mrs. DeLuca may agree with you as your friend, she has no power in this situation."

The gratitude I feel toward Wilder for removing my mom from the line of fire catches me by surprise.

Mr. Buenaventura sighs like this conversation is taking a toll on him. "I think it best we shelve this for now. Unless we all want our food to get cold and our evening to spoil."

Mrs. Buenaventura hesitates, then resigns with a sigh. "I suppose you're right, Francesco." She shifts her gaze to my mother. "Again, I do apologize for all of this."

"No need to apologize," my mother says, and even though she's witnessed many Buenaventura spats, her tone tells me this one is different.

Mrs. Buenaventura's smile reappears. "Right . . . now who needs more wine?"

And just like that, the conversation shifts back to its usual tales of Buenaventura adventures. Wilder excuses himself right after dinner and Liv wags her eyebrows at me and sends me a text that reads, *I WON*. While I want to tell her she's categorically wrong, Wilder's behavior tonight threw me, made me see his commitment to the bakery in a whole new light, and I'd be lying if I said I knew what to make of it.

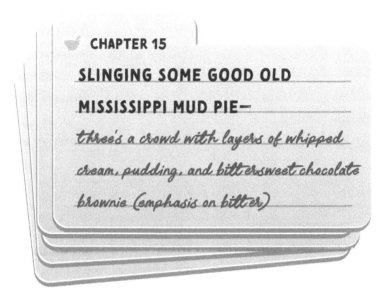

## CHAPTER 15

## SLINGING SOME GOOD OLD
## MISSISSIPPI MUD PIE—
*three's a crowd with layers of whipped cream, pudding, and bittersweet chocolate brownie (emphasis on bitter)*

All morning I've been replaying last night's events. After dinner, I tried to bring up the bakery with Mom to make sure she was okay, but all she said was, "I understand why they would want him to work for the family company." And since that was dangerously close to striking at my own guilt, I let the conversation go.

But Wilder? What the heck does he get out of it? I turn around, for what feels like the twentieth time, to stare at his back while he kneads dough. And the worst part is that I'm looking at him a little differently, less death wish, more curiosity.

"You might feel better if you said whatever's bothering you," Wilder says, and even though he doesn't turn around, I snap my head back to my peanut butter and jelly mousse cupcakes, pretending I wasn't just staring at him.

"Who said anything's bothering me?" I reply, but my voice winds up sounding like an animated kid's narrator.

"I've lost count," he says, and I can hear his smile, "but

you've sighed enough this morning to give a heartbroken high schooler some serious competition."

My eyes widen. "I have not," I say, which only makes me sound more immature.

He glances over his shoulder. "The offer still stands, if you'd like to confide in me."

He sounds so genuine that I hesitate, realizing part of me wants to do just that. I frown.

"Why did you say all that stuff last night about the bakery?" I ask, hoping he can make sense of it for me.

He stops kneading his dough, turning in my direction like he's prepared to give this his full attention.

"I just don't get it," I continue. "You told your family you would work with them. So then why are you here?"

"Because I want to be." He looks so sure of himself that I only get more confused. "Do you remember when we were kids and we used to have bake-offs here every Sunday?" he asks like there's any chance I forgot. "I've traveled quite a bit since then, studied with world-renowned pastry chefs, I even started a bakery in London, but I gave it up."

"Why?" I ask, my curiosity piqued.

"Because," he says, and pauses like he's remembering something, "none of it was this place."

For a moment, the silence that hangs between us is overwhelming. I don't know why, but I didn't expect Wilder to answer with such sincerity. It throws me, and in a flash of sentimental stupidity, I feel that same inexplicable pull toward him I used to as a teenager.

*I plod across the grassy square toward the bakery, my pompomed hat drawn tight over my ears and my hands shoved deep into my coat pockets. Jake tries to hold my hand, but I tell him my fingers are too cold, which is mostly true.*

"Almost time for the holiday market. You excited?" he asks, his cheeks lifted in a smile.

I attempt to smile back, but it feels underwhelming. "I'm basically the market's best customer."

He chuckles and we're about to cross the street to the bakery when Jake slips his arm around my waist. "Well, get ready then, because two Sundays from now I'm buying you the biggest fried dough Haverberry has ever seen." He pulls me in for a kiss.

Before I can consider it, I turn my cheek to him.

He releases me from the embrace, his smile disappearing. "Did I do something I don't know about?"

"What? No," I say, embarrassed I rejected him, and not even sure why. I glance toward the bakery as an excuse like Mrs. Varma or my dad might see us through the window.

"Okay," he says, "then how about we go someplace where I can kiss you. Let's go to the diner."

I scrunch up my nose. "The diner has terrible hot chocolate . . . like the worst."

He nods like he knew I was going to lodge that objection. "Then let's go to the bakery. We'll get our hot chocolates to go and take them down to the beach."

I shake my head. "Too cold."

He frowns. "Would you rather I dropped you at home?"

"Not at all. Why would you ask that?"

"You just seem . . . I don't know . . . not too stoked to be hanging out with me?"

I break eye contact. "Everything's fine."

He gives me a look like come on. "Is this because of the other night?"

My heart pounds. "No."

"Because if you weren't ready—"

"I was ready." But even as I say the words, my stomach knots *up. And suddenly I'm angry at myself. Why am I making things weird? Not to mention that just last week I was actually proud of myself for leaning into something new, finally moving on and doing something for me.*

*I scratch my forehead under the edge of my hat. "I don't know. Maybe I wasn't ready."*

*Jake exhales. "I get it. We don't have to rush."*

*"Thanks," I say, but somehow, I don't feel any better.*

*And by the way he's staring at me, he knows it. "Just tell me what to do here. You know I'm not great at all the emotional stuff."*

*"I don't know," I admit. "I'm just . . ." I bring my hands up and drop them again. "I'm confused, ya know?"*

*His eyebrows push together. "Confused in general, or confused about me?"*

*"In general," I say, and for a brief second, I consider telling him the uncomfortable truth that when I lost Wilder, I lost a piece of myself, and I never really found it again. And that I feel the hole acutely—a constant ache that shifts the moment I try to locate it, like an electron in light. It's always there with me, following me like my shadow, showing back up just when I think it's finally disappeared.*

*But I can't say those things, so instead, I slip my hand into his. "You know what? How about we drive over to Middleton and eat Mexican food until we pop?"*

*"I'm so in," he says, his smile finally returning.*

*And this time when he kisses me, I kiss him back, shoving my doubts into the back of my mind, trying to ignore the prickling sensation of nervous energy that tells me something is still wrong. But the feeling doesn't go away. It seeps out around the edges, spilling into my body language and turning my reasons into excuses. I find myself doing bizarre things like ducking around the corner when I spot him in the hall or intentionally lagging behind in class so I*

*don't cross paths with him. And three weeks later, for reasons nei-*
*ther of us understand, I break up with him.*

I stare at Wilder, aware that I should end this conversation.
I've spent a lot of years closing Wilder off in my mind, locking
him in a drawer with my old love letters. But instead, I just stare
at him, waiting for him to finish his thought.

"It's actually funny," he says, laughing at himself, "how
much time I've invested in trying to recreate the feeling I had
when I was baking here."

*Don't, Maddi. Keep it business only*—"Then why did you
stay in Europe for so long?"

He sighs. "Denial? Avoidance? Bettering myself? Take your
pick."

I break eye contact, his answer veering too close to my own
truth.

"And you?" he asks. "What kept you away?"

"I just didn't want to be here," I say, adopting the shrugging act a beat too late.

He watches me, reading my expressions the way he used to.
"You always loved this town."

"I changed my mind."

"I don't believe that."

We stare at each other, neither of us conceding, my heart
smacking against my rib cage uncomfortably.

"What are you doing, Wilder?" I ask.

"I'm not sure I understand the question."

"Right now, I mean, why are you talking about these things?"

He waits a beat like he's trying to figure out his delivery.
"I thought it might be easier working here if we attempted to
be friends."

I almost laugh, except it's decidedly unfunny. "Friends?"

"Yes," he says with confidence. "I'd really like it if we were."

I blink at him. And for a split second, my body betrays me and delights in the idea. I scowl at us both. "I'll think about it."

His smile is so genuine that I deeply regret starting this conversation.

"Fair enough," he says, far too happy about it.

But before I can reply, his phone rings. He stares at it a moment. "Hello?" he says, and turns away from our conversation. After a handful of yesses and nos, he says, "I don't really think—" but the voice on the other end cuts him off, and as it gets louder, it sounds female.

I don't find out who it is because he leaves the kitchen. Which makes me wonder if it's his mom. Are they fighting about the bakery? And while I don't really care if Wilder fights with his parents, I do worry about what it might mean for my mom. Could this possibly interfere with her friendship with the Buenaventuras? I'd hate to see that happen, especially now that she's lost my dad.

I glance through the round window in the kitchen door and catch a glimpse of Wilder frowning. But he quickly moves out of view and so I return to my frosting. When he comes in ten minutes later, he doesn't say a word and even though I want to ask, I don't—it's none of my business after all.

The rest of the morning passes quietly, each of us consumed with our tasks. I almost bring up Dad's will a dozen times, but every time I'm about to, I feel crappy that I'm trying to get out of the agreement he's fighting so hard to keep. I'm working up to it again as I take off my apron, only before I get the words out, Wilder speaks.

"Are you in a rush?" he asks.

I consider telling him yes, but instead, I shake my head.

He smiles. "Glad to hear it because I'd really like to show you something."

"What kind of something?"

"The kind I think you'll like."

I hesitate, about to say *no* simply because he's being so vague, but reconsider—it might give me an opportunity to have the will conversation. "Yeah, okay."

His smile lights up his face and he takes off his apron, trading it for his coat.

"Wait, where is this thing?" I say, realizing it's not as simple as I supposed it to be.

"In town," he replies, and I reflexively reject the idea. His gaze shifts to amusement. "Unless walking a couple of blocks with me makes you nervous?"

I roll my eyes. "You don't scare me, Wilder."

His mouth pulls up a little farther. "Funny, because you scare me."

My eyes flit to his, and for just a second, I find myself enjoying the way he's looking at me. He doesn't wait for my response, he just pushes the door open for me. We say a quick goodbye to Albert in the front of the bakery, and as I get my fingers in my soft white gloves, we walk outside.

The sun is out, the snow is glittering across the square, and the sidewalks are packed with enthusiastic holiday shoppers. There's an electricity to the air—the first day of Hanukkah and the Saturday before Christmas—a giddy feeling that magic might be real, and the possibilities are endless.

I breathe in deeply, the scent of fresh snow filling my lungs, a little woodsy like the damp bark of a pine forest and slightly metallic like the frost that forms on the outside of a drink shaker.

I glance at Wilder as we weave our way around the square and I'm surprised to find him watching me. "What?" I say, a twinge embarrassed by the grin I know is on my face.

"Nothing . . . I just forgot how much you love winter."

"Nobody loves winter, Wilder," I correct him, but I can't keep the happiness out of my voice. "I live in perpetual summer in LA . . . it's ideal."

"Uh-huh," he says, not buying it for a second. "You once woke me up at 2:00 a.m. and dragged me outside in my pajamas because it was snowing. And not even the first snow of the year, it was at least the third."

"True," I say, not losing my grin, "but only because the pond in your backyard was finally frozen and I wanted to ice-skate on it."

He lets out a quiet laugh and shakes his head, and I find myself laughing with him.

Only my laugh gets cut short as we round the corner toward the park. It suddenly occurs to me where we're going. "The thing you want to show me is in the holiday market?" I say, my breath coming up short as the memories of that place wash over me.

His gaze turns questioning. "Is that a bad thing?"

"Oh, no, I mean, that's fine," I say, trying to cover my reaction, not wanting to explain what I'm feeling or why.

"You sure?" he asks again because unlike most people, Wilder never let anything go. He called me out on even the stupidest of white lies, pressed me when it was clear I was shutting down and folding in on myself. And for a long time, I relied on him for that, to draw me out and talk away whatever was bothering me. It was one of the things I missed most about him when things fell apart; I hated being alone in my head with no one to scare away the bad.

And in a moment of reckless honesty, I say, "The holiday market just has . . . a lot of memories."

His expression turns thoughtful. "I understand," he says in a way that makes me think he really does; he knew my father better than almost anyone. "If you want—"

"No, it's fine," I say, now feeling a little silly, and walking forward once more. "I want to go." And as I say the words, I realize they're true. I've been here a week and a half, and I've been so worried about what people might say or do that I haven't gone to the one place I love the most. And as we cross through the wrought iron archway onto the snow-laden green bustling with stalls, I lift my chin.

Fried dough and warm chocolate scent the air, making my stomach rumble and my mouth water. The market is abuzz with people and laughter and there is so much wintry goodness that I fear my heart might actually explode.

"Follow me," Wilder says, as he leads me past the spiced apple cider booth and through the crowd.

I look everywhere at once, trying to soak it all in and store it away like a pretty dream for later. But as Wilder slows, I look ahead and come to a stop so fast that I actually hear brakes screeching in my head.

There, in front of me is the Nothing Batter Bakery booth, and for once in my life, I don't know what to say. I move forward, slowly, carefully, like I might blink and find out it's just an illusion, an alluring memory from my childhood that's come to haunt me with its joy.

My gaze flits along the edge of the booth wound with sprigs of berries, branches of pine, and fairy lights up to the handmade fabric awning my mother custom ordered in Paris when I was seven. There are bags of peppermint bark tied with bows, sweet ricotta filled zeppole dusted with powdered sugar, and cannoli decorated with snowflake sprinkles—all the things Dad and I used to make.

Wilder says something to Jenna, who's currently manning the booth dressed like a sexy elf, while I attempt to remember how to breathe.

"My dad—" I say, and stop, taken by surprise by the flood of emotion. "He would have loved this."

Wilder smiles a slow, sad smile. "He always talked about starting the booth again when you came home, and I just thought . . ." Now he stops, realizing what he implied. "I'm sorry, I shouldn't have said—"

"No," I say, a little too firmly, my eyes watering of their own accord. "I know it's my fault he discontinued the booth. I know—" I swallow, trying to regain control of the wobble that is seeping into my voice.

Wilder shakes his head. "It's not your fault, Maddi. You have every right to live your own life."

I look away. While it's a nice thing to say, it's only words. It can't undo what's done. "This was really thoughtful, Wilder. And I'm sure it was no easy task getting a booth on such short notice."

He smiles. "You're telling me. I practically promised the market committee my firstborn child to convince them to give it to me for the day. Albert and I spent all of yesterday and most of last night baking to pull it off."

My eyes widen. The big mysterious obligation Wilder had yesterday was *the booth*? But I thought his parents said it was his anniversary with Kate?

"Here ya go!" Jenna says with an extra dash of pep and a big wink as she hands me a small plate. On it is a steaming hot lava cake drizzled with what smells like a mulled wine reduction—my favorite dessert since always and one the booth has never carried before.

"No way!" I say in utter disbelief.

He grins. "Thanks, Jenna."

"Yes, thank you. Seriously," I parrot.

"Not a prob," she says before she returns to the line of customers.

I stare gluttonously at my dessert, not hesitating to scoop up a bite of the deliciousness.

"What do you think?" he asks.

I groan. "Okay fine, you keep these beauties coming and maaaybe we can be friends."

He laughs. "You should grab an extra one for Spence."

I perk up at the sound of his name. "Holy shit. Spence is going to love this booth. We have to go—" I stop, realizing that I was just including Wilder in my life like that were normal.

"Pick him up?" Wilder asks. "I think that's a great idea."

I give him the side-eye. "You do?"

"Yes, I do. You and I went mad over this place when we were nine. And I'd really like the chance to meet him properly."

I don't know whether it's Wilder's kindness or being drunk on chocolate, but it actually sounds fun. "Okay, fuck it, let's go get—" Only I don't finish my sentence because as we turn around, Kate's standing behind us in her camel peacoat and beret, looking just shy of livid.

"Really?" she says to Wilder, readjusting her bag on her shoulder. "*This* is what you had to do this afternoon that was so important you canceled our plans?" She flicks her hand in my direction and I flinch.

Wilder sighs like he's exhausted. "Kate, I really don't think—"

"Don't you dare try to diminish this," Kate snaps, her voice raising and catching the attention of the people around us. "We've been dating for a *year*; I know you, Wilder. Don't think I didn't just see the way you were looking at Maddi!"

Oh shit. No, no, no. There is a very long list of reasons that cannot be true. I take a step back, the crowd around us now definitely listening to Kate's tirade.

Wilder's face has gone stone-cold, calm in a way only he

can muster. "I'm not certain what you think you saw, but I'm also not having this discussion with you here. This bakery is my business and whether you like it or not, Maddi is my business partner."

"I'm just gonna—" I start to say I'm leaving, but Kate steamrolls right over me with an angry laugh.

"Business? You call some small-town nothing bakery your *business*? Your family owns half the town, Wilder. You're a *Buenaventura*. Don't pretend this matters. Call it what it is—dumping way too much energy into trying to fuck the one girl who got away. Watch out, Maddi, because as soon as he gets what he wants, he'll move on. Oh wait, you already know that, don't you?"

The blood drains from my cheeks and I open my mouth to tell her she can go screw herself, but I don't. Because I'm not standing in the middle of the holiday market fighting over Wilder. I refuse. So, I walk away. I walk past them both and into the crowd.

Wilder calls my name, but I don't turn around, all the joy I felt a moment ago trampled by what I always knew to be true, that whatever good this place holds, it holds more shit than it's worth. My only regret is not asking Wilder for the will earlier in the day.

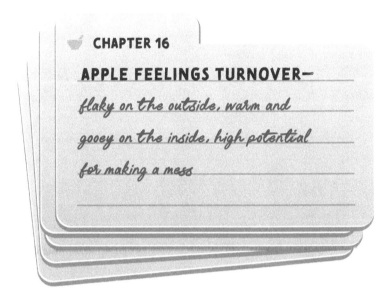

## CHAPTER 16

### APPLE FEELINGS TURNOVER—

*flaky on the outside, warm and*
*gooey on the inside, high potential*
*for making a mess*

My elbows rest on my knees, and my legs hang over the side of my bed. I dig my Christmas llama socks into the rug. But no amount of massaging my temples seems to be easing my stewing. So I stand up, shaking myself out, but the anxious buzzing in my chest will not subside. I just keep hearing Kate's words over and over, like a mantra of my own foolish hopefulness. And the thing is, I don't think I'd have cared so much a day ago. I mean, I'd have been pissed, don't get me wrong, but having her say those things only moments after seeing the bakery booth was like a stake to the heart.

*I know everything changes after a breakup. I mean, I've already been through that ordeal with Wilder. But I just didn't realize how lonely it would be without Jake, how awkward I would feel in my everyday life. School now feels like a place I don't belong. At lunch, Jake sits with some of our friends and Wilder sits with the rest. To Wilder's credit, he offered our old table to me, but I refused it. It'd* only make things worse, framing him as some sort of martyr. So I sit by myself, staring out the window and just waiting for the days to pass until winter break.

Unlike my weekdays, however, my weekends have been full of life. The holiday market is in full swing, and I've been working in our booth with my dad from morning until night. After school, I go by the bakery and help him with the extra baking to restock.

My dad wipes the counter clean around my mess, handing me a package of bags for the peppermint bark that's cooled on the rack. "I notice we're all on our own this year with the booth," he says, like by not saying Wilder's name he can ease me into talking about him.

"Uh, yeah," I say. "I think he's been busy with all his finals and whatnot."

My dad nods, throwing a hand towel over his shoulder. "He came by to see me the other day."

My head whips up from my bowl. "What? Why?"

Dad stands just a few feet down the counter, twisting the lid off the brown sugar container. "He wanted to offer his help, in case we were shorthanded."

"What did you say?" I ask, my words rushed.

He pours the sugar into a bowl that is balanced on a small scale. "I told him you would let him know if we did."

All the air leaves my lungs in a heavy exhale. "Okay good. Thanks," I say, my heart decelerating.

Then in a rare moment of chattiness, my father continues the conversation, something that only really happens here in our bakery, which has some magical power to bring him out of his usual quietude. "I'm not trying to pry, but if you want to talk about it, I'd be happy to listen."

The offer hits me hard. I've often felt these past few weeks that I've been silently screaming into the void and it's as though he just heard my SOS. "Everything's fine—" I say reflexively and stop,

*swallowing my words and the swell of emotion that follows. "Ac-*
*tually . . . everything isn't fine." I put down my spoon, my head*
*hanging over my bowl. I peek in his direction and find that he's*
*come to stand next to me.*

*He places his hand on my shoulder. And even though we're*
*not a huggy family, I turn, wrapping my arms around him. He*
*smells of vanilla and cinnamon, a scent he often trails through our*
*house when he comes home from work, and when he hugs me back,*
*I press my face into his shoulder like an old familiar blanket that*
*has the power to blot out fear.*

*"I lost my best friend," I say into his shirt, my eyes blurring*
*with tears. "The one person who really—" I stop before I say* loved
*me. "And I can't fix it. It's just broken, smashed to bits."*

*"Shhh," he says against my head, his short beard catching in my*
*hair. "He's not lost. He's still there. You'll see. Sometimes it takes*
*people a while to find their way back to one another, especially when*
*they're as close as the two of you. The more you care, the more you*
*hurt. But I can promise you that one day you'll look back on this*
*and realize that it's all okay, that everything worked out for the best."*

*I nod against his chest, wanting to believe him, to bolster myself*
*with the confidence in his voice and the sturdiness of his embrace.*
*We stand like that for a long while, me crying myself out and him*
*shushing away the sadness. It's the first time since I was little that*
*I remember him holding me like this. And for a moment, I think*
*maybe he's right—maybe the people who truly care about you do*
*show up just when you need them.*

My phone buzzes on my bed and I turn around to face
it, fully expecting that it'll be a text from Spence telling me to
come downstairs. But no.

Unknown Number: Hey, Maddi. It's
Wilder.

I instantly look up and around my room like there's a hidden camera and someone's pranking me.

> Wilder: I got your number from Liv. I
> hope you don't mind.

I stare at the texts. Is this really what he thinks he should be doing? Texting me right after his girlfriend tore him a new one?

> Wilder: I'd really like to talk to you.

I exhale audibly, typing out *Then talk*, my thumb poised over the send button without actually pressing it. And as if he could read my mind, he says:

> Wilder: In person, if that's okay. I'm
> not a phone guy. Truth be told, I hate
> text.

Of course you do; I'm surprised you even own a cell phone because it clashes with your European aristocratic vibe. I purse my lips together, erasing my text and pushing my hair back from my forehead. I can't shake the feeling that I'm in dangerous waters. If everyone has a destiny, ours is to have the most complicated relationship of all time, one that can only end in disaster and somehow include very public humiliation on my end.

I should say no. I'll see him at the bakery in the morning anyway. What difference will half a day make? But at the same time, I understand his urgency to clear the air; it's something we failed at spectacularly when we were teens.

> Me: What are you thinking?

Wilder: I could pick you up around
eight if you're free?

"Mom?" Spence says, popping his head in the room. I whip around so fast you'd think I got caught eating his candy.

"Yeah?" I say, my voice a little too high-pitched.

"Wanna come play a board game with me and Grandma? I keep telling her that there are lots of digital games we can play, but she's insisting on finding Balderdash."

I smile. Balderdash was my favorite as a kid. She actively disliked it as I remember, which makes it just a little bit cute that she's digging it out now.

"Let's do it," I say enthusiastically.

I quickly type a response to Wilder and toss my phone on my bed, leaving it there while I join Spence.

Me: See you then.

Please, please don't let me regret this.

*The morning after the conversation with my dad, I wake up early, still feeling the safety of his reassurance wrapped around me like a hug. I grab the water glass on my bedside table and chug it, remembering the Advil Wilder left me five weeks ago. I haven't drank since. Truth is, I haven't been to a party since or any social event, really. And in a moment of clarity, I realize how stupid that is.*

*I swing my legs out of bed, feeling lighter than I have in months. It's Sunday, which means booth day, and I'm actually starting to wonder if my dad is right, if maybe things aren't as bleak as I thought they were. It's funny how one small thing, like a well-timed hug or an understanding comment, can change a person's perspective. It makes me wonder how many things could shift if we were more generous with one another.*

*And in a moment of true optimism, I pluck the portable phone off my nightstand. Before I can psych myself out, I dial Wilder's number, the landline that only rings in his room, and when I hear his sleepy voice on the other end, my stomach drops to my toes.*

*"Wilder?" I say, even though it's obviously him.*

*"Maddi?" he replies, his blankets rustling like he just sat straight up in bed. "Is everything okay?"*

*"Yeah," I say, staring out my window and digging my toes into the rug. "Everything's fine. Or at least I think it will be. I was just wondering . . . do you want to come help at the booth today?"*

*"Wait, really?"*

*For a flash of an instant, I feel silly. "I mean, only if you want—"*

*"I want to," he says so assuredly that some of my doubt drops away.*

*"Okay then, see you there?" I say, cutting the conversation short so neither of us has the chance to change our minds.*

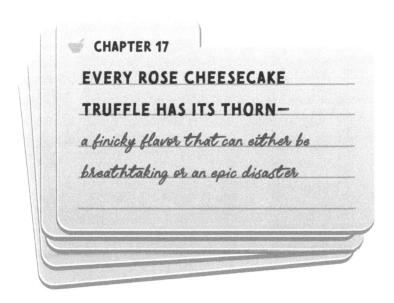

## CHAPTER 17

## EVERY ROSE CHEESECAKE
## TRUFFLE HAS ITS THORN—
*a finicky flavor that can either be breathtaking or an epic disaster*

As the minutes march toward eight o'clock, my stomach ties itself in knots. Why did I agree to this? I stick my thumbnail in my mouth and pull it back out, glancing once more toward the living room window.

"So, can I come?" Spence asks for the many-ith time, plopping down on the couch next to me and stealing half my blanket.

"Not this time, little dude. But next time for sure," I say, even though I don't anticipate there being a next time.

He sighs dramatically and rests his head on my shoulder. "Fiiiine. But if you go to the bakery, please bring something delicious home with you."

I smile against the top of his head. "You got it."

He sits up then, and I immediately miss the snuggle. "So, what's the deal with Wilder anyway?"

"Deal?" I say, even though I've said these exact words on more than one occasion. Spence really is my mini-me.

"You know what I mean," he says.

"It's kinda complicated," I say, not sure I even understand the whole of it. "But essentially, we grew up together. We were best friends when we were kids. If you can believe it, we spent more time together than you, Max, and Nando."

He looks skeptical. "So what happened?"

I shrug. "We got in a big fight. Lots of them, actually. And it was right before I moved out to California, so we never resolved it."

"Did you ever say sorry?"

I smile, wishing things were as uncomplicated as all that. "More like he didn't."

"Well, he should."

"I agree."

"And you'd forgive him?"

The question catches me off guard. No one has ever asked me that. "Uh, yeah, I guess so."

"Why do you sound unsure?"

"Because not all fights can be resolved with an apology."

He looks at me like I'm flat-out wrong. "That's not what you told me. You said that the only thing people can really do when they've messed up is apologize. Punishing them for their mistakes never solved any problems."

I laugh. "So, you just memorize my words and then use them against me?"

"I listen."

I pull him in and smother his cheek with kisses. "Oh, how I love that brain of yours."

He pushes me away with a big grin. "Get in line," he says like he's a celebrity, and dusts off his shoulder.

We both laugh, but mine is cut short when I glimpse a truck pulling into Mom's driveway. Spence follows my eyeline and instantly springs up.

"Dad!" he declares, sending a flash of anxiety through me. I check my phone. There are no messages from Jake asking if he can stop by. And to make matters worse, it's 7:55 p.m.

I stand, following Spence to the door, which he flings open for Jake.

"Come in! Come in!" Spence says, all aglow.

Jake knocks the snow off his boots and steps into the foyer. "I was driving home and I found this on the floor of my truck." He pulls Spence's headphone adapter out of his pocket. "Thought it might be important."

Spence's face lights up. "I was looking for that!"

"Thanks," I say on his behalf, relieved that's the only reason he stopped by.

"But while I'm here," Jake says as though he could sense my thoughts and decided to push his luck. "Have you guys had dessert yet? Your mom tells me I need to do way better than root beer floats before she'll agree to join us."

Spence bounces in response. "Oh, she can't join us, she's going out with Wilder. But yeeeess to dessert!" he says.

So, this wasn't just a casual stop-by of goodwill.

And with impeccably bad timing, the doorbell rings. It's Jake who answers.

"Wilder," he says with a distinct lack of enthusiasm, stepping aside so he can come in.

"Jake," Wilder replies, and suddenly the small foyer feels very crowded.

In Wilder's hand is a large to-go cup, which he offers to Spence. "I know you and I haven't had a chance to hang out yet, but I figured if you're anything like your mom when she was a kid, you might want this."

Spence pulls the lid off. "Hot chocolate? With toasted marshmallow cream! Wow, thanks!"

For just a moment, Jake's expression goes from unamused to surly. I guess he finds Wilder's hot chocolate about as entertaining as Mom finds public nudity.

"I'm surprised to see you here, Wilder," Jake says.

"I could definitely say the same about you," Wilder replies, seemingly friendly in front of Spence even though I recognize his veiled insult for what it is.

I jump in to defuse the tension. "Yes well, we better be go—"

"I'm shocked you and Maddi are on speaking terms after what happened at the market today," Jake adds to one-up him.

I instantly feel ill. If Jake of all people knows about Kate's tirade, then who doesn't?

"What happened at the market?" Spence asks, aware that there's a conversation going on he doesn't understand.

I give Jake and Wilder a look like *I will murder you both in your sleep if you repeat what happened in front of my kid.* Also, screw you, Jake, for bringing it up like that.

Wilder opens his mouth to reply, but my mother enters. I find it very hard to believe she didn't hear the end of that conversation.

"I see we have guests," Mom says. "Can I offer you all a glass of wine or some tea?"

Oh, hell no. And let these two duke it out verbally for the next hour? I'm about two seconds away from throwing them both out a window.

"Wilder and I were actually on our way out," I say, now squeezing around them to the closet and grabbing my coat. "But thanks, Mom."

"And Dad and I are going to get dessert," Spence echoes, clearly not wanting to miss his opportunity to drown himself in sugar.

"Okay then," she says. "Maybe another time. You all have

fun." She smiles, but when she looks at me, her eyes convey a silent communication that feels a little like gloating that I'm once again cavorting with the Buenaventuras. I decide to ignore it.

I hand Spence his coat and gloves and pull his hat over his head.

"*Mom*," he says like I'm fussing.

But when I give him a kiss on the cheek, he doesn't resist. "Have fun and text me."

"I will," he promises, and I open the door, ready to get out of here before Wilder and Jake pull out their dicks and lasso the furniture.

Spence and Jake follow us out, and when Wilder opens my car door for me, I can feel Jake's eyes on my back. If Spence weren't here, I would yell at them both. Besides, the whole thing is idiotic. Neither of them is interested in me.

As soon as Wilder closes his door, I give him a pointed look. "Why is being in this town like reliving high school? Does no one grow up?"

He looks over his shoulder as he reverses out of my driveway. "No," he says, and his answer throws me enough that some of my frustration dissipates. "It's not that people don't mature," he adds, "but I think a lot of what we tell ourselves about adulthood is categorically false."

I raise an intrigued eyebrow.

"For instance," he says, "there's no magical age where you figure it all out. Even my parents don't have everything figured out. In fact, I've met a lot of adults I'd consider more juvenile than Spence."

I grunt. "Okay, yeah, I guess you have a point. But whatever problem you have with Jake, you need to keep it in check, especially when my kid is around."

"You're right. I apologize," he says with no resistance whatsoever.

"Okay then. You're forgiven," I say, remembering what Spence said about apologies.

"May I ask, though, how many times has Jake visited you in California?"

The question takes me by surprise. "Never, but that's not the point."

"Isn't it? Don't you think he should do better than that?" Wilder asks, his voice losing its usual calm.

"Um, yes, I do. But I didn't know you did."

"He has a beautiful son he never sees. I don't know how you even stand him."

I shrug, trying to play it off, even though I've said the same thing many times when I was frustrated. But now I'm looking at Wilder a little differently, seeing his conflict with Jake in a new light as being more about Jake as a person and less about their rivalry.

For a couple of long seconds, we fall into silence. And in the absence of conversation, nervousness creeps back in.

"So, where are we going exactly?" I ask.

"You'll see," he says with a hint of a smile.

"Okay, just checking, but . . . we're not going to your house, are we?" I say, regretting agreeing to this invitation with zero details.

He glances at me with a curious look.

"What?" I say, feeling self-conscious.

"Nothing," he replies, and I can tell it's definitely not nothing.

"All I'm saying is that one run-in with Kate is enough for the day." I feel the need to explain even though I hate that it makes me sound like I'm scared of her. I'm not. Well, maybe I am a little. "I'd rather her not discover me in your living room, where you undoubtedly have a fireplace, and therefore andirons for her to wield against me."

He raises an eyebrow. "Did you think I'd invite you over if Kate were there?"

I can't read his tone, and the unknowing makes me frown. "Well, I can't imagine she'd like it if I was over."

"No, I imagine she wouldn't," he says, and I get the distinct impression he's amused by something. "But I'm not taking you to *my* house."

As he takes the next turn, I realize why he emphasized *my*—we're not, in fact, headed for his house; we're headed for his parents'. "Uh, Wilder—" I start, gearing up to tell him that I'm not exactly excited about seeing them, either, and trying to figure out how to phrase it without offending him. It's bad enough my mom's insisting we go to their Christmas Eve party.

"Don't worry. They aren't home," he says, anticipating me.

"Oh," is all I reply, and then proceed to stare at the side of his face. What the hell are you up to, Wilder Buenaventura?

He parks his car in his parents' giant driveway and gets out. He doesn't try to fill the silence, and so stubbornly, I stay quiet, too. I just follow him up the steps to the front door as he unlocks it.

"Keep your coat and boots on," he says and wipes his feet briefly on the mat.

Maybe we're just picking something up and leaving again? When he doesn't head for the library or the living room, I assume I must be right.

Instead, we walk down the hall together and pass through the kitchen to the back mudroom. The floor is tiled in a rusty burgundy to hide the debris tracked in from people's boots. There are rows of cubbies for shoes, a giant hat rack, and a coat closet. He stops, lifting the lid of the old trunk that doubles as a bench, and it instantly dawns on me what he has in mind.

"Ice-skating?" I breathe, a smile forming before I can smother it.

He smiles back. "I hear the pond just froze over."

For a split second, a thrill runs through me. But as my wits return, the feeling sours. The truth is, I do want to go ice-skating; that sounds every kind of perfect. But not with Wilder and not like this.

"That's it, Wilder," I say, now truly flustered. "Enough with the thoughtful surprises."

And he actually has the nerve to smile. "You always loved surprises."

"I do! That's not the point."

"Then what is the point?"

I want to shake my fist at him. "Why on earth are you bringing me ice-skating at your parents' house late at night—"

"It's 8:18."

"You know what I mean," I say, getting progressively more worked up, the anxiety of the day seeping into my voice. "As much as I absolutely hate to agree with your girlfriend, don't you think this is pushing things too far?"

"Kate's not my girlfriend," he says, his voice subdued as ever. "We broke up the day after the benefit."

I stare at him blankly, not computing. I even open my mouth and close it again.

He waits.

"I'm sorry, did you just say you broke up?" I flip back through my interactions with them, with her, trying to make sense of it. "But your parents said it was your anniversary the other night at dinner."

"They made an assumption, one I didn't correct because I didn't want to have that discussion in front of you and your mom."

And now I feel like an absolute idiot. Not only do I sound like I care, but everything I previously thought is skewed by this new lens. "Are you sure she knows you're broken up? Because it didn't seem like it in the market."

For the first time during this conversation, he appears put out. "While I don't think it's generous to reveal the details of our personal relationship, I will say that this isn't the first time we've broken up, and the fact that she's acting like the breakup isn't real is likely due to the fact that we've gotten back together in the past."

I'm not sure how to respond. I know some people have on-again-off-again relationships. And even though Kate is still highly questionable, it at least puts her jealousy in perspective. But then it occurs to me that he broke up with her the same day my mom read the will, and my heart starts pounding like a bass drum.

"Now," he says when I don't continue. "Would you like to go ice-skating with me?"

If I thought I was nervous before, it pales in comparison to my current state of jitters. My mind spins. Did he break up with Kate because he thought I was staying in Haverberry?

*As the day winds down, I watch Wilder help our last customer at the booth, surprised that he actually stayed until evening. We had an hour or so of awkwardness this morning, but as the day progressed, we fell into a familiar rhythm, handing each other things before the other asked, and sharing treats from neighboring stalls after bathroom breaks. It felt weirdly normal.*

*"Why don't you two go on and I'll close up here," my dad says, and I start to protest. "Nope. I insist. You made my day a breeze, and while I plan on paying you both handsomely for your efforts, I would also be very annoyed if you didn't let me pack up."*

*"I can give you a ride home if you want, Mads?" Wilder offers and I nod.*

*I kiss my dad on the cheek, and we pick our way through the closing market, saying our goodbyes to the other vendors. But as we leave the park, plodding along the sidewalk, we fall into companionable silence, like we're both afraid to shatter the unspoken truce. Our winter boots crunch stray pieces of salt as we go.*

"Today was fun," he says, when we're a full block away.

"It really was," I agree.

"Maybe . . ." he hesitates, shoving his hands in his coat pockets. "Maybe I could come help out next weekend?"

I turn to him, shocked by how nervous he seems. "Sure," I say in an easy tone. "I mean, if we can keep from fighting for that long."

"I'd like to try," he replies way too earnestly.

I sigh. "Me, too." And for the second time in forty-eight hours, I feel like maybe that's possible.

He smiles. "How would you feel about not going home right away? We could always sit in the square and watch the tree for a bit?"

I give him the side-eye. "You, Wilder Buenaventura, want to watch the tree?"

His smirk appears. "I hear that's a fun thing to do."

I laugh as we enter the square. "Liar. I legit have to drag you here every year."

He grins as we cross into the green. "So that's a no then?"

I purse my lips. "It's not a no. But only because I haven't done it yet this year."

He chuckles and holds his hand out toward the bench. As we sit, I get a whiff of his firewood scent.

The tree of course is magnificent, with sparkling white lights and garlands of red, big glittery ornaments, and a huge glowing star. It never fails to lift my spirits.

"I got into Vassar," I say.

"Wait, what?" he replies, his face lighting up. "When did you find out?"

I look at my gloved hands. "Two days ago. Early decision."

"You know that's a huge deal, right?"

"My parents are excited."

"Obviously. As they should be. I can't believe you didn't tell me," he says, but stops short.

*We're both quiet for a second.*

*"No, I know why you didn't tell me. And I know that's on me."*

*My eyes flit to his, but he looks away, almost like he's angry with himself.*

*"Are you still thinking about going to the Culinary Institute?" I hate that I ask, and even more so, I hate the hopefulness in my tone like I'm trying to prove to myself that his mother was wrong that day in the supermarket, that he wasn't applying because of me but because it was his choice.*

*"Actually," he says, looking at his hands. "I'm aiming for Oxford. If not, then LSE."*

*"England?" I say, almost choking on the word.*

*"Yes," is all he says, still not meeting my eyes.*

*I look away, hurt bubbling up in me again as I realize Mrs. Buenaventura was right that my dream wasn't his dream. He must sense the tension, because he shifts the conversation to easier things, like Matt Mazzeo asking Jenna out with a striptease in the cafeteria that included the words "Now that you've seen the goods, you know the man is from the woods," which is so dumb it's actually kinda good. We smile, we laugh, and for the first time in forever, we do not fight.*

*"Where would you live, if you could live anywhere in the world?" he asks, after we've sat on that bench for so long our butts are numb and our cheeks are bright red, both of us aware it's well past time to go home.*

*"Right here," I say.*

*"Nowhere else? Not even Alaska where you could live in winter most of the year?"*

*I laugh. "While I do actually think that sounds amazing, I'd still choose here. But if the sky's the limit, I'd transplant one of those cozy English cottages, the romantic ones with the old stone walls and the thatched roofs."*

*He smiles. "Not some big estate?"*

*I shake my head. "Don't get me wrong, I wouldn't want my cottage to be teeny tiny, but I also don't love the idea of all that open space. Feels cold, ya know? Like those big echoey foyers, or your parents' formal living room where the furniture is pristine and spaced out. No one is ever really comfortable in places like that."*

*He nods. "One of the many reasons I'm always in our library."*

*And in a rare moment of no bullshit, I say, "What do you think, Wilder, do you think we can actually get past this? Or is it all too fucked up?"*

*He looks at me then with so much intensity that I hold my breath. "I'm counting on it, Mads. I don't know what I'll do if we don't."*

*I nod, not really trusting myself to push farther. Because right now, this moment is enough.*

Wilder and I lace up our skates on the bench next to the small pond in Wilder's backyard. Snow covers the grass in a sparkly blanket, punctuated by old brambly trees and the occasional shrubbery. The moon is out, casting a luminous glow over the reflective white.

He broke up with Kate when I came home, organized the booth because he knew it would matter to me, and now this. For a second, Kate's comment about Wilder trying to get me back plays in my head. And the worst part is, I hold onto it, pulling it to my chest like a hot water bottle, clinging to the cozy warmth.

I sneak a glance at Wilder, bent over his skates while he ties the laces, hair tumbling over his forehead, and my stomach does a loop-da-loop.

No.

Just no.

I'm not thinking these things. I REFUSE.

I frown at the glittery pond, attempting to make it less romantic, but the stupid thing is perfect. So, I turn to Wilder, my brain desperately trying to make sense of the situation we're in. And what if there's no hidden meaning here? What if he's just being nice? People are allowed to be nice. Even the ones who I supposedly hate.

"Wilder . . . why are you doing this?" I ask, only my voice doesn't embody the unattached quality I was aiming for.

"Why am I doing what?"

"This," I say, gesturing at the gorgeous scenery that inspires me to throw my arms in the air and sing.

He sits up, his look turning thoughtful. "I thought the reason would be obvious," he says, the corners of his mouth lifting up ever so slightly.

Which apparently is all it takes for my heart to slam against my ribs like a gladiator trying to knock the other guy off his feet. If he says any of the crazy things I've been thinking in my head, I will be forced to deck him. Deck him or jump him. NO. *Not* jump him. Excuse me God, universe, anyone who is listening, I'd like another brain; I'll pay for express shipping.

"I wanted to apologize," he continues, and relief floods me in a whoosh. At least I think it's relief?

Is this who you are now, Maddi? So far out of the dating game that someone takes you to a pretty pond and you think they're proposing? What kind of special deluded are you? He just wants to apologize—a perfectly normal gesture from your *business partner.*

Wilder watches me like he can see that I'm fretting and he wants to fix it. "I regret that Kate said those things to you today. In a way, it's my fault. I thought it would be easier on her if I let her come to terms with our breakup in her own time. But it doesn't seem to be playing out that way. Quite the opposite, really. And while that's not your problem, there's no reason you should be made to feel uncomfortable. While I can't control Kate, I can cut contact with her, which is what I've done."

I sit there staring at him. He looks like Wilder. He's got tousled hair, aristocratic features, and a smirk that makes you want to know his secrets. But seriously, who the fuck is this person?

"Maddi?" he says when I don't reply.

"Uh, thank you, I think?" I say, and even though I've had arms all my life, I have no idea what to do with the things. I stand, hoping movement will help.

He stands with me. "I should be the one thanking you for not cursing me out on the spot."

"I thought about it, believe me," I admit, picking my way carefully through the snow on my skates.

"I wouldn't have blamed you," he says as we approach the pond, offering me his hand.

Thoughts scrambled, I take the thing, using it to balance as I step onto the ice. And fuck me if I don't get a whiff of his scent, a delicious blend of fireplace and cinnamon . . . and lawless sex. What? STOP IT RIGHT THIS VERY MOMENT, ASSHOLE BRAIN!

Only in my current state of having a wee mental scramble, I hold onto his hand for two seconds too long.

And when he smiles about my choice, I yank my fingers back, blurting out, "I'm not . . . it doesn't mean anything that I took your hand." Then I die a little bit inside.

I push off and he pushes off with me.

He laughs loudly enough to set my face on fire, both of us gliding in easy strokes. "I didn't think it meant anything. I know you only accepted it to be polite."

My embarrassment ratchets up to infinity, and I very diligently study Bob Ross's landscape for the good sense I seem to have lost, hoping I'll find it somewhere among the "happy little trees."

"I'm sorry, am I making you uncomfortable? That wasn't my intention," he says, which only makes it a hundred times worse.

At a loss for any believable reply that isn't the truth, I say, "Honestly? I don't know how to act around you right now."

For a second his expression leans toward concern. "Because you're still angry with me?"

My eyes flit to his. "Because I'm nervous."

His brow momentarily dips in confusion. "Nervous?"

"Yes, nervous."

He hesitates like he's not sure, which only makes me feel more foolish. Did I get it wrong? Am I just reading into things?

I do the ice-skating equivalent of hitting the brakes. He stops a few feet after me, turning to face me.

He looks down and then back up like he suddenly got shy. "I just . . . wanted to do something nice for you."

"See that's exactly what I mean," I say, waving at him like he's some sort of personal weakness—the perfect slice of pumpkin pie staring at me in the fridge late at night. "Breaking up with Kate, surprising me . . ."

He hesitates like he's arguing with himself.

"Tell me why you invited me here, Wilder," I say, completely lost in my need to understand. I'm crossing a line, pushing him over it is more like it. And I can't seem to stop myself; I'm that cartoon character who puts the brakes on too late and winds up just sliding right off a cliff and splatting at the bottom.

"I wanted you here," he says like it matters, pushing his hair back from his forehead. "Simple as that. I've wanted to spend time with you ever since I saw you at the benefit."

For a wisp of a moment, I lean into his words, grab ahold of them like a lifeline. But that only makes things more confusing, threatens to shatter the barrier I've so carefully constructed be-tween me and Wilder.

It's too much. And even though some very persistent part of me wants to believe him, I just can't. "You acted like you couldn't have been more disappointed to see me the night of the benefit. You told Liv she shouldn't have invited me."

"No," he says like I've got it categorically wrong. "I said she didn't warn me."

His denial only winds me tighter.

"You told her she made the night uncomfortable. You can't tell me that wasn't about me."

He shakes his head. "I only said that because she knew I was in the process of breaking up with Kate and throwing you into the mix was going to complicate it. As you experienced."

For a second, I just stare at him, unable to process what he's saying. Liv knew he was breaking up with Kate? Is that why she made that bet with me? But that makes no sense, not if he made the decision to do it before I even arrived. And now I feel extra stupid for thinking that their breakup had something to do with me, and more importantly, for *saying* it to *him*.

Whatever fire was blazing inside of me suddenly squelches, and I wish I could disappear, just crawl right the fuck under a bush.

"Maddi?" he says when I don't respond.

But I just stand there, barely looking at him, embarrassment eclipsing all else. "I should probably get home," I reply, because it's the only thing to say at this point.

## CHAPTER 18

### BABY BUN-DT CAKE—

*complicated designs that are nearly*
*impossible to get out of the tin*

All morning I've told myself on repeat that I'm going to ignore how much yesterday affected me. That Wilder and I are business partners. That's all. We don't need to ice-skate and he certainly doesn't need to make grand gestures like the booth. This is business. Just business.

Yet as I carve a path through the bakery and open the kitchen door, my stomach jumps and twitches like a piece of microwave popcorn. Wilder is already there even though it's only 3:58 a.m., and the moment I lay eyes on him, I feel that uncontrollable pull.

He looks up from his work, an inviting smile on his face. "Good morning," he says, which I grant you is as bland a greeting as they get, but to me translates to *I remember what you look like in the goddamn moonlit snow.*

I immediately avert my gaze. "Good morning," I parrot, swallowing the words and feeling even more absurd. It'd be really great if I could stop acting like a lunatic.

"I made you some coffee," he says, and my eyes find his once more, searching for any lingering frustration. But I find none. He looks the way he does every morning, freshly showered and happy.

Wilder walks over to me as I hang my coat and scarf on the hook, carrying a steaming mug topped with whipped cream, and when I take it from him, his fingers accidentally graze mine. We both notice, and my already chaotic pulse jumps.

I clear my throat. "Thanks."

"You're welcome," he replies, still standing in front of me like a wall of pheromones with a hint of smokiness.

I take a sip, licking the excess foam off my mouth, and his eyes immediately move to my lips. A warning sounds in my head followed by naughty images of whipped cream.

I skirt around him, grabbing my apron, and hoping like hell he can't tell what I'm thinking by looking at me. "Mocha?" I ask.

"Indeed."

To my great relief, he doesn't call me on my weirdness or try to talk about what happened last night. Instead, he returns to his pecan pie. But even though his back is to me, I can feel him over there.

So I dive into my work, hypervigilant and committed to concentrating on anything that isn't him. And for the next couple of hours, he gives me space. Albert comes in and opens the front of the bakery, and still Wilder and I continue our quiet rhythms, which is great. Except it's not, because I find myself looking at him more and more, his normalcy now driving me nuts.

"Wilder?" I say, when it feels like one more second of silence is going to make my head explode.

"Yes, Maddi," he says, turning to face me, a hint of hopefulness in his tone.

"I was wondering if . . . you wanted to go over some of the accounting soon, just to, you know, see where we stand?" Just me bringing our relationship back to business, I think, mentally patting myself on the back.

"I'd be happy to," he says. "I'm actually in the process of getting everything digitized so it's easier."

"Right. Good," I say, realizing that he's already thought of this and that I'm ten steps behind. He's embracing the bakery while I'm still acting like I'm a guest in it.

"I think I should have it all converted shortly after the holidays if you want to go over it then?" he offers, and while it sounds perfectly reasonable, I hesitate, because it brings to light the one thing I haven't dealt with—am I leaving after Christmas or am I staying? And if I'm staying, for how long?

"Works for me," I say, and turn back around, now consumed with a whole other slew of worries, aware that I'm running out of time to make a decision.

As the hours wind down toward eleven, Wilder's phone buzzes relentlessly. And when I find him frowning at it, I want to ask: *Is it your mom? Is it Kate? Is it your ex-fiancée from France deciding to pop in to make things even more interesting?*

The last half hour seems to stretch forever. I keep starting to say something, convinced that I should clear the air, only to conclude that any attempt I make is going to increase the awkwardness. When we finally hang up our aprons, I'm bathed with relief.

Although now that I'm faced with separating from him, our interaction feels incomplete, all the things neither of us said hanging in the air like specters.

But before I can open my mouth, he says, "I won't be in tomorrow."

My stomach drops like a lead weight. "Oh," I say, pretty sure my disappointment is showing on my face.

He pulls down his coat, slipping his arms into it. "I have to help my family set up for the party." But his reasonable explanation doesn't make me feel better. He's out tomorrow. And then we're both out for the holidays. So, the next time I see him will be at his parents' Christmas Eve party.

"Sounds good," I lie. "Have a good one." Whatever the hell that means.

"You, too," he says, and for a second, it seems like he's going to say something more but decides against it.

And he's gone.

I stand there staring at the door he just walked through, dumbfounded at how we could go from the booth and ice-skating yesterday to polite colleagues today. I know this is what I wanted, hoped for even, so why do I feel like I'm sinking?

*The Monday morning after the holiday market, I wake up sick. Maybe it was staying out too late in the cold with Wilder, or just overdoing it with sweets, but I'm so nauseated that I throw up my breakfast. Twice.*

*So, I stay home from school, my mom bringing me juice in bed. But the weird part is that I don't have a fever or muscle aches. And even though I'm queasy, I'm also hungry. Very hungry.*

*I make my way into the bathroom for the umpteenth time this morning and stare at myself in the mirror, trying to decide whether I'm actually sick or if there was just something wrong with my eggs when I catch a glimpse of my tampon box in the reflection. I turn, frowning at it, trying to remember when I last had my period. I'm certain I had it sometime recently, didn't I? Why don't I know this?*

*My frown deepens and my nausea turns to a different kind of uneasiness. I'm sure it's nothing, I tell myself. I only had sex with Jake once, and we used a condom. The chances are slim to none. But I can't stop staring at that box and the longer I stand there the more unsure I become. And now that the question's in my head, it floods my thoughts, seeping into the crevices of doubt.*

*"Screw this," I say in a huff and exit my bathroom, grabbing*

*my sweatshirt off my vanity chair and pulling it over my pajamas.
I tell Mom I'm going to CVS to get some stuff to help my stomach.
To which she tells me nothing helps the stomach flu, and I tell her
I'm going anyway.*

*I'm relieved to find CVS mostly empty, but still, I don't linger
in the aisles. I grab a box of saltines, a couple of bottles of coconut
water, and two pregnancy tests. But as I near the cash register and
old Mrs. Lambert behind it, I start to panic. Why didn't I drive a
town over where no one knows me; why didn't I just shove the tests
down my pants and make a run for it? It's too late, though. She
sees me and I see her see me, and so I place my stuff on the counter,
feeling much sicker than I did a minute ago.*

*Her gray eyebrows rise when she spots the pregnancy tests, and
during a personal episode I can only describe as brain implosion,
I say, "Those are for my mom. Wish her luck." And I don't stop
there. I continue because clearly I haven't hit my limit of fuckery
for the day. "I never imagined she wanted another, but I guess I'm
just that much of a joy that she can't stand the idea of me going to
college. You know?"*

*"Oh," Mrs. Lambert says, and her suspicion turns to shock.*

*We stop talking then. She gives me my receipt and I hightail
it out of there, hoping and praying to every god in the universe
that the CVS burns down, and Mrs. Lambert has a sudden urge
to move back to France.*

*But the moment I get home I forget all about my crap perfor-
mance, and instead, lock myself in my bathroom. I chug a coconut
water and wait. It only takes four minutes before I get the urge.
And seven seconds of peeing before my life takes a hard left.*

*Two effing pink lines.*

*I drop the thing on the ground like it was diseased, tearing
into the second applicator. I tap my foot on the floor, chug another
bottle of coconut water, and half an hour later I get exactly the same*

188 **ADRIANA MATHER**

result. The nausea, which was forcefully present an hour prior is suddenly missing, leaving only shock and fear in its wake. I slide down onto the tiled floor, my back up against the cold bathtub, the pink lines on the sticks staring at me like harbingers of doom.

I don't cry. I don't know why really. I just sit there, still, waiting for it to go away, for me to blink and jump the rails into a parallel timeline, one where I wasn't victim to that thirteen percent chance of condom failure I learned about in sex ed. I don't pace. I don't scream. And I don't try to bury the tests in the bottom of the trash.

I sit there for so long that my butt goes numb on the tiled floor. And when my mom knocks, I don't scramble, trying to clean up the bathroom. All I say is a dull, "Yeah?"

"Are you decent?" she asks through the wood.

But I don't know how to answer that question. Am I? Have I lost my decency? Did I ever have it in the first place?

"Madeline? Are you okay in there?" she continues when I don't reply.

No, Mom, I'm not, not even a little.

She jiggles the locked door handle. "Do you need my help?" she asks, her voice rising with worry.

Maybe it's the offer of help, or maybe it's that she sounds so concerned, but something inside me splinters, breaking my stillness and tumbling out in a mess of hot tears. Big heaving sobs. I stand up, my hands shaking. Please, Mom, help me.

I turn the lock, pulling open the door. Her eyes widen and her mouth makes an O. She assesses me for damage while my heart pours down my cheeks.

She pulls me close, wrapping me in her arms as I weep against her shoulder. She's so warm; her arms are so secure—I wonder if I can stay here, if I can just bury my face in her neck, would it all go away?

"Where does it hurt? Do you need a doctor?" she asks, rubbing my back. "Tell me what's—" But her voice stops there, just drops off a cliff, and I know that she's seen the tests on the floor behind me.

*She lets go of me, the cold seeping back into the space between us. Her eyes move to my face. "Tell me those aren't what I think they are." Her voice is so low it's barely audible. "Tell me you're not . . ."*

*Mom can't even muster the words. But she doesn't need to and neither do I because there has never been anything more obvious. I'm pregnant.*

*She hesitates, moving incrementally forward as though she might pull me back to her, hold me like she used to when I was little. And as she moves toward me, my hands lift to meet her. "Please," I hear myself whimper.*

*But she turns around, hand on forehead, moving instead to my bedroom. "How could you be so careless? How could you do this to our family?"*

*Our family,* her *embarrassment.*

*"I didn't mean—" I start and stop.*

*She rounds on me, her expression a showcase of disappointment and fear. And I realize that I've finally done it, the thing she's always been afraid of—I've disgraced her.*

*I wipe my eyes with the back of my hands, and we stare at each other. Physically three feet apart but separated by miles in every way that counts.*

*"This is going to break your father's heart," she says, pressing her hand into her chest. "I can't . . . I don't know what to say to you. How could you?"*

*"I don't know, Mom," I say slowly, the cold moving from my body to my voice. "How could I look for affection outside this house? It's a mystery," I reply, and I don't know why I say it. Maybe it's because I'm overwhelmed and she's making it worse, or because the thought of my father being disappointed in me is so awful that I resent her for saying it, or maybe I just want to hurt her the way she's hurting me.*

*"Excuse me?"*

*"You heard me," I say, sniffling.*

*Her eyes narrow. "Tell me you didn't do this on purpose. Tell me it's not Wilder—"*

*And that's where I break. "Get out!" I shriek, surprising us both. "Get out! Get out! Get out!" My voice is so loud that I don't know if she tries to say something to calm me down. But I don't stop until she's gone.*

## CHAPTER 19

## LOVING GROOM'S CAKE—

*gooey flourless chocolate cake with fresh raspberries, modest and simple and perfect*

My mother is in a strangely good mood when I get home from the bakery. She has brunch prepared and she's talking animatedly with Spence at the breakfast table in the kitchen about the horse-drawn sleigh rides Mr. Hamza orchestrates on Christmas Eve.

"We used to go every year," I say, taking a seat with them. "It was my favorite holiday activity."

"Can we go?" Spence asks, shoveling frittata into his mouth. "Can we do it again this year?"

I defer to my mom, aware of what it means to her. And even though she hesitates, she nods. "If you both want to."

"We really do!" Spence says, all enthusiasm.

A small laugh escapes my mother's lips. "Your grandfather would always dress up in a suit," she says, remembering. "And I'd wear a red velvet dress. He said that when we were old enough and our hair was white, children would think we were Mr. and Mrs. Claus. It was a silly little thing, but we enjoyed it."

I smile along with her. I always loved that ritual.

"Why did you dress up?" Spence asks, and I look at my mother.

"Your grandfather proposed to me on Christmas Eve," she replies, her smile both happy and sad, and my heart clenches right along with her. "We were very young, mind you. And we'd only known each other a few months. I was just out of college when I met your grandfather, and on a weeklong skiing trip with my girlfriends. We were staying at a friend's bungalow up in Vermont. And in the little mountain town we were situated in, there was the cutest Italian bakery you ever saw. I went there every day; their cannoli were that good. But if I'm telling the truth, I was more interested in the cute boy who was serving them."

"Grandpa worked there?" Spence asks, and it makes me smile that he's so interested.

"He did," my mom says, sipping her tea. "It was actually his father's bakery. In fact, your grandfather comes from a long line of bakers."

"So, it's in our genes," he says, in his *I'm making adult conversation* voice.

"That's right," my mother replies, briefly looking at me.

"What happened next? Did Grandpa ask you out?"

She raises an amused eyebrow. "He did, and you know what he said?"

Spence shakes his head.

"After I'd come in the third day in a row, he brought us our pastries and coffees and then turned to my two girlfriends. He said, 'Ladies, I'd be grateful if I could have a moment with Eleanor.'" She shakes her head. "And you can only imagine my surprise because I had no idea he knew my name. Not that my friends hadn't said it many times during our visits, but I didn't know he was paying attention. I was flattered."

Spence leans forward. I, too, find myself gravitating toward her story, one I haven't heard since I was around his age.

"Now of course my friends looked at me for approval, and I nodded. And even though I was never one to be shy, I remember being so nervous when they got up and he sat down. To make matters worse, he didn't speak for the first minute." She presses her lips together like she's stifling a chuckle. "So, I lifted my chin and said, 'Did you come over here just to stare at me?' Well, that did it. He put his elbows on the table and smiled. And I swear on everything, that man could smile."

My chest lifts a little, my breath catching.

"He said, 'Eleanor, I'm not a talker. Never was. So, I don't know how to do this other than just to tell you straight. I'd really like to take you out.'" She leans toward us, conspiratorially. "Now since I was raised in Boston, a city girl, it certainly wasn't the first time a boy showed interest. I wanted more than that. 'Give me one good reason I should say yes,' I replied. But if I expected this country boy to falter, he did no such thing. He looked me right in the eye and said, 'I've lived here all my life, and even though it's a small place, I've seen thousands of tourists come and go, more pretty girls than you could ever imagine. But I'm telling you now that I've never seen one as beautiful as you. And while I understand that what you look like is only a fraction of who you are, I'd really like the opportunity to know the rest of you.'"

I find myself grinning, and Spence has actually stopped eating to listen.

"I laughed then, more surprised than anything. You see, it's not that I was unattractive, I was pretty enough I suppose, but I was never the prettiest girl in the room. In fact, the girl whose bungalow I was staying at, the one who was no more than ten feet from where I sat that very moment? She was the type boys would lose their wits over, just crumble into a blubbering mess of flattery and roses right at her feet. And so, I said yes. Now that I think of it, I didn't even know his name when I agreed."

"And then he proposed?" Spence asks, sipping his orange juice.

Mom nods. "We dated for two months, almost no time at all, really. But we were crazy about each other. And when he took me on a sleigh ride in Boston on Christmas Eve, he didn't even have a ring. He said later that he hadn't meant to propose that night, but that when he saw me in my red dress, he knew he didn't want to wait, that whatever life we had left he wanted to spend it together. We were married for thirty-three years."

Her words hit me hard, like a sweep to the legs I never saw coming. And I find myself blinking away moisture in the corners of my eyes.

My phone buzzes then. Three times in a row. I pull it out of my pocket, hoping to distract myself from the sudden emotion.

> Jake: Uh, Maddi . . . is there something you forgot to tell me?
>
> Jake: Something big?
>
> Jake: Something about the bakery?

For a split second, I panic, like somehow everyone already knows about the confusing feelings I've been having for Wilder. But an instant later, I realize what he's saying.

> Me: Do you mean the inheritance?
>
> Jake: I do.

Jake: But what I'm wondering is why
you didn't tell me yourself.

I can't tell over text what his tone is, but I know if our po-
sitions were reversed, I'd be a little miffed. I'm just not used to
including him in my life that way, not that that's an excuse.

"Mom?" Spence says, and I realize he must have said my
name more than once. Both he and my mother are staring at me.

"Sorry. I was just answering a message."

"From Dad?" Spence says. "What did he say?"

Shit. He must have seen my phone. "He just wants to ask
me about something. I'll be back in a sec." I get up and walk
out of the kitchen before either of them can object. I grab my
coat from the closet and step onto the stoop, pressing send on
Jake's name. He answers on the first ring.

"Well, hey there," he says, and it sounds like I'm on speak-
erphone in his truck.

"Hey," I reply, slipping my arms into my coat sleeves. "So,
about the bakery . . . What did you hear exactly?"

"That your father left it to you *and Wilder*? And that you're
moving back here?" he says, and even over the phone I can hear
he has mixed feelings about it.

"That's partly true," I say, walking down the driveway.

"Which part?" he asks, but before I can answer, he adds,
"Are you home? You sound like you're outside."

I nod like he could see the gesture. "I'm standing in my
driveway."

"Oh, got it. So, this truth . . ."

I walk along the edge of the plowed snow. "Well, my dad
did leave the bakery to me and Wilder. And his will does spec-
ify that we have to work there for a year full-time, but I'm not
sure I'm moving back."

"Huh," is all he says, and goes quiet for a few seconds. "Why?" I shrug. "Because I like our life in California, and I'm not certain I want to upend it." But the truth is even if I were willing to, even if I could get past the tangle of emotions I feel about my father's bakery, living in the one place I know I'll never be enough is not something I can do.

Only instead of answering, his truck pulls into Mom's driveway. I can't help it; I panic a little. I went outside to bring this conversation away from the house, not draw him closer.

*I find Jake on the football field after school, throwing a ball with a few of his buddies. And in a way it seems fitting—I've become a high school cliché in every way.*

*He sees me coming, but he doesn't pause his game. Even when I stop right next to him, he doesn't acknowledge me.*

*"Jake," I say, "I need to talk to you."*

*He tosses the ball, barely glancing at me. "I wouldn't stand there if I were you. Benny has shit aim. He might bean you."*

*"I'm serious. I need to talk to you," I say, not impressed with his attempt to ignore me, and also not blaming him for it.*

*"So am I," he says. "I'm surprised they even let Benny on the team."*

*To which Benny yells, "Dude, my dick can throw better than you."*

*"Jake, it's important," I try again.*

*He shrugs me off, turning once again to his friends and catching the ball. Panic starts to set in. It took me four full days to leave my house, my bedroom really. And pulling up to this school, looking for Jake's truck, waiting for Wilder's car to leave before I'd get out, took everything I had. My resolve is wearing thin, my upset materializing before I can stop it.*

*I wipe my eyes, turning around and trying to hide my face as I walk away. And worse still, I can feel his friends watching me.*

*But before I reach the edge of the field, Jake jogs to catch up with me.*

I stop, looking up at him and sniffling, wishing I'd just stayed in my bedroom where I could be messy without any observers.

"So, what's this important thing you need to tell me?" he says, a little concern seeping past the hard edge he had a minute ago.

I fidget with my coat, working up to it. "Can we go somewhere?"

He shakes his head. "I'm giving Benny a ride home. But it wouldn't matter anyway because I'm busy today."

I exhale, folding my arms around myself. In my head, I pictured marching up to him and telling him I was pregnant flat out, but in real life, it feels nearly impossible.

He looks from me to his friends and back again. "Maddi?"

And while I understand why he's not enthused to spend time with me, I also wish there was a little bit of residual kindness to buffer this moment.

"I'm pregnant," I say quietly.

The pink stain the cold air left on his cheeks nearly disappears. "Wait, what?"

"I'm pregnant," I say again, and this time the word backs up on me, sending a wave of tingles through my sinuses.

"Fuck, really? I mean, are you sure?" he says, and it's like a punch to the gut. I didn't expect him to be excited about it or even happy. But his panic only makes me feel worse, like somehow, I did this to him, instead of it being a mutual decision.

"I'm sure," I say.

He pushes back his hair with both hands and walks a few feet away in a loop before turning back to me. "And you think it's mine?"

For some reason, I never saw this one coming, which I suppose again makes me not only a cliché but a giant chump. And now I'm mad. "Are you seriously asking me that?"

"Come on, Maddi, you know you and Wilder never got over one another. I saw you two at the booth together last weekend."

*I want to strangle him, just grab him by the neck and thrash him about like an alligator.* "I said I was pregnant, not a lying cheater. I don't know why I expected something better from you. Something less bro-y, but I guess that's just who you are."

His expression hardens. "Did you think I was gonna be happy about this? Jump for joy and go out and buy a stroller because my ex-girlfriend who dumped me suddenly shows up and tells me she's pregnant?"

*The ball bounces off Benny's chest a half second after Jake stops speaking like he didn't even try to catch it. Great. Now his friends know, and the whole school is sure to follow. Can this moment get any more perfect?*

"Really, Jake?"

"It's not my fault you came to tell me on the goddamn football field," he fires back, which only makes me angrier. I turn around. Screw this. I did what I had to do and now I'm leaving.

He grabs my arm as I walk away, but I slip out of his grip.

"Don't touch me," I say, so worked up I might actually explode. And he doesn't. He just lets me walk away.

Jake gets out of his truck and closes the door. "Actually, what I meant was why did your dad leave the bakery to Wilder?"

My worry transforms into frustration. That's his pressing question? Not a plea that if we do stay, he'll be able to see more of his son?

"I don't know," I say flatly.

"That annoys you?"

"A little, yeah," I say.

"My question? Or that you have to work with Wilder?" he continues, and I give him a hard look.

"Why are you even asking about Wilder?"

"Why would I not?"

"Because Wilder isn't the point."

He shakes his head. "I really don't get you, Maddi."

"What do you mean?"

He hesitates like he knows it's a bad idea to continue. "Look, do whatever you want, but all I'm gonna say is that every time you get involved with him, you get hurt."

I stand there for a second, getting my annoyance in check and resisting the urge to disagree. He's not exactly wrong. And there's no way in hell I'm going to utter the words *This time is different*, because I'm not an idiot, and also because that would be admitting something was going on between us . . . which it's not. Mostly.

Instead, I go with: "Is that all you came by to say? Because if so, your concern is noted."

Only he's Jake, so he laughs. "Wow, Maddi, I didn't realize you'd be in this deep already. I have to hand it to Wilder, he's smooth."

I press my lips together, biting back my reaction. "I, too, have some questions, Jake, *while you're here*. Mainly, why don't you care as much about asking if Spence is staying as you do about if I'm somehow getting friendly with Wilder?"

His smile falls. "That was shitty."

I want to say, *Which part? The fact that I pointed it out or the truth of it?* But I don't because I'm not trying to fight with him and have him avoid Spence in the process. "Look, I know you've been trying. You've been spending a lot of time with Spence and he's really loving it."

"As am I," he interjects.

"And that makes me really happy," I continue, which is true. "But I think it'd be better if we didn't try to relive our teen years. They were painful enough the first time around." Now, if I could just take this advice myself that would be great.

He nods, looking out into the snowy front yard and back

at me. "Sorry, Maddi. I don't know why it made me so crazy when I heard. You're right. It's none of my business."

I sigh. Apologetic Jake is like a golden retriever giving you sad eyes; it's basically impossible to stay mad.

"It's fine," I say. "You should have seen my reaction when Mom read the will."

A hint of his smile returns. "I can only imagine."

"If Spence wasn't there, I might have lit the house on fire, starting with Wilder."

"I don't doubt that for a second," he says with a laugh and pauses. "And Maddi, you're right, my first question should have been about Spence. He really is a cool little guy."

"The coolest," I agree.

"And well, I know you haven't made up your mind . . . but I, for one, would like it if you two decided to move back."

I'm about to answer but I don't get the chance.

"What do you mean move back?" Spence says from behind me, the front door clicking shut like an exclamation mark.

Whatever relief I just felt is obliterated in a flash. I whip around as Spence skips down the steps to join us.

"Mom?" he says, looking up at me. Jake has the good sense to let me answer.

Shit. This is not how I wanted Spence to find out. It was supposed to come from me in a controlled way, and while I realize the fault is solely mine, I also thought I was doing the right thing, making it less complicated by waiting. But now . . .

I scratch my eyebrow, all my worries about making the right decision barreling in. "So, you remember how I told you that Grandma wanted to talk to me about Grandpa's will?"

He nods. "Yeah, you did that like a week and a half ago."

"Right, well it had to do with the bakery, which is why I've started going there in the mornings."

His eyebrows push together. "Okay . . ." he says like he's thinking about it.

"The thing is," I start, "your grandfather decided he wanted me and Wilder to have it."

"Wait, Grandpa left you the bakery?" Spence asks and there's a warning in his tone.

"Half of it, yes."

"Grandpa left you the bakery *and you didn't tell me?*" he says like I betrayed him.

"It's complicated."

"Saying, *Hey Spence, you know that dream I've always had about owning a bakery, well now I do*, is complicated?"

Jake laughs before he catches himself and tries to cover it with a cough. "Sorry, but wow is he your kid."

Spence, however, isn't looking at his dad and he certainly isn't laughing; he's staring at me.

"What's complicated is that in order to keep the bakery I have to work there for a year," I say, and his face shifts from hurt to shock.

"Wait, *what?!*"

I close my eyes for a split second, acutely feeling the hole I've dug. "Your grandpa specified in his will that in order to claim the inheritance, I have to live in Haverberry for a year."

I can feel his panic, even before I see it in his expression. "You mean we. *We* have to live in Haverberry for a year."

"Yes, you're right."

"Why wouldn't you tell me this? How could you keep this a secret? What about my friends; what about my school?" He's so upset that his little chin starts to shake. "Were you just going to make this decision without me?"

"No, I was going to talk to you about it," I say, realizing how lame those words sound in retrospect.

His face scrunches and he sniffs, wiping his nose with the back of his hand. "I don't believe you."

"Spence—" I start, well aware we're headed for a total meltdown. I reach out to comfort him.

But he moves out of my grasp. "Don't," he says, voice wavering, stepping back even farther. "You're lying. You promised you'd never lie!" He makes for the door, jogging up the steps and slipping inside. He doesn't scream at me or call me names and he doesn't slam the door, which in a way makes it worse. He's the most reasonable nine-year-old in the world and his disappointment strikes harder than anything else.

"I feel bad. I didn't know he didn't know," Jake says, but I shake my head.

"Thanks, but this mess is mine," I say, heading for the door.

I say a fast goodbye to Jake, and he gets in his truck. Only when I go back inside, Spence isn't upstairs face-planted on the bed or burrowed under a pillow, he's on the couch with my mother, crying into her shoulder, and the visual gives me a start. It's not that I expect her to be standoffish, but I can't help but notice that she's warmer with him than she ever was with me, stroking his head and shushing him.

"Spence?" I say, softening my voice as I walk into the living room. "Want to come upstairs and talk to me about what just happened? I'd really like to explain."

He shakes his head and my heart sinks. There have only been a couple of times that he's refused to speak to me, and I know from past experiences that pushing him to do so only makes things worse.

But then he says the thing I never thought I'd hear in a million years. "I want to talk to Grandma."

I stand there for a long moment, not sure how to react.

"I've got him," my mom confirms.

And the realization that I'm the one out of place in the room, leaves me feeling upside down. "Okay," I say, trying to keep the upset out of my voice. "I'm here whenever you're ready."

I turn around, making my way into the kitchen, where I pace for the next twenty minutes, punctuated by shoving a cookie in my mouth and staring out the window uncomfortably. My thoughts flit to Liv and the will I've yet to obtain, wondering if maybe there's a solution there that'll make this easier. And by the time Mom and Spence show up in the doorway, her arm around his shoulder and Spence wiping his face on his sleeve, I'm dead set on that course of action.

"Spence?" I say, opening my arms, and he leaves my mother's side, his head hanging, walking straight into my embrace. I bend down, holding him tight.

While Spence is mature, he's also just a little boy, one who is deeply sensitive. And I'm his world. It's been just the two of us his entire life.

I look up at my mother from where I hold Spence. "Mom, could you get the addendum for me? I want to be able to explain it to him."

"Of course," she says with a nod, and relief floods me. I asked her and we're not having a blowup; at least there's that.

A handful of seconds after my mother leaves, he pulls away from me, his face puffy. "I'd really like to talk to you now."

"Great, because I really want to hear whatever you have to say," I reply, motioning for him to sit with me at the small breakfast table.

He slides into the seat next to mine, taking a few seconds to collect his thoughts. "The thing is," he says, "I really don't want to leave my friends in California."

I nod, my head dipping a little with the motion. "Totally

understandable." While the adult world isn't fair, its blowback on the kid world is even less so. "I'm sorry I didn't tell you—"

"That really hurt my feelings," he says with emphasis.

"I know, Spence. I feel terrible. I should have been up-front with you, even if I didn't have a clear solution."

"Grandma said that the bakery is really important to you because it was Grandpa's and that you'd regret it if you lost it," he says, and my hackles go up. Now she's guilting my kid?

"Yes, the bakery is important to me, but that's not something you need to figure out. That one is on me," I assure him.

"And then there's Dad," he says with a pinch of hope that gives me pause. "I guess it'd be kinda great to live near him."

I hesitate. It's not that Jake hasn't been showing up these past couple of weeks, but the chances of that lasting are slim to nil. I hadn't put much thought into it, probably because I never seriously considered staying, but now that I hear Spence say it, it might be the number one reason to leave. While we lived in California, Jake's absence could be written off as geography, but that excuse disappears when he's a five-minute drive away.

"What I'm saying is," Spence continues, "the more I think about it, maybe it wouldn't be so bad to live here." For a moment, I think I misheard him, but he continues, "Being near family actually sounds really nice."

The air suddenly shifts and the room spins, my own opinion so deeply opposed to his that they don't even share the same atmosphere. I stare at him for a long moment, trying to slow my galloping pulse. "I know moving isn't your first choice—" I start, but he cuts me off.

"Actually, I think it is. I think we should do it."

I freeze. I expected a lot of things from this conversation, but this absolutely wasn't one of them. Shouldn't I be relieved right now that I don't have a crying kid who vows to never leave his friends? But relief is not what I'm experiencing—cold terror might be more like it. It squarely puts me in the "no" camp all by myself, with my mother, Spence, and everyone else standing on the other side of the line.

"Yes, well, it might not be as clear-cut as here or California," I hear myself say, trying to regain my balance and searching for anything that will steady me. "There might be another option. I'm looking for one."

His head tilts like he heard something that interests him. "What do you mean?"

"I mean, maybe we can go back and forth or maybe I can figure out a way to operate the bakery part of the time from California?" I hear the desperation in my voice, feel the resistance in my very being. Jake will disappoint Spence. I'll be forced to live with my mother until I can get on my feet. The bakery. The guilt. The memories. My dad. This goddamn town. Wilder, a dangerous amount of Wilder.

"But how?" he asks.

"You remember Liv?"

"The woman whose car you hit?"

I nod. "I'm going to have her look at the will and see if there are any loopholes in the wording." I don't know why I'm telling him this; I know I shouldn't get his hopes up before I know, but I can't seem to stop myself. I'm like a large dog that sat down mid-walk, stubbornly refusing to budge, clinging to the sidewalk, and pronouncing it my new home.

But before Spence replies, his eyes move from me to something behind me, and my stomach fills with dread over what I just said because I know what I'll find there, or rather who.

Only I'm not prepared for how upset she looks. Outrage and hurt mix on Mom's face in such an obvious way that my unsettled feeling turns to tumult. And it's made worse by the fact that she's carrying the will.

"Mom—" I start, regret coursing through me, but she cuts me off.

"Don't," she says, and her tone shuts me right up. She puts the addendum on the counter with a thwack.

I stand. "Mom, I didn't mean—"

The look on her face makes me want to hide under the tablecloth. "Didn't mean for what? For me to overhear the truth?"

I close my mouth because she's spot-on, even if my delivery would have been softer.

But she's not done. "Didn't mean for me to know that you're telling our closest friends behind my back that you can't wait to leave? That you've gone so far as to implore their help in getting away from me? Or maybe the fact that you hit Liv's car? Let me ask you, did you make reparations for that? Did you fix her Aston Martin?"

All the color drains from my face. Whatever I imagined her reaction to be, this cuts much deeper because it's true.

Spence stands up, looking back and forth between us. "I think I'm gonna let you two talk," he says, and even though I have no desire for him to overhear this, the thought of him leaving jolts me with panic. As long as he's here, we're forced to temper our conversation. But he slips past my mom, shooting me a look over his shoulder like *you better fix this*, leaving me to my self-made peril.

My anxiety rockets into space. I don't speak to my mom right away. I know that anything I say is only going to make this worse—that I wouldn't even know how to tell her the thousand reasons I'm terrified to move here because I barely understand them myself.

I catch the muffled sound of Spence closing the bedroom

door upstairs, and I know she hears it, too, by the way she glances toward the doorway.

"You know, previously when you said you didn't want to stay, I gave you the benefit of the doubt. She's in shock, I thought. But now?" She starts slowly like it's taking a monumental feat of control to explain the obvious to me.

"Mom," I say, "please don't do this."

"Do what, Madeline? Have an adult conversation about the topic at hand? Because you've been here for what? Ten days now? And all you seem to be doing is avoiding it. I've tried to give you your space, but really, this cannot go on. Despite the fact that your father's dying wish was for you to have his bakery, you cannot give up one year of your very important life in California to make him happy?"

Her words split me right down the middle, and my self-control momentarily slips. "This isn't about Dad. And I'm sorry you don't like it, but this is about making the best decision for me and my son, and in order to make it properly, I need time."

"Really?" she says like she's not convinced. "And would that best decision you cite also include financial stability? Because despite the fact that you try to cover it, I can clearly see you're struggling. This bakery would mean a lifetime of security."

No one in the world knows how to push my buttons the way my mother does.

"First of all," I say, my nerves raw, "I've never asked you for anything. Not once since I moved out. I've taken care of myself for the past ten years and I can continue to do so."

She nods like I'm so predictable. "Ah yes, we're back to this. What terrible parents we were. How could we be so cruel to you? How could we offer to have you and the baby live with us only to have you throw our generosity in our faces?"

I'm trembling now, sick with the deluge of emotion that's simmering below the surface. "Generosity?" I say, shaking my head. "Is that how you remember it? Because as I recall you treated me like you wished I'd disappear so that you didn't have to deal with me. Did you really think I wanted to stay in a house where I'd be reminded every day that I was a disappointment? Do you remember what you said the day you got a call from one of the women in your ladies' club asking if the rumor was true? You said into the phone, and I quote, 'We're devastated. I can barely look at her.'"

"Did you expect me to be happy? To be overjoyed that my only child was throwing away her future?"

I don't know why I thought she might feel bad hearing those words repeated back to her. I should know better by now.

But instead of countering, I pull out my phone and snap a picture of the will, dropping it back on the counter, and sending the picture in a wordless text to Liv.

"Don't worry, Mom, with any luck I'll be gone in a few days, and you won't have to deal with me."

"Deal with you?" she says like I've completely missed the point. "It's obvious to me now that there's no getting through to you, Madeline. You think I'm trying to control you, that your father was? One day you're going to wake up and realize that your own worst enemy is you, only by then it'll be too late."

My eyes widen. I'm about to refute her statement, the way she's painting me as rigid and unyielding, but for one horrible second, I'm not sure she's wrong. And the doubt twists inside of me, confusing what I know to be true and turning my response to ash on my tongue.

She shakes her head like it's all too much. "I'd thought your father's bakery would be a welcome gift, a way to honor his legacy that would bring you joy. But I can see that it's nothing but a burden for you, anchoring you to a place and to people you can't stand being around."

Her words are like arrows punching holes in my armor, inflicting damage to the softest parts of me. "Mom," I say again, this time quieter, the awful sting of guilt overriding everything else.

She takes a breath, leveling me in her gaze. "No, I think you were right all along, you should go back to California."

Death blow.

I open my mouth, but she's already turning and leaving the room, the air noticeably chilling in the wake of her departure.

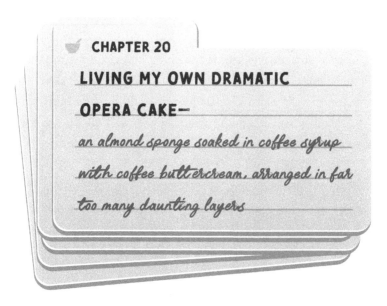

## CHAPTER 20

## LIVING MY OWN DRAMATIC

## OPERA CAKE—

*an almond sponge soaked in coffee syrup with coffee buttercream, arranged in far too many daunting layers*

Mom leaves the house after our fight without a goodbye. I text her when it nears dinnertime to ask if she wants me to make her something, but all she says is that we should eat without her. And that's the end of our communication, which of course worries Spence, and we wind up spending the whole meal talking about her. I assure him that everything is going to be fine, even though I'm not entirely sure.

When she finally does return home in the evening, she's weighed down with shopping bags. The hurt on her face is no longer visible, but she also does a good job of not looking directly at me. Shortly after, she goes up to her bedroom and closes the door. Spence takes his computer to the living room to video chat with his friends and I proceed to stare at my bedroom ceiling, feeling like a failure of a parent and a failure of a daughter. How did this all get so screwed up so quickly, and just when I thought I was getting a handle on things?

My phone buzzes and I snatch it up, hoping it'll magically provide an answer to my many messes.

> Liv: Sorry. Been busy with the gf.
> Headed back to Haverberry soon. But
> I just wanted to let you know that I
> had a quick look at that will and I'm
> sorry to say that I'm not seeing the
> loophole I know you were hoping for.
> I'll look again of course when I have
> more time, but so far it feels pretty
> tightly worded.

The hope I was holding onto with my desperate clutchy little fingers vanishes in an instant and all I'm left with is a hollow feeling.

I sit up, texting Liv a quick thanks, and before I close out of my messages, I spot Wilder's name. I don't know why, but I open the thread, reading through his texts from last night. My mind replays everything that's happened recently—how emotional it was to see the booth after all these years, how hard it must have been for Wilder to pull off on such short notice, and how moved I was before Kate showed up. And then there was the apology ice-skating that spiraled into awkwardness. I try to sort my way through it, how much of it was my fault, how much of it was his, why it went south so fast, but it's one of those balled-up necklaces you find at the bottom of your purse that you consider just throwing out as opposed to untangling.

The longer I stare at Wilder's texts the antsier I become. And worse still, a wisp of an idea starts to creep in, one born out of the futile need to control something. I actually start to think maybe I should get in touch with him, just clear the air the way I wasn't able to this morning. That if I solve one relationship that maybe the others will follow.

I purse my lips, my shoulders lifting with the tension of having to decide. I go so far as to type out a message just as an experiment.

**Me: What are you doing right now?**

I stare at it, my thumb hovering over the send button.

*Stop. Are you just trying to make things more complicated?* I ask myself, throwing my phone on the bed with a huff. But before I even realize I'm doing it, I'm getting up and moving toward my vanity, pulling out the journal I promised myself I had divorced from meaning. The worst part is I know exactly what I'm looking for—the picture I tried to throw out on multiple occasions and failed, eventually stashing it so I wouldn't have to look at it in the frame on my vanity. Even as I lift it out of the drawer, I tell myself to put it down.

But no. I open the journal, my fingers pulling the photograph free from the pages, and a thrill zings through me hinged somewhere between excitement and the need to close my eyes and scream for my life.

I stare down at a younger version of me and Wilder on the beach, arms thrown around each other, skin tanned from hours in the sun and hair dripping from the wave that had crashed over us a minute prior, wearing the type of joy in our expressions that is so pure you can't help but smile in return.

I turn it over, running my thumb over the inscription on the back. There in Wilder's neat cursive are the words: *Promise me, Mads, that you'll recognize me in our next life, even if you're a cat and I'm a dog. Even if I can't hold you like I am in this picture, I just want to be near you.*

For one bright flash of a second, I consider if that's what he's doing now with the booth and the ice-skating—trying to be near me. But as soon as I think it, embarrassment envelops me like too-hot bath water, burning my most vulnerable areas. Of course not; he's simply trying to make this situation livable, nothing more. And even if he was, say making a bigger move than just civility, look at how it turned out last time. Broken trust, friendship in the gutter, an inordinate amount of pain. And this time the bakery hangs in the balance. Plus, it's not only my heart in the equation now, but Spence's, too. So, good, it's decided then. Clean. Easy. Business only. Nothing to see here, folks.

Just two old lover-enemies learning to coexist.

Exactly.

While also baking passionately in the den of their childhood memories.

Um? NO.

And one of them smells like pastry and fire and is a tasty British-Argentinian snack.

SERIOUSLY brain, we're back here?

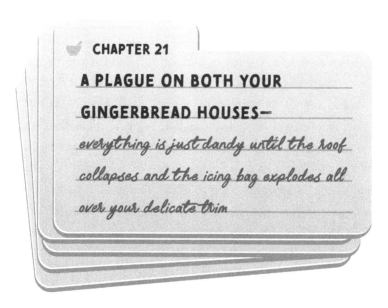

## CHAPTER 21

# A PLAGUE ON BOTH YOUR GINGERBREAD HOUSES—

*everything is just dandy until the roof collapses and the icing bag explodes all over your delicate trim*

Morning baking duties with Albert are pleasant and relaxed. Now that we've gotten used to each other, he tells me stories about his grandkids, and I tell him stories about Spence. He's the easy sort to be around who's just as happy in silence as conversation, who laughs at his own jokes and calls his dough a *cheeky little fellow*.

When the hour gets reasonable-ish, I send Liv a text. It's odd to admit, considering I've only been back a couple of weeks, but I noticed her absence this past weekend.

> Me: Soooo

And to my surprise, she responds right away.

> Liv: Good morning, gorgeous.

Me: Did not expect you to be awake.

Liv: Sleep? Me? Nah. Way too
awesome for sleep.

Me: Well I'm glad you're awake
because I have a question.

Liv: Wow, this is a lot of build up. How
bad is it?

Me: Haha. You tell me?

Me: Did you or did you not know
that Wilder broke up with Kate
when you made that bet with
me?

Liv: Mmmmm. I like where this is
going. Yes, I did know. But tell me . . .
why are you asking?

I stare at my phone. Where does she get this level of confidence, and can I borrow some?

Me: And you wouldn't consider that
cheating on our bet?

Liv: Not even a little. Does that
mean you're admitting I won?

Me: Nothing is decided yet.

Liv: You know I'm grinning, right?
That if you can't admit I won after
that booth Wilder practically killed
himself setting up for you, then
you're in way deeper than I thought.
Should I be picking out names for
your soon to be children? Liv Jr. has a
delightful ring to it, don't you think?

I laugh out loud, earning a curious glance from Albert.

Me: Yes, he set up that booth, but
probably just to ensure I didn't
murder him one fine morning and
bake him into a pie. Besides, he
was planning on breaking up with
Kate before I arrived. That had
nothing to do with me.

Liv: And what if he knew you were
coming home when he made that
decision?

I read her text twice. I'd be lying if I said I wasn't wondering that considering how close our families are, even though I
would never have asked it outright.

Me: Did he actually tell you his
breakup had anything to do
with me?

Liv: Haha. Well played. No, he did not.
But the circumstances are suspect.

Me: Shrugging

Liv: Grinning

Me: Are you working today?

Liv: Off for the holidays. Did you
miss me?

Me: Like a lot.

Liv: Good. Put on your drinking boots,
Maddi, because you're with me
tonight.

I hesitate, not entirely trusting myself to drink with her again.

Me: Count me in. But ONE drink
only. And it'll have to be on the
9:30ish side because I have some
stuff I need to resolve with my kid.

Liv: Whatever you wish, madame.

Me: Text me the details.

Liv: You got it.

Albert and I take turns shoveling delicious treats into the ovens, and as the morning winds on, my thoughts drift to my dad. Not to say that I haven't been thinking about him since the moment I set foot in Haverberry, but it's mostly been an amorphous cloud of guilt and mourning whose downpour I was trying to dodge. Maybe it's Albert's age or the fact that he hums as he mixes like my dad used to, or maybe it's just being in this space day after day. Whatever it is, I'm starting to see wisps of Dad here and images of me as a young girl bouncing from station to station, following him around and clinging to his every word.

Not long after Albert moves to the counter at the front of the bakery, I venture to Dad's desk, sliding the middle drawer open and running my fingers over the stationery he always used. Inside still smells faintly of the lavender satchels Mom put in all our clothing drawers. I never asked why she put them in his desk of all places, but now that I think of it, it may have been Dad bringing a piece of her to work with him. He adored her, a type of love and dedication that should only be followed by *and then they lived happily ever after*. While I usually see her faults—her controlling perfectionism that bound me tighter than a straightjacket—he only saw her virtues. It used to upset me as a kid, the way she could do no wrong in his eyes, but as an adult, there's something beautiful about the way he cared for her. And for a moment, I consider how devastating his absence must be for Mom, losing the person who unfailingly saw her as her best and brightest self.

*I'm afraid I built Wilder's friendship up in my head, telling myself that as long as I had him as a touchstone, I could weather the fallout my pregnancy caused in other areas of my life. But the truth is, we're still shaky, me and him, and the pregnancy has made things infinitely touchier.*

*I'm showing now, and it makes going to school feel like I'm an exhibit at the zoo. No one has gotten used to it, least of all me. And the pregnancy hormones have me on edge and disgruntled. It feels like there's no place I can simply be, and an insistent ache is forming in my innermost being that the town I desperately love seems to be rejecting me on some very basic level.*

*Here I am walking down the hall, just trying to get to my car, with people stealing glances at me for the five billionth time today. I tug my arms around my chest like a shield, trying to ignore the banners that float over my head announcing senior prom.*

*"Hold up," Jake says, appearing next to me.*

*"I'm kinda in a rush," I say, even though I have nowhere to be.*

*"Okay, then I'll walk you to your car," he says easily as though we haven't had an infinite amount of awkwardness these past few months.*

*"Do whatever you want," I reply.*

*"That good a day, huh?" he says like he can somehow defuse the tension by just being chill enough.*

*"What do you want, Jake?" I ask as we push through the front doors of the school. It's one of those jarringly gorgeous May days, where the air is a perfect seventy degrees, the sun is warm and inviting, and the entire green world is abuzz.*

*"I just thought maybe we could hang out," he says, and I steal a glance at him as I walk off the cement path onto the lawn. Despite my better judgment, I stop and look at him. "Just drive to the beach or something like we used to," he continues with a shrug.*

*"Why?" I ask, not hiding my shock.*

*"Because I'd like to spend time with you," he says, and now I'm really confused.*

*"Jake, you've been avoiding me like I was contagious for the past four months."*

*He looks down at his shoes. "I haven't been avoiding you."*

*My eyebrows shoot up like a warning.*

"Okay, maybe I've been avoiding you," he admits. "But all that stuff with our families was awkward as hell. I didn't know how to deal with it, ya know?"

"Yes, I do. I was there. But I can't not deal with it." I point at my growing belly and give him a *what are you going to say to that look*.

He shifts his weight from foot to foot. "Do you know if it's going to be a girl or a boy?"

I open my mouth, flabbergasted. "Nope."

"Fingers crossed for a boy," he says, and I'm starting to think he had a stroke.

"Don't do that, Jake."

"What?"

"That. I know you don't want this. Hell, I don't want it, either. But you're going to Florida for college. Your life is proceeding as planned. I'm deferring Vassar and staying here."

"I'm gonna be involved, Maddi," he says, but the tone in his voice further betrays his hesitancy.

"How about this?" I say, not willing to be riled on the front lawn of the school, especially since people are not so subtly staring. "I promise not to lie to you, if you promise not to lie to me. One time offer. We don't need to fight. But don't you dare pretend that you want to be involved or that you want to spend time with me when you don't. Because honestly? I can't have one more person let me down right now."

He scratches the back of his neck, considering it. "Yeah, okay," he agrees but doesn't deflate. "And as long as we're on this honesty kick, there's something I've been meaning to ask you."

"Go for it," I say, even though I was hoping I'd be on my way to my car by now.

A smile appears on his face. "Will you go to prom with me?"

I stand there for a good three seconds at a total loss. "Wait, what?"

"I'd really like it if you did."

"Jake, I—" I start, but he cuts me off.

"So what if you're pregnant? You don't need to drink. I won't drink with you. It might be fun."

I open my mouth and close it again, completely thrown. An awkward laugh escapes my lips. "I think you and I have very different definitions of fun."

"Cheesy prom clothes, bad food, and even worse music that we can dance stupidly to?"

I give him the side-eye. Why is this not sounding totally insane right now?

"Look, I know prom is lame, but maybe it's fun lame? And if you turn me down, that's cool. But I just want to make sure you're not turning me down because of these idiots." He sweeps his hand at the lawn full of people. "Who can all stop staring by the way," he says, raising his voice. "Yup, you and you." He points around the green. "Can all definitely mind your own business."

And for a split second, a sliver of weight lifts off my shoulders and I feel like I can breathe.

Jake's gaze returns to me. "So, what do you say, Maddi, wanna go to prom with me?"

Which is the exact moment Wilder appears by my side.

"You've got to be kidding me," Wilder says.

Jake takes a breath. "Actually no. I'm not kidding. And truthfully, dude, this is between me and Maddi."

Wilder's expression goes stone-cold. "Not sure where to start on that one, Jake. Except to say that there is no you and Maddi because you've been completely absent these past five months."

My face burns. There is something shocking about hearing Wilder's anger even though I said some version of the same thing.

"You really want Maddi to stay home on prom night while everyone else is out partying?"

I'm about to jump in and tell Jake to piss off, that Wilder has been the one and only person to stand by me through all of this, but Wilder hesitates and so do I.

"Oh wait," Jake says. "You didn't tell her, did you?" He laughs but it's for emphasis rather than humor. "You're seriously standing here lecturing me about being shitty while you keep your prom date a secret from your supposed best friend?"

My eyes flit from Wilder to Jake and back. "Wilder?"

Wilder shakes his head and gives Jake a look like he's going to murder him. Then he turns to me, but before he says a word, I know the answer.

"At least have the balls to tell her you made plans without her," Jake continues, and I can feel myself shrinking. "What did you say to Matt in the locker room today? That there was no way you could squeeze in his cousin 'cause your limo is at capacity?"

My chest constricts. Jake's words grate on my biggest insecurity, a palpable fear that everyone has abandoned me and that Wilder secretly wants to do the same. That he's being nice, but that it's nothing more than good-mannered pity. And what's worse is that he let me be humiliated by it, allowing me to think that the solidarity Jake referenced earlier was something Wilder and I branded. I suddenly feel small and unwanted, like I was living in one deluded reality while Wilder was solidly in another.

"Maddi," Wilder starts, a conflicted look replacing his usual calm.

My temper flares. "Don't," I say forcefully, clutching onto my anger for fear that I'm going to crumble in front of all these people. Instead, I turn to Jake. "I'll go to prom with you."

They both open their mouths to respond, but I stop them with my hand.

"Now, I'm leaving. And if either one of you says one more thing about my personal life in front of this school, I'll never talk to you again." And with that, I storm off toward my Prius, hoping I get there before I start crying.

## CHAPTER 22

### DARK CHOCOLATE CROW PIE—
*served with a dollop of whipped humiliation and a shard of cocoa nibs praline*

The afternoon and evening are infinitely less dramatic than the day before, but the tension between me and Mom is still thrumming below the surface, and I can tell Spence is worrying about it. So, I suggest we make a whole slew of Christmas treats, including Mom's favorite eggnog cookies to cheer her up.

Mom goes shopping once again, which is the most I've seen her leave the house since we arrived. Spence gives her our "apology" cookies when she returns, and she oohs and aahs over them. But when he tells her I made them with him, she brushes past my involvement and pulls him into the living room to show him some of her spoils, including a wreath for the front door and an early present for him. While I'm thrilled to see the worry lines eased on my kid's face, I fear I'm developing my own. It's not that being on bad terms with my mother is anything new, but this level of friction is reminiscent of those horrific weeks before I moved to California. And it's bringing back that old itch to run as far from her as I possibly can, whatever the personal cost.

After an awkward few minutes of standing in the living room doorway where it becomes obvious I'm a third wheel, I retreat to the kitchen, cleaning up from our dinner and day of baking. By the time I finish, I've made a promise to myself that I won't let this fight fester, that I'll speak with her the moment Spence heads to bed.

And I do. I intercept her in the foyer about to ascend the staircase with her nighttime glass of water.

"Mom?" I say, my voice less confident than I'd like.

She sighs. "What is it, Madeline?"

"I just . . ." I begin, feeling strange and unsure. If hugs were rare in this family, discussing feelings was even more so. There was an unspoken rule that after a fight both parties would separate for an undisclosed amount of time, never delving into the shadowy details and instead pretending it never happened in the first place. When the fight was really bad, barbed tones and stiff postures were an aftershock, but even those would eventually fade into the gray area of general resentment. "I was hoping we could talk."

She glances at the stairs. "I think we've both done enough talking for the time being."

"I'd really like to clear the air," I say, my tone relaying how bad I feel.

"Yes, well, I'm exhausted," she says. "It'll have to wait."

And even though I promised myself I wouldn't, I get mad. Why can't she just say yes? I would never deny Spence the space to talk.

"Was that all?" she asks when I don't respond.

"I'm going out with Liv," I say, careful not to let my frustration seep into my voice. "I'm just letting you know."

"Right. And now you have," she replies, her tone shifting a degree cooler.

For a moment I'm confused by her reaction; she's always delighted when I spend time with the Buenaventuras. But then it occurs to me that it was Liv I named as my cohort in the will disparagement. I wince, but she doesn't see it. She's already walking up the stairs and away from me, holding up the skirt of her nightgown in one hand.

I stare after her, but she doesn't look back. Why is this always so hard? Why can't we have a conversation without it being a screaming match or an evidence locker of disappointments?

I stand at the bottom of the stairs for far too long, thinking about all the things she said regarding my rigid abhorrence of this place and my rejection of Dad's wishes. And the sick feeling rushes back in. I never decided to hate Haverberry. As a kid I loved it more than anything in the world; the rejection was very much the other way around—Haverberry abandoned me long before I ever left. But once again, doubt takes hold, wrapping its long fingers around my heart and giving a warning squeeze.

I look up at the foyer ceiling for answers I'll never find, instead deciding to go up and check on Spence. I find him in bed all curled up in his Grinch onesie, eyes closed with a movie playing on his laptop, mouth hanging open. The clock on the bedside table reads 9:01, which is early for him, but it was a big day of holiday baking, and the sleep will do him good. I close his laptop and kiss him on the forehead, texting Liv that I'm ready to get that drink.

She tells me to meet her at the Beach Shack, which isn't a shack at all, but a beachfront bar and restaurant that's decorated with driftwood and shells. And even though it takes me all of ten minutes to brush through my hair, throw on a sweater, and drive the 1.5-mile distance, her car is in the parking lot when

I arrive, the scratch I inflicted on it no longer visible. My guilt reemerges, easing only slightly when I push through the door into the cheery room.

The Beach Shack smells of coconut tanning oil and earthy wicker furniture. The back wall is made of glass, leading to a patio that's closed for the winter and trails directly into the sand. And instead of bar nuts, the tables are populated by baskets of handmade salty potato chips that make my mouth water.

Liv is seated at a table near the giant picture window, looking like the cover of a magazine in an emerald-green blouse that has a large Edwardian-esque ruffled collar and a pair of high-waisted black pants with gold sailor's buttons.

"Maddi!" Liv exclaims as I near the table. She stands to kiss me on the cheek.

I take the cushioned seat across from her where there is already a cocktail waiting for me, something amber-colored in a lowball glass, the kind reserved for strong drinks.

"So, tell me, how's Haverberry's favorite baker today?" she asks in an upbeat tone.

I hesitate. While I know it's just a friendly greeting, her words bring me right back to my argument with my mom and by extension, my awkwardness with Wilder.

"Oh," she says before I get a chance to respond. "It's one of those days, huh?"

"It's most definitely one of those days," I agree and grab my drink, which I discover is a riff on an Old Fashioned only infused with spices and something fruity like blackberry.

"Anything I can help with?" Liv asks, and I sip my drink again.

I'm about to brush off her question in the name of good old DeLuca avoidance, but for some reason, it isn't sitting right, like an old coat that's too tight in the shoulders. "Remember when you said that I might not want to poke into that addendum?"

Liv puts down her drink like she's preparing for something that's going to require her full attention.

"I was just wondering," I say, a little embarrassed by how needy this all sounds; I've never been good at asking for help. "Do you think I'm doing the wrong thing here?"

"In trying to leave?" she asks, and I nod. Liv goes quiet for a moment, giving it some thought. "Truth? I don't know."

And even though her response is gentle, it hits me hard. Liv wouldn't lie to me, that much I know.

I sip my drink, embracing the tingly burn it creates in the back of my throat. "I'm telling you, I woke up yesterday feeling like I knew exactly what I wanted and who I was, and now I feel like I have no idea, like maybe I can't see myself clearly at all."

She pushes her silky sheet of hair behind her ear. "Shit, Mads, I feel that way at least once a week."

My eyes whip to her in surprise, ready to call bullshit.

"What?" she says. "It's true."

"Liv, you display more decisive confidence in five minutes than most people do in a lifetime."

She purses her lips, debating whatever she's going to say next and leaning her elbows on the table to level me in her gaze. "Exhibit A: You know my company? That very very challenging company that takes all my time? The one I built from the ground up and still doesn't do the things I want it to? Well, as you might imagine, I have trouble allocating responsibility, preferring instead to micromanage the shit out of everything. And while that never bothered me before, lately I've been feeling like I'm missing out on something."

"Missing out on what?" I ask, grasping at her candor and the camaraderie she's offering.

Liv swishes her drink. "Like maaaybe I want more of a personal life than I let on. Maybe I care more about my relationship with Claudette than I admitted the other day." She shakes her head like hearing it out loud only makes it more confounding. "And I don't know why I'm even telling you this. Either the cheer of the holidays finally thawed my scrooge soul, or I really am desperate as fuck. Hard to tell."

I flash her an understanding smile, ready as always to support everyone's vulnerability except my own. "I'm glad you told me. And it's a good thing, Liv, not a bad one."

"The same way people keep telling you inheriting the bakery is a good thing, not a confusing pile of emotional shit?" she replies.

"Okay, I see your point," I admit, and give her a sympathetic look. "You want my opinion?"

"No, but I know you're going to give it to me anyway."

"You're right. I am," I say, aware that even though she's protesting, she wouldn't have brought it up unless she wanted feedback. "I think you have way, way too much to offer not to share it with another person."

"Yeah, well, love has never been easy for me. Even saying the word makes me feel itchy. Maybe it's the fact that our parents employed nannies to raise us for the first thirteen years of our lives, or maybe it's just something faulty in my wiring. But fuck if it doesn't make me want to run."

"Are you in love with Claudette?" I ask.

Her eyes meet mine. "I have no idea what to do with that question," she says, which is all the affirmation I need.

"You make time for her," I say with a small smile. "You make time for people who are important to you."

"Easier said than done."

"Isn't that the truth," I agree, once again feeling like this conversation is edging against something I don't want to look at.

*Wilder finds me perched on a boulder at the very end of the beach. The waves lap at the multitude of small rocks congregated* on the shore. *The town doesn't sweep the sand this far down the main drag and so the winter rocks pile into heaps, making it impossible to walk on barefoot. Good for finding beach glass and even better for being alone.*

"Hey," he says. "Can we talk?"

*While some part of me reflexively warms that Wilder came to find me, I know I'm still too revved up and wish he'd given me space so that I could come to the conversation with some semblance of calm. But I don't say that, because now that he's here, I don't want him to go. Instead, I just nod at the ocean as he sits on the boulder next to me.*

"So, Jake . . ." he starts.

*My stomach clenches, knowing there's no way to have this conversation without teetering on the edge of all the things we've been ignoring these past months in favor of peace.*

"I just want to make sure you're not going to prom with him because you're mad at me," he continues.

"Wait, what?" *This isn't about Wilder lying to me, it's about his rivalry with Jake? And now that I look at him, I see his usual calm is absent.*

"He's not a good guy, Mads. I don't want you getting hurt because—" *But he doesn't get a chance to finish because I cut him off.*

"As opposed to you, who are such a sterling individual that you planned a whole prom limo without ever telling me?" *I say, now fired up in exactly the way I didn't want.*

*But this time he's not balancing me out with his comforting steady tone, he's matching my frustration.* "Look, it's not like that. Asking Elaina just—"

"Elaina?" *I say, my sinking feeling increasing. She's a gorgeous Cuban-American with a wicked sense of humor and a kind streak a mile long. It's impossible not to like her.* "Are you seriously going to try to tell me that you asked her and then forgot? It just slipped your mind for . . . How long has it been exactly?"

*He leans his elbows on his knees, momentarily looking at his hands. "A week."*

*I swallow, trying to hold back the wave of hurt and failing, my hormones tap dancing on my nerves. "Tell me, Wilder. Did you hope I just wouldn't find out so you wouldn't feel obligated to perform some sort of charity and invite your pregnant friend as a tagalong?"*

*"Hey," he says, looking up. "That's not what's going on. I could never be embarrassed by you. I don't know how you could even think that."*

*"Maybe because you're acting like I'm a third-tier friend."*

*He hesitates, annoyed at me or himself, maybe both. "Look, things were finally going well with us. I just didn't want to complicate it by . . . You want the truth? I was actually working up to telling Elaina I can't go with her."*

*I stare at him, my upset spiraling into something unruly. Since I've gotten pregnant, it's as if I vibrate at a more intense frequency, unable to shrug off slights or pull back the reins. It's one of the reasons I've kept to myself so much. But right now, Wilder is poking at my biggest insecurity, the one I try to hide more vehemently than all the rest, the nagging voice that keeps telling me I've changed for the worse and that no one will ever love me the same way because of it.*

*"Fuck your pity," I fire back. "Don't you dare break it off because of me. You think I wouldn't be happy you had a prom date, that I was incapable of handling that news?" I know I'm not doing myself any favors, but it's too late; I'm strapped to the board and headed down the slope at a dizzying speed, backward.*

*"Come on, Mads. You know I don't mean it that way."*

*"No, actually I don't."*

*He gives me a look like* Please *don't do this.*

*"Tell me, why would you having a prom date complicate things, as you so clearly claimed?"*

He huffs but doesn't answer, which increases my fire tenfold. This is what we always come to, him and me, a place in a conversation where he just shuts down and lets me dangle with my emotions all on my own. And today I'm not having it.

"Is it because you think I'm still in love with you?" I say, my tone barbed and dangerous. "Because, if that's the case, I can tell you with the utmost certainty that I most definitely am not."

He looks out at the ocean, his expression hardening. And I know without a doubt that his emotional drawbridge is lifting, sealing me out.

"Great. Silence," I say. "I want to say that I'm surprised, but I guess I should have expected this from someone whose mother told them to break up with me."

Wilder goes so still that I think he might have ceased breathing. "What did you just say?"

"You heard me."

He looks like he's falling even though he hasn't moved an inch. The color drains from his face and then is replaced by tensed muscles. "You have no idea what you're talking about."

"Then explain it to me!" I say, giving him one last chance, imploring him to tell me something that makes sense, something that explains why after seventeen years of friendship he's suddenly decided to close part of his life off to me.

"Just let it be, Maddi."

"And if I can't?" I say, drawing a line in the sand, and even as I do I kind of wish I didn't.

"Then I guess you can't," is all he says. And even though he's sitting next to me, I feel him slipping away, our truce evaporating into the air like a misty memory.

"Okay then," Liv says, rolling her glass between her palms, "as long as we're doing whatever this honesty thing is, let me ask you something. Is the bakery important to you?"

My heart stutters like it hit the brakes too hard. "That's not—"

"The same thing?" Liv says, finishing my sentence. "Because I would argue that it is."

I frown.

"Look Mads," she says, "I know this is tough as shit for you. I'm not diminishing that. But just like you gave me advice, I'm going to give you some. Don't let what happened all those years ago take away something that might be really good for you now."

I stare at her, wanting to argue, to tell her she doesn't actually know what happened all those years ago because she wasn't there. But I know that's unfair and more importantly, I know she's saying it because she cares. "I kind of hate you," I say, in a tone that suggests the opposite.

"Well good, then I'm on brand."

We both reach for our drinks.

"You know what?" Liv says, swallowing. "I have an idea."

I give her the side-eye. "Why does that make me nervous?"

"Because you know it's going to be on point?"

I'm unconvinced.

"Remember that bet we made? I would argue that I won," she says, and as I open my mouth to protest, she lifts her hand. "And you, I'm certain would argue that you did. So why don't we call it a draw?"

"Okay," I say slowly, not sure what I'm agreeing to. "I think I can get on board with that."

"Great. Because then we both get to pick a prize."

Curveball.

"Why didn't I see that coming?"

"I really can't answer that for you, Mads. It was broadcast like a mile away."

I want to laugh, but I'm not sure I'm going to think whatever she chooses is funny. "What kind of prize?"

"Considering our conversation—"

I cut her off. "No, definitely nothing related to our conversation."

A small smirk appears on her red lips. "Considering our conversation, I think we should each choose something that'll be good for the other, something that might help us solve these issues we don't know how to deal with. Not something broad like *spend more time with my girlfriend* or *really think about what the bakery means*, but something tangible, like a one-off event just to dip our toes in and see how it feels."

I stare at her, chewing on the inside of my cheek, both intrigued and wary.

"What do you say? Are you brave enough to run a little experiment with me? Are you still that daring girl who once roller-skated across the teachers' lunch table because Matt Mazzeo said she didn't have the balls?"

I huff. "Don't do that. You know I can't say no to a dare."

"How about this, if you're worried, you can go first. Pick whatever you want, and I promise mine won't be worse." But by the way she's looking at me, we both know she's got me, that she's pushing all the right buttons.

I glare at her in response. "A one-off event, right?"

Liv's smile widens in victory. "Yup."

"Okay then," I say. "Give me a minute here."

"Take all the time you need," she says, reclining in her chair and popping a potato chip in her mouth.

But it only takes me a moment to run through everything I know about her and her girlfriend, one detail in particular standing out above the rest from that dinner I had at her house last week. "Okay, Liv . . . Invite your girlfriend home for the holidays."

The calm composure she brandished a minute ago vanishes

as she sits up so fast, she chokes on her chip. "Wow. You went right for the throat."

"What?" I say, the picture of innocence. "Even if she's spending the holidays with her family, it'll let her know how much you want to be with her. She'll think it's sweet and considering tomorrow is Christmas Eve, it's a low-risk ask."

Liv shakes her head. "She's *not* spending the holidays with her family. She's in the city."

"Oh," I say, instantly realizing that what I thought was nothing more than a thoughtful gesture is something much bigger, and worse still—I'm the one setting the bar for Liv's rebuttal. "If you want me to pick something else—"

"I do," Liv says.

"Okay," I say, ready to oblige and get us both out of the hot seat. But something stops me. Maybe it's the conflicted look on Liv's face or the way she seemed so sad when she talked about loving Claudette. "If you're really sure."

"Are you trying to reverse psychology me? Because I invented that game."

"Actually, no," I say. "Hand to heart. I'm just making sure that you're not going to spend the holidays thinking about her and wishing she were here but are just too scared to actually tell her that."

Liv opens her mouth and closes it again.

"Liv?"

She purses her lips, clearly warring with herself. "Fuck you, Madeline DeLuca. I'll do it. But I want to be clear that it's under duress and also that I'm taking responsibility for being the imbecile who came up with this plan."

"You don't have to—" I start.

"No, the fact that I don't want to is exactly why I have to. In fact, I'm going to drive to the city tonight, ask her in person," she says, and I can't help but admire her resolve.

"Tonight? But it's nearly ten."

"Yup, which is why I'm going to have to cut this evening short," she says, and takes the last sip of her drink. "But not before I give you your assignment."

I wince, deeply regretting picking something so big for Liv. What kind of stupid am I?

She assesses me. "Here's the thing . . . I was thinking about having you write a letter to your dad about the bakery, something that would be just for you, to sort out your feelings."

"That actually sounds—" I don't get to say *reasonable* before she continues.

"But now I'm thinking that's not quite right, that like me, you're happy enough to keep your emotions in your head where you can manage the living hell out of them. So instead, I want you to have an honest conversation about the bakery . . . with my brother."

I gulp. "I don't think—"

"I want you to tell him how you really feel about the place, lay it all out in the open. No one loves that bakery more than you two. He'll understand better than anyone. And maybe you'll get that clarity you're after, or at least put your decision about leaving in perspective."

I take a beat, feeling all kinds of uncomfortable. I can barely talk to Wilder about little things much less bare complicated feelings I don't understand myself. I'm about to tell her no, that she has to pick something else, but before I can formulate a response, she's typing into her phone.

"Tonight," she adds, and I just about slide off my chair. "I'm texting him to come here now. That way we both get this done before we come to our senses and call the whole thing off."

I rub my hands down my face, hoping Wilder's busy or maybe his phone fell in the toilet. "Liv, this really isn't a good—"

"He's on his way," she says, and looks up at me. "And yeah, it turns out this was a shit idea of the highest caliber, but there you have it. We're in it now and who knows, maybe it's exactly what we both need."

"While I love that you're trying to look at the bright side here, I'm just not there yet. I'm pretty sure I'd like to hide under this table."

She laughs. "Give me a couple of hours and I'll be right there with you, cursing us both."

## CHAPTER 23

### HEART RACING LIKE A HUMMINGBIRD

**CAKE** — *layers of coconut, pineapple, and bananas, cream cheese frosting over cinnamon-scented cake, not sure if I'm in love or having a heart attack*

Wilder takes no time at all to show up at the Beach Shack, either that or my sense of time is warped because my adrenaline is pumping like a burst water main. And as he walks in the door, I know I'm not up to this task. Vague references to wrongs disguised as biting wit? That I can do. Straightforward communication about my true feelings and insecurities? Fuck outta here with that. Especially considering everything that's happened recently, which I've spent more time analyzing than I'll ever admit.

I watch Wilder cross the room. Actually, everyone does. His dark wavy hair outlines his face in a tragically beautiful way, like a painting of some grand duke in a museum come to life. He wears a gray sweater over a black-and-white pinstriped button-down that's rolled up at the cuffs, his wool coat and scarf thrown over his arm. But under the polished getup, there is also something softer, something around the eyes and the way he holds his mouth that makes you feel like he was thinking specifically about you.

Wilder, seemingly not noticing the attention, heads straight for us. And when his gaze meets mine, he smiles.

And that's all it takes, one smile and my heart starts pounding like a lovestruck teen. In self-defense, I shrink an inch in my chair.

"That's my cue," Liv says just as Wilder approaches. She stands, giving me a fast kiss on the cheek and then pats her brother's arm. "Take care of our girl."

Wilder looks at me and then back at his sister. "You weren't kidding about being in a rush," he says. "What's this emergency?"

Liv gathers up her coat and purse. "Ask me tomorrow when I get back from the city. And wish me luck!"

Wilder's expression turns knowing like he can sense something important must be happening with Claudette, but Liv doesn't see it because she's already carving a path through the crowd.

Wilder's gaze returns to me. "Maddi," he says with a hint of a smile, making my name sound important.

"Wilder," I manage, now deeply regretting finishing my cocktail.

He notes my empty glass. "Can I get you anything from the bar?"

I'm about to say "yes and please" to the liquid confidence, but then think better of it, considering I drove here. But the idea of sitting in this cheery seashelled room staring into his well-constructed face and baring my soul with no alcohol also sounds impossible. "Not sure I should," I say with deep regret.

"Dare I ask what you and my sister are up to this time?" Wilder takes the seat across from mine, focusing in a way that assures me I have his full attention. He doesn't scan the room to see who he knows, or glance at the menu. He just stares directly into my eyes, his scent drifting toward me like a fishhook.

I shake my head, searching for the wits I once possessed. "Believe me, I wish I knew. I think Liv and I have lost our minds."

A smile turns up the corners of his mouth. "I seem to remember that was a common occurrence growing up, you two concocting some absolutely terrible idea that was sure to give one or all of our parents a stroke."

"Remind me again," I say, elongating the words, happy for the diversion into easier subjects. "Who it was that decided to borrow his dad's boat without asking and without checking the fuel tank before we left, marooning us on White Sands Island for eight hours before your parents realized what happened and sent out the National Guard?"

He chuckles. "Liv?"

Now I laugh, too, the sound catching me off guard.

A guy with a black waiter's apron stops at our table. I instantly recognize him—Benny, one of Jake's old football buddies. I guess I'd been so consumed with my conversation with Liv that I hadn't noticed him earlier.

"Hey man," Benny says, clapping Wilder on the shoulder, and as his eyes drift to me, they widen. "No way! Maddi DeLuca? I heard you were home."

"I'm here all right," I say, not sure if that's a good thing.

"It's been what? Like a decade? That's wild," he says, but before I can respond, he continues. "Hey, how did everything work out? I mean with your kid and everything? Last time I saw you, you were close to popping."

I take a breath. It's not that I'm surprised by the idiocy of this question or the enthusiasm with which he asked it, but it's just been a long day. And while I feel like I have a better tolerance for this type of thing than I did two weeks ago, it exhausts me just the same.

Wilder's face goes stone-cold. "Hey, Benny?" he asks before

I get a chance to formulate a response. "How did everything work out with your divorce? The last time I saw you, you were moving out."

I steal a very surprised look at Wilder. He didn't just say that, did he?

Benny's face falls. "Shit, sorry man," he says, giving Wilder a defeated look. "I get your point, but way harsh."

"I'm not the one you should apologize to," Wilder replies, and my shock deepens.

Benny looks at me. "Sorry, Maddi. No offense meant."

"No offense taken," I say, actually feeling a little bad for him. I haven't seen Wilder lash out like that since seventh grade when Max Westman told me I'd be prettier if I had bigger boobs. "And to answer your question, my son is wonderful. The best, really."

Benny perks up, fully on board with rerouting the conversation. "You should bring him down to the beach this summer. I'll give him a surfing lesson," he offers, and something about it gets me. Yes, Benny started in an off-putting way, but in retrospect, I think it was more out of curiosity than malice. And it gives me pause, making me wonder how many other interactions I may have misinterpreted for judgment since I've been back.

"I think he would love that," I say.

Benny grins. "Then it's a plan." He pulls a pen from behind his ear. "So, what can I get you guys?"

Wilder gestures to me.

"Just water, please," I say.

"Same," Wilder agrees. "And a big basket of fries, with all the dipping sauces."

I give him a look, wondering if he simply wanted a snack or if he's appealing to my love of condiments.

Benny takes leave of us with a nod, and once again it's just me and Wilder. For a moment we're both quiet.

"You didn't have to do that," I say.

"The fries? They really are amazing, and they hand make all their sauces, so."

I give him a look like *you know what I mean*.

A small knowing smile appears on his lips, and he scratches the back of his neck. "Truth? I just didn't want you to think Benny's attitude was a shared one."

"Oh," I say, shifting in my seat, not expecting him to explain.

But he doesn't stop there. "Don't take this the wrong way, but I know you care what the people in this town think," he says, and I can feel my shoulders rise an inch.

"I think you're confusing me with my mother," I say, trying to exit the conversation as fast as possible.

Wilder shakes his head. "I don't mean the way your mother does. I mean that you're sensitive when it comes to this place. That you care. And I didn't want you to feel like people think badly of you here, because they don't. Everyone's just excited you're back, even if they express it badly."

I stare at him, my heart thumping like a persistent headache, as he casually voices my insecurity. "That's not . . . I don't—" I stop, drawing in air and releasing it again. "Don't do that," I say instead, feeling exposed. "Don't act like you know what I'm thinking."

Benny shows back up then, placing the water and two cups on the table, filling them both as we say a quick thank you.

Benny walks away and Wilder picks up where we left off. "I'm not your enemy, Maddi. At least I don't want to be."

It's so close to what my mother said yesterday that I balk, my impossibly fast pulse sounding all the alarms. And I can't understand how we got back here, how five minutes with Wilder and I'm on the defensive like I was a career footballer.

"I don't think you're my enemy," I manage, my voice less confident.

"Don't you?" he asks, and it sounds so genuine that I hesitate. Because he's not exactly wrong.

"It's just . . ." I start. "When I saw you in my dad's bakery. I don't know. I . . ." I trail off, not sure I can vocalize how jarring that was, how it was something I once wished for so badly that seeing it all these years later in this distorted context felt like a betrayal.

The worry line between his eyebrows appears. "Is that the problem?" he asks. "Is that what you want? For me to give up the bakery?"

My eyes find his, more shocked than anything. I know I haven't exactly hidden how annoyed I was that he was in my father's will, but that was when I was angry, cut to the core that Wilder somehow became favored over me with my own parents. "I know you wouldn't do that."

He looks briefly out the window and then back to me. "If it's what you really want, if it meant you would stay, then yes . . . I would," he says, and suddenly I can't breathe. I hear his words, but I don't understand them. Didn't he tell me just the other day that the bakery was and is his dream, that no matter what he did or where he went in the world that it didn't make him happy the way Nothing Batter does?

"Wilder—" I say, barely managing his name. I rub my forehead, unable to ignore the huge sacrifice he's willing to make for me. And the longer I look at him, the worse my overwhelm gets. My breath comes unevenly and everything feels tight, like someone placed a giant anvil directly on my chest. "I don't want you to give up the bakery. You love it." I swallow. "And the bakery should be loved. My dad—" I stop, unable to get out the words *would have wanted it that way*.

The look of worry on his face only fans the flames of my shame. The awful truth now hangs between us, that Wilder loved the bakery when I couldn't, that even now he's willing to disappoint his family and fight them tooth and nail just to run it. *That* is probably why my dad left him half of it because Wilder was right that day in my dining room when he said the difference between us was that he wanted it.

I shake my head, unable to look at him, terrified my thoughts are showing on my face and that I'll break down in the middle of the goddamn Beach Shack. "I'm sorry," I say, leaving becoming a visceral need. "But I don't think I can do this. I think I need to go." I'll just tell Liv I didn't have it in me, that I decided a long time ago to shut all this out. And that to bear that kind of weight again, to risk shattering my heart a second time, is not something I'm capable of.

"Maddi," Wilder says, but I'm already out of my chair gathering my things.

"I don't want to ruin your night," I say, barely able to look at him, trying to escape before my emotions get the better of me. "You ordered fries. You should enjoy them."

But he's standing with me, pulling money out of his wallet, and placing it on the table with what appears to be a very generous tip for Benny.

I hadn't even considered the check. "Let me pay—"

But he shakes his head. "I got this one," he says, still being way too generous about the fact that I'm bolting. "I'll walk you out."

I put my coat on as we make our way through the crowd, my unease growing with every step. By the time we actually make it to the parking lot, I'm not only feeling ridiculous, but I'm disappointed in myself.

"See you tomorrow night?" Wilder says, generously giving me an out, and even though I can see that he wants to say more, he doesn't push it—another kindness, which only makes me feel worse.

And so, I stand there frozen in place a handful of feet from my car, watching him walk away. I should let him go. Nothing

I'm going to say is going to make anything better. I'll only confuse things more. But his offer to give up the bakery for me rails
in my mind, twisting what I thought I knew about him and
making me doubt myself. Was Mom right that I'm my own
worst enemy? Am I pushing Wilder away for no reason?

*Jake picks me up for prom, but we don't take pictures on my
staircase or stand in awkward poses in the backyard next to the
rose bushes. There isn't the bit where my dad puts his arm around
me and tells me how beautiful I look. Spoiler: I look like a baby
blue chiffon mushroom. And there's no sweet moment in front of
the mirror where my mom gives me her pearls and tells me to enjoy
myself. Instead, they both look worried, and Mom asks me if I really
want to do this, if it's a good idea.*

*Jake honks his horn in my driveway, and I leave without fan-
fare, nothing like my junior prom when I went with Wilder. Even
our arrival at The Black-Eyed Susan is underwhelming. We just
pull leisurely into a parking spot and Jake says, "You ready?"*

*But the moment I slide out of his truck, the air buzzes with
energy. The place is already packed, and the swell of music reaches
the parking lot. And to tell the truth, I'm not ready. The closer we
get to the door, the more I think my mom might have been right.
That it's just going to be another occasion for people to talk about
how sad I must be that I screwed up my life. Jake, however, seems
relaxed and happy as always.*

*"You cool?" he asks as we take the stairs toward the door.*

*"Yup," I tell him, even though I'm not. I'm highly considering
doing the pregnant version of bolting (fast waddling?).*

*He seems to take my affirmation at face value, his smile never
wavering. "Let's get a picture," he says as we step inside the Love
Under the Sea themed room that shimmers turquoise and has
moving water and fish projected on the ceiling. Jake gestures to
the blue coral archway encased in twinkle lights and fake bubbles.*

"I'm not sure I need to memorialize this moment," I say, touching my belly that sticks out farther than my boobs.

"Sure you do," he says. "It's all part of the fun."

While I don't agree, I'm also not about to make a big deal about it. So, we step under the archway and the photographer asks us to smile. Jake puts one arm around my shoulders and uses his other hand to point to my belly, a huge grin on his face. For a split second, it's nice to have someone look excited about the baby after months of reinforced disappointment. But it's like too-sweet frosting that hurts your teeth and cracks your tongue; Jake isn't going to be there, not when it matters. He'll be off at college doing keg stands while I'll be up all night with baby drool in my hair. I try to push the thought away, to not resent the fact that he made the same decision I did and yet I'm the one shouldering the burden.

We make our way through the front room into the main dining room, which is centered around a huge dance floor, above which flowing gauzy fabric is suspended in the air, adding to the moving water effect.

I spot Wilder across the room, laughing with friends, and his tux makes him look mature in a flattering way. For a second, I regret our fight this past week, wishing I could just walk up to him and crack a joke or tell him how weird my parents were before I left the house. But I've never known how to let things roll off my back; instead, I carry all the slights with me, accumulating pebbles until they become an impossibly heavy boulder.

Which is the exact moment Jake slips his hand into mine. "Should we dance?"

I take a second. "Um," I say, gently slipping my hand out of his, not sure how to respond. It's hard not to notice that he moved closer in conjunction with Wilder coming into view. Plus, I'm not trying to reconcile romantically with Jake. Things are complicated enough as it is.

But I'm saved from having to figure it out by Raff, who claps Jake on the back.

"*There you are, man. We were waiting for you,*" Raff says, all smiles. "*Hey, Maddi.*"

"*Hey,*" I say.

*And suddenly Matt is there, too. "Are you kidding me with this place? Have you seen what my lady Jenna did with these decorations? She's a fucking Picasso."*

*Raff grunts a laugh. "You know Picasso was an abstract art—"* He stops, reconsidering his audience. "*You're right, Matt, fucking Picasso-esque.*"

*I grin and Matt goes on about how he wishes he could have thrown the after-party, but his dads weren't convinced. "Speaking of partying,"* Matt says to Jake with an obvious elbow nudge. He hands Jake his drink, which is most definitely spiked.

*Without hesitation, Jake takes a sip. I know it must be strong the way his mouth puckers. And I have a small sinking feeling. It's not that I particularly care if Jake wants to drink, it's that he was the one who said he wasn't going to, that we'd have solidarity. Plus, he's driving, which leaves me in the greatly undesirable position of policing him in a way I shouldn't have to. When did I become categorically unfun? Is this my life now?*

*Jake hands the drink to Raff, who sips it and passes it back to Matt. In about three seconds flat they're all making jokes and heckling each other. And while I'm happy Jake's having a good time, it's hard not to feel like I don't belong in that fun, not the way I used to.*

"*I'll be back,*" I say to Jake, gesturing to the refreshment table across the room.

*As I walk away, people follow me with their eyes. I can hear their whispers—*Can you believe she and Jake came together *and* Is that a good idea in her condition? *I'm immediately exhausted, just worn the heck out by the monotony of it. The worst part is, I half agree with them.*

*I reach the table and make my way to the bowl of lemonade, where Mr. Pitzer ladles some into a blue paper cup. I nod my thanks, but before I can turn around, the scent of fireplace drifts my way.*

*"I'd love one, too," Wilder says to Mr. Pitzer, whose frown remains permanently fixed under his mustache.*

*My head whips to Wilder, surprised he came right for me. It's not that we're not on speaking terms, but ever since our fight on the beach there has been tension and space, like we're carefully stepping around each other, trying to avoid the bomb we know is hidden somewhere in the dark.*

*He's wearing an easy smile, a look I rarely see on him these days. "It's a shame the decorating committee was underfunded," he says, sipping his lemonade and glancing at the floor to ceiling glittering water décor that is way over-the-top. His dark wavy hair, which looks like it was initially combed, is just this side of tousled, and somehow it makes him appear more dashing than not.*

*I find myself comforted by his joke and its nod to normalcy. "I'm deeply regretting wearing blue. I feel like a prop. A baby whale or maybe a bloated dolphin?"*

*"First, no. You're beautiful. And second, so is that baby," he says, never dropping his smile.*

*My eyes widen. I could hug him. He can't know how much I needed that boost, or maybe he does and that's why he said it. A warm feeling pools in my stomach. And instead of brushing him off or rolling my eyes the way I normally would, I say, "Thanks, Wilder," in a way that lets him know I mean it.*

*"Always, Maddi," he says, and as if we were the leads in an '80s movie, a slow song starts. And when he doesn't break eye contact, my stomach dips in a way it hasn't in many months, just as the baby kicks, like the baby is responding favorably to his presence.*

*I look down, reflexively touching my belly.*

*Wilder looks down, too.*

*"The baby's kicking," I explain.*

*"May I?" he asks, holding his hand out.*

*I nod, taking his wrist and placing his hand where mine just was. And with luck, the little one kicks right into his palm.*

*He looks up, wonderment in his eyes. "That's incredible," he says, and I know it's the hormones, but I get a little misty-eyed.*

*Wilder leaves his hand on my stomach until the kicks die down, and for a long second, we just stare at each other. And I'm not sure why, but it feels like we're both thinking about how things might have been different.*

*"Hey, Mads?" he starts with a weighted tone, and it almost seems like he's nervous, an emotion so rare for Wilder that it gives me pause. "Will you dance with me?"*

*For a second, I don't know how to react, unsure what he's actually asking. Is this a friend dance, or a "hey let's squash this fight" dance, or is it something more?*

*But as if fate were conspiring against us, the slow song ends. We both glance at the DJ, and I say, "Next one?"*

*"Most definitely," he agrees.*

*But the next one I'm in the bathroom with my baby-squished bladder. And the one after that? Well, let's just say I wish I'd made my exit fifteen minutes prior.*

Wilder grabs the handle of his car door, and a surge of panic jolts through me. If I let him walk away, everything will be unsaid and unfinished the way it always is. We'll be right back in our holding pattern of missed connections.

"Wilder, wait," I say, the panic edging into my voice. "Don't go."

He looks up, and as his eyes find mine, time stretches before me like pulled taffy. He opens his mouth to respond, but I stop him as I walk closer.

"Wait. Let me get this out or I'm going to lose my nerve," I say, wading through my fear to get to something true. "You're not just here randomly tonight because Liv needed to rush to the city."

Wilder's eyebrows push together.

"Liv and I made a deal."

"A deal?" he asks, unsure.

I nod. "That I would talk to you about the bakery."

His perplexed expression doesn't waver.

"And I'm probably going to say this wrong," I start, in an attempt to acknowledge my terrible communication skills. "But as you may have noticed, I've been confused about the bakery lately. And I got into a terrible fight with my mom about leaving during which she told me that if I hate this place so much that I should just move back to California. Liv suggested that I ask you—" I stop short because what should be a simple re quest to hash things out feels like an uphill trek sans oxygen. I haven't asked Wilder for help, haven't confided in him in any real way since we were teens. I swallow, breaking eye contact and rubbing my eyebrow even though it doesn't itch. "I think you might be the only person who understands how complicated my relationship with the bakery is."

When I venture a look at him, his expression has softened. "I'd love to talk to you about the bakery," he says, and I can tell he really means it, that he's flattered.

"Great," I say, even though my instinct is to run.

"Would you like to take a walk?" he asks, and I follow his eyeline to the beach.

I nod. Movement sounds far better than standing next to our cars.

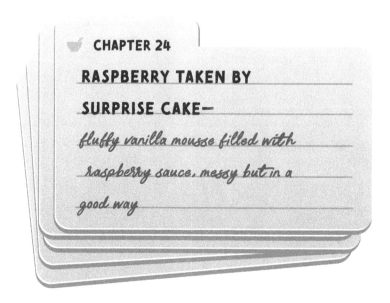

## CHAPTER 24

### RASPBERRY TAKEN BY
### SURPRISE CAKE—
*fluffy vanilla mousse filled with raspberry sauce, messy but in a good way*

For a moment, Wilder and I walk in silence. I put my gloves on as we make our way from the parking lot onto the sand. The beach is calm and the water laps lazily at the shore. The air smells of smoothed rocks and damp sand while the moon casts a long bright line across the sparkling ocean. It's so pretty that I don't mind the cold.

We take a handful of steps before I figure out what I want to say, and he kindly gives me space to do it. "I know you always got along with my father," I start, figuring it's the best way to ease into the bakery itself.

"I did," he says with a happy nod. "Believe it or not I missed the bakery almost immediately when I went away to college." He pauses a split second like he feels shy. "I actually wrote your dad letters."

I stop dead in my tracks, and he stops a step later, turning to face me. "You wrote to him?" I repeat, my voice bright with surprise.

His eyes dip momentarily before meeting my gaze. "Actually . . . I wrote him once a month for eight years."

"What?" I say barely above a whisper, not able to process it. Wilder wrote my father letters for *eight years*?

Wilder's shyness doesn't dissipate, only exacerbating my shock. "It started when I was at university. I was studying business, but I would bake on the weekends, and so I used to write him questions about recipes and ask his advice."

I stare at Wilder, trying to make sense of it. "But afterward you went to Cordon Bleu . . . if anything, you probably knew techniques he didn't."

A nostalgic look appears on his face like he's remembering. "I did it because I enjoyed it."

And just like that, the oppressive weight of guilt resumes. But as my initial reaction fades, something softer creeps in—the thought of how much my dad probably enjoyed this correspondence. Wilder knew, like I did, that my father was a relic from a simpler time. He loved his routine and his small circle of people; he didn't text or make much use of email. I can picture him opening Wilder's letters at his desk, putting on his reading glasses, and setting about his response enthusiastically. And while part of me wishes I had thought of this, I don't begrudge them for sharing it without me.

He sighs like he's debating going on, and I'm grateful when he does. "You know how we used to say that we were born to the wrong parents? That you were much more unapologetically yourself like mine and I more reserved like yours?"

I nod.

He wears a small sad smile. "Your father understood me in a way, maybe because we both kept our feelings too close to the chest, or maybe because we were both rather singular in our focus sometimes. But I always felt close to him. And . . ." He looks briefly out at the ocean and then back at me. "It made me feel like I was still connected to the bakery, among other things."

*Among other things.* I break eye contact, my heart thumping. And for the first time, I see Wilder, too, has residual grief over the loss of my father. "You made the window display, didn't you?" I start, my mouth suddenly dry and my voice quieter.

He smiles. "I took a chocolate course in Switzerland," he says, like that explains it.

I've taken multiple chocolate courses and I couldn't manage that display with three months and a magic wand. Also, there's the bit about the display including details of things that are important to me, but I don't say that. "You did it before you even owned the bakery."

"I did," he says like he understands I'm asking for an explanation. "Owning the bakery is an honor. But even when I didn't, I loved it just the same."

A lump forms in my throat. *Owning the bakery is an honor.* The truth of it hits me so hard that I feel a tingle in my throat, working its way up to the bridge of my nose, my chest rising and falling too quickly. I stand there for a long moment, unable to respond.

"Maddi?" he says, searching my face with concern.

I exhale one long breath, desperately trying to pull back my reaction. "It's fine. I'm fine."

"You know it's okay not to be fine, right?" he says so gently that my chin actually shakes. "That there's no right way to be when you lose someone."

And even though I agree with him in the larger, vaguer sense, I absolutely do not agree as far as it relates to this moment. Having a tough conversation is one thing, losing control in front of Wilder is another.

He waits, giving me the space I need to collect myself. And in a way that makes it worse.

"You're doing that nice thing again," I say, trying to shift the tone.

But his voice is comforting and steady like he knows I need that. "As opposed to being rude and unfeeling?"

"Exactly," I agree. "If you were acting like the villain I've built you up to be in my head, I'd be able to brush you off right now." But the moment I say it, I feel bad.

Wilder nods like I'm confirming what he always suspected.

"It's not that you're a villain . . ." I say, trying to step it back. "It's just," I pause, not actually sure anymore who Wilder is in my life.

"Complicated?" he offers.

"Definitely that," I say, but it still feels stingy. Here he is showing up for me in exactly the way I need and I'm trying to write it off as a fluke, just waiting until he does something terrible so I can be right about him. I tuck a few stray hairs behind my ear. "I'm being unfair."

"You're being honest."

I shake my head. "See there you go again. Stop being so generous with me," I say, unsure what to make of either of us.

"What if I don't want to stop?" he says.

I open my mouth to respond, but nothing comes out.

Unlike me, he doesn't shy away from the conversation. "What if I think you got the raw end of a very bad deal all those years ago, and that you deserve as much generosity as I can give you?"

It's getting increasingly hard to look at him. "Wilder," I start and stop. "It wasn't your . . ." I'm about to say fault, but isn't that what I've been telling myself all these years, that without my bond with Wilder that this town became unbearable, an oppressive weight of rejection and loneliness? I rub my hands over my face, suddenly flustered. "You're doing that thing . . ."

I say, exasperated. "That Wilder thing, where you show up at the perfect moment and say exactly what I need to hear. The thing that always pulled me back from the metaphorical edge when we were teens. The thing that—" I stop abruptly, realizing I was about to say *made me fall in love with you.*

I think he must get the idea, though, because he goes still like he needs a moment to consider his response.

But something in me doesn't want to stop, doesn't want to hold back the things I've so carefully hidden. Some part of me is just plain exhausted. And I'm suddenly seeing my agreement with Liv differently, not so much as an opportunity to hash things out, but as a way to voice the things in my past that I don't have the strength to carry anymore.

*Returning from my umpteenth bathroom trip, I spot Jake on the edge of the dance floor with Benny.*

*"Hey," I say, figuring this is as good a time as any to tell him I'm going home and will (not so) regretfully miss the after-party. I'll just blame it on being pregnant and tired and he won't take it personally. It's not that Jake has been a great date, but in a way, I get it. I can't have the kind of fun he wants to, jumping all over the dance floor and sneaking drinks from Matt's flask.*

*But the moment I walk up to him, the music changes to a slow song and the DJ says, "This one is for all you couples out there, the last one of the night."*

*We both look up at the DJ booth, now perfectly stuck in the awkward gray area of do or don't.*

*"Shall we?" Jake says after a beat. He holds his hand out to me.*

*For a second, I hesitate, remembering my promise to Wilder. But it's not like I can bring that up now; it'd be a disaster. Plus, I've barely danced with Jake at all, and to deny him this would be unkind. So, I place my hand in his and walk onto the dance floor. I'm sure Wilder is dancing with Elaina anyway. It's definitely less awkward this way, I think, trying to convince myself that some small part of me isn't disappointed.*

*Jake eyes me as he puts one hand on my nonexistent waist. "Everything okay?"*

*"Definitely," I say, as we sway back and forth at a distance because of my belly. Even so, at this proximity, I catch a whiff of alcohol on his breath and it's stronger than I expected. For a flash of a second, I get frustrated, but I let it go. I'm leaving anyway, so it doesn't matter. Let him have fun.*

*Jake doesn't look convinced. "If you say so."*

*I give him a questioning look. "Huh?"*

*Jake shrugs. "Nothing," he says, but after another full rotation, he continues anyway. "It's just that you've been out of sorts since we got here."*

*For a second, I'm confused. I actually thought I was doing a pretty good job of being pleasant and trying not to cramp his night. "Jake, I'm pregnant. I can't do—"*

*"No, I know," he says. "I don't mean that. You've just been sort of . . . well, sulky."*

*I press my lips together, trying to suppress the flare of hormones that makes me take that the wrong way. But considering the looseness in his voice, and his whiskey-scented breath, I decide once again to let it go.*

*"Now you're mad?" he asks like I'm just proving his point. "I just meant that you've been so quiet, ya know? Not like your usual self."*

*And this gets me, stings disproportionately, because he's right. I stop dancing. "No, I haven't been my usual self," I say, matter-of-factly. "But it isn't just tonight. And you'd know that if you'd spent any time with me these past few months."*

*Jake rubs his hand over his face. "Okay, Maddi, you're probably right," he says like I'm being unreasonable but he's too magnanimous to point it out, which really fires me up. Doesn't he know how hard it is for me to even be here like this, how alone I've felt these past few months, how I can't ever just* be *anymore? Maybe he doesn't know the extent of it, but he can't be totally oblivious, either. Not to mention that I've been doing my damnedest to not interfere with his good time tonight. But even though I want to stomp on his foot, I don't.*

*"Look, I know this isn't the perfect situation," I say, keeping my voice calm, trying to factor in that he's probably saying half of this because of the whiskey. "I'll admit that I'm not the best prom date. And to be truthful, I'm exhausted. So, I think it'll just be easier on everyone if I go home and let you go to the after-party with your friends."*

*Jake takes a breath like he should have expected this. "Fine. I'll drive you home if that's what you want."*

*"Thanks, but no need to give me a ride," I say, relieved that we're going to call it quits instead of trying to press on with this failed experiment. I'm about to tell him I'll just grab a taxi, but he responds before I get the chance.*

*"I guess Wilder beat me to it, huh," he says like it was inevitable. "I don't know why I'm surprised."*

*I open my mouth, taken aback. Suddenly his off mood and all his comments about me not having fun take on a new light. He thinks this is about Wilder? But I don't want to get into the weeds with him on that one while he's tipsy; all I can do at this point is be honest. "It's not that. I'm not accepting the ride because you've been drinking."*

*He stares at me. "Seriously?" He laughs. "I only had a few sips."*

*And here we are, exactly where I don't want to be.*

*Which is the moment Wilder appears next to us, and by the look on his face I get the sense he overheard the last part of that conversation.*

"Can I cut in?" he asks, even though we're not dancing.

"No, you can't," Jake says before I can get out a response.

"Good thing I wasn't asking you," Wilder fires back.

"Don't you have a date somewhere that you should be paying attention to instead of talking mine up?" Jake says, and I can feel this situation unraveling, both of them pulling the loose strings with all their might.

Wilder doesn't hesitate. "Not my problem you're insecure. You want Maddi's attention? Earn it."

"Oh, that's rich, coming from the guy who likes to pretend he's perfect, but then screws Maddi over at every turn."

And whatever hope I had of getting out of this place without incident, begins to slip away. The people around us are starting to take notice.

Something changes in Wilder's face then, and his calm façade splinters, anger spiking in its place. "You want to talk about screwing people over? What about that baby, Jake?" he says, pointing at my belly. "Are you going to step up and be a man or are you going to run to Florida next year like a little bitch?"

All the blood rushes to my head and for a second, I see spots. Their voices have gotten louder and the people near us have all but stopped dancing to watch.

Jake's fury is plain on his face, and it feels like a line has been crossed, one there's no retreating from. Can't they see they're making it worse? That when this all shakes out it'll be me who bears the social weight of it.

"Guys—" I start, but Jake is much louder.

"Go fuck yourself, Wilder. You think I'm the only one responsible for all of this? Maddi didn't even ask me if I wanted to keep it, you know that? She just made the decision by herself."

I blanch, my eyes involuntarily watering. And even though I know his anger is directed at Wilder, it feels like a shot at me.

*But Jake's not done, whether it's the alcohol or pent-up frustration from tonight and the months before it (probably both), I don't know. "Let's be honest. This isn't about the baby or college or anything else. What has always pissed you off is that Maddi chose me over you. And the part you can't get over? She loved it."*

*To say his words are humiliating is a vast understatement. He took me out at the knees without warning, a clean shot, demeaning whatever affection we shared and transmuting it into rivalry. Look everyone, it's pregnant Maddi, the girl both Wilder and Jake screwed.*

*Only Jake doesn't get another word out because Wilder punches him right in the face, a loud crack that sends Jake stumbling backward and splits his lip.*

*My hands fly up, palms out. "Stop!" I yell, but they're not listening to me.*

*Jake is running at Wilder, and when they collide, they slam onto the dance floor, scattering the couples around them and alerting the teachers on the periphery. I feel the tears on my cheeks before I even know I'm crying, and I turn around, running from the room.*

I stare at Wilder, my chest buzzing like an imbalanced washing machine. "Here's the thing, Wilder," I say, my voice shockingly normal for how upside down I feel. "I've spent a lot of years blocking you out. Many, many years. Because whether I want to admit it or not, you and the bakery were my touchstones when I lived here; I knew that if I had you both that—" I cut myself off, realizing I'm entering uncharted territory, that I'm about to say things I can't unsay. But in a moment of Liv-inspired bravery, I throw my caution into the ocean, letting the tide carry it far, far away. "That as long as I had you both, I'd be okay. And while I'm moved that you remained so close to my father, I'm not sure I'm capable of opening up like that again, of really loving the bakery again. It feels . . ."

Wilder's chest rises and falls. "Scary," he says, not as a question but a statement.

"Terrifying," I agree.

"I understand," he says, and I can tell he feels it, too. We both go quiet for a moment. "But is that a good enough reason?"

I stare at him, unsure how to respond. "Are you asking me if my fear is justified?" I say, a little confused.

"I'm asking if you're going to let it stop you from doing something that might bring you joy."

His question rattles me, but before I can sort out why, he's speaking again.

"You used to rotate around that bakery like it was the sun, Maddi. I would argue that half the reason I love it is because your love was so strong that it was impossible not to."

I push against his words as though I could somehow shove them back in his direction like an unwanted plate of food.

But he's not done. "If I'm being honest, there is no bakery without you." He pauses weightily like he knows that whatever he says next is going to matter. "You and Charles were the heart of that place, the thing that gave it its magic."

*The day after prom passes excruciatingly slowly. Thankfully the bakery's plentiful Easter business leaves me so busy that I can't obsess over what happened. Dad and I move around each other in familiar patterns, trading ingredients, stopping periodically so he can teach me a new piping technique.*

*"You're really getting good at that," he says, leaning over my shoulder where I create a buttercream rose on top of a lemon curd-filled cupcake. "I'm proud of you."*

*His approval hits me hard, the word* proud *lodging a lump in my throat that constricts my chest. I nod at my cupcake, not wanting him to see how much it affects me.*

*He pats me on the shoulder before returning to his coffee-flavored* panna cotta drizzled with bittersweet chocolate, and my thoughts drift to the day he held me while I cried. I can't help but wonder if he would do the same now; if I showed him how much I've been struggling, would he rub my back and tell me things will work out?

"Dad?" I say, desperately wanting to find my way back to him.

"Yes, Maddi?" he says, pausing his work.

"Do you want me here? In the bakery?" It's the only thing I can think to ask because I have no idea how to ask him if he still loves me the way he used to.

He turns around to face me, his forehead creasing slightly.

"I mean, I know I've been spending a lot of time here. I just wanted to make sure that was okay." And I instantly hate myself for modifying my question, for downplaying even that.

He runs his hand over his short beard. "Of course," he says, his voice quieter than normal. "You're always welcome here."

But that doesn't feel like enough, doesn't dull the ache of my larger fear. If anything, it makes it worse, the promise of reassurance that never fully comes to pass.

For a moment we stare at each other, both of us clearly out of our element, the seconds expanding like millennia. My heart pounds long, sad beats in my chest, my piping bag limp in my hand. And when it seems he won't continue, I turn back around, my hope burning out, like the supernova of a dying star.

Hearing my dad's name coupled with my own sends me spinning. My throat tingles and I look toward the ocean, refusing to allow moisture to build in my eyes. Maybe there was a time when I believed the bakery was magic, that it could make anything better, but I was wrong and so is Wilder. "It's been fine without me all these years; I'm sure it will continue to be so."

Wilder shakes his head like I'm missing the point. "But will you be fine?"

My eyes whip to his face, ready to tell him I most certainly will, but he's faster.

"I'm not saying you won't be okay. You're the strongest person I know. What I'm asking is, will you regret not giving it a second chance?"

My chest clenches, like I'm trying to physically block his words with an invisible force field. "I know you're doing what I asked you to—talking to me about the bakery, asking the hard questions. But the thing is, I'm not the same girl I once was. And you're here now. Dad obviously thought you were just as capable of running it as I was, probably more so."

For a second, he looks surprised. "Is that what you think? That your dad somehow doubted you? Because I can promise you, Maddi, he never did. You were in every letter he ever wrote me. Updates on the progress you made in LA, how he looked forward to you bringing those skills back to the bakery eventually, how he was glad that when he was gone that he would have something to give you that mattered."

All of a sudden, there's no air—a giant beach and not one drop of oxygen. The tightness in my chest transforms into a thudding ache. I can't look at him. "I doubt that," I say, trying to convince us both.

His eyebrows push together. "Why would I lie to you?"

I throw my arms to the side, overarticulating and hiding behind my bluster. "Because you're being nice. Because my dad never wrote to me about those things. He never wrote to me, full stop. Because he didn't—" I cut myself off before I say *love me that way, not the way he loved my mother with that unconditional grace he always afforded her.*

Wilder's expression softens, and I kind of hate him for the gentleness and the way it starts to erode my shield. "For someone so smart, you don't see yourself clearly."

"Are you saying I don't know how my father felt about me?" I say, desperately clutching to my perceived rightness in order to fend off my unsteady chin. "Because I remember his disappointment. I remember he didn't stand up for me. Not once. And I very much remember that neither of my parents came after me when I left for California. They just let me go. I'm pretty sure they were relieved."

"Yes, he failed you then. We all did." His persistent gentleness pokes at my weak spot, and his admission tightens my throat so acutely that my eyes brim. "And I can only guess at the hurts and struggles you've endured since. But this is it, Mads. Right here, right now is the moment in your life where you get to make peace with some of it. And it's not perfect. It never will be. And maybe it's not enough, but your father loved you. I can tell you that as a fact. He loved you fiercely and he wanted more than anything for you to be happy."

His words work their way into my chest, clutching at my heart. The tears in my eyes spill over and I can't stop them.

Wilder wraps his arms around me then, pulling me into him, and his kindness only makes me cry harder. Chest rattling sobs and messy tears spill out of me with such ferocity that my breath hitches and my eyes squeeze shut. I vibrate in his arms with the force of my grief—grief for my dad, for what will never be, for the time I can't get back, for all the things I can never make right.

"I miss him," I admit, the words tearing out of me, taking a piece of me with them as they go. "I really, really miss him."

"I miss him, too," he says, his own sadness an echo of my own.

He rests his cheek against the top of my head, and rubs comforting circles on my back. But he doesn't try to stop my tears or tell me to look on the bright side by giving some magical piece of advice, he just steadies me, hanging right out in my pain and not flinching from it. And it cracks something inside of me, exposing a long-forgotten vulnerability, one I once worked tirelessly to erase.

Wilder holds me for a long time until my shoulders settle and my cheeks dry. Even when we both know that he could release me, he holds me still. And I don't try to pull away. I just lean my head on his chest, listening to his heartbeat, allowing myself to be comforted.

"Thank you," I say after some time, my voice a little raw.

"No, thank you," he says into my hair. "For trusting me with it."

I nod against him, touched by his words, and now I do pull back.

He lets me go, but before I step fully away, he brings his hand to my face, gently brushing my cheek where tears once flowed.

And as our eyes meet, it's as if something snaps into alignment—an invisible thread that was once severed, rejoins, locking us both in place. The sensation is so intense that I feel it move through me like a pulse of heat, as though some integral part of me just found its way home.

He lowers his hand, his cheeks lightly flushed. "I'm sorry, I shouldn't have done that," he says. "I've just never—"

Hearing the tenderness of Wilder's voice, and the intimacy it suggests, steals the breath from my lungs. My heart sets to hammering in my ribs. But I just stand there, too close.

"Never what?" I ask.

He shakes his head, like whatever he was going to say is so true that it pains him.

But I can't let it go, caught up in the moment and the way he showed up for me. "Never what, Wilder?" I ask again, barely above a whisper.

Wilder looks into my eyes, his own softening in the dim light. "I've never seen anyone so beautiful," he finally says, and it hits me hard.

Because I know when Wilder means something, and he means this, and not in the way that people tell you your hair is pretty, or your dress looks nice. For fuck's sake, I'm certain my cheeks are a blotchy swollen mess. But he says it like he means me, my very person, all that I am.

I don't move away, don't brush his comment off with an awkward thank you, telling him it's late and I need to get home. I just stare up into his eyes, searching them for the longing I saw a moment ago, knowing I'm tempting fate and not really giving a damn.

He smiles a small, sweet look that sends me right over the edge. And now I'm wondering, is it really fair to walk around in the world with a face like that? Just smiling here and there at unsuspecting people who are sure to lose all their good sense in some desperate attempt to gain another?

"Wilder," I breathe.

"Maddi," he replies, the invisible tether pulling us closer.

He reaches up to brush the stray hairs back from my forehead and to plant a kiss there like he used to.

But when his gaze returns to mine, he appears torn. "I should probably walk you to your car."

And for a split second, I don't think, I just feel. "Is that what you want?"

Wilder gives me an almost sad smile. "To walk away from you? I've never wanted that."

His delivery is so sure that my self-control slips out of my grasp, my mouth running full speed away from my common sense. "Then don't."

For a second, he seems surprised, but as he searches my face

for understanding, whatever caution he was wrestling with vanishes. He reaches out to caress me once more, his touch gentle
but confident, reminding me how many times his skin has met
mine, the sensation of him heightened by years of separation
and newness.

For just a moment, I second-guess myself, positive I've lost
hold of my senses, tossed them out to sea with a deranged cackle.
Can I actually be the one standing here instigating this, swiping
my hand over the flame and telling myself if I do it just right, I
won't get burned? I should turn my face; I should break eye contact. Because I know if I do, he'll drop his hand, and everything
will go back to normal. Except no, nothing is normal between
me and Wilder; it never has been. We've either been too attached
or too separated, coiled lovingly around one another, or snapping like alligators. I know this the same way I know how to
write my name, reflexively. It just is. And so are we. And right
now, I'm not looking away.

Wilder tilts my chin up toward his, running his fingers
through my hair to the nape of my neck, his other arm looping
behind my back drawing me closer to his body. And as his lips
find mine, there's no hesitancy. That's the thing about Wilder,
he kisses like he means it, leaning into me, pulling at me with
the tips of his fingers like there is no such thing as close enough,
only hunger and breath.

My hands move through those soft waves and down his neck
to his taut shoulders, over the familiarity of him. His fingers press
pleasantly into my hips below my coat and catch under the edge
of my sweater, trailing heat and a flurry of tingles where his palms
touch my bare skin. And I remember. I remember why the first
time I kissed him I knew. Wilder has a pull, a gravity to him that
is so intense that you don't even realize you're in it until you're
tangled up in his arms, lost in his warmth, utterly mesmerized.

He takes his time, his kisses both sure and gentle, working his hands along my back, generating so much heat that I want to shrug off my winter coat and push him right into the sand. But I don't and neither does he. Because we both know that we've already crossed a line, that the feeling of being locked together is too evocative, and if we don't pull back, we're both going to soar right over the cliff happily embracing our own emotional demise. Maybe we already have.

So, when it feels impossible to stop, we do, looking at each other for a long painful moment that makes my breath come fast and his stare intensify.

"You should probably walk me to my car now," I say, the words sticking as I force them out in an attempt to sever the connection.

He exhales like he feels the loss of me viscerally. "Of course."

When we return to the parking lot, he opens my car door, flashing me an uninhibited smile, one I haven't seen since we were kids. It makes me doubt my decision to go even more.

"Goodnight, Maddi," he says, and the mere sound of his voice, slow and intentional, makes my thighs burn.

Just like that, I know I'm in trouble, that I'm not going to be able to forget our conversation or the way he felt pressed against my body. That it's becoming clear that Liv was right, that Wilder still cares about me more than I ever thought possible, and that maybe I care about him more than I ever dared to admit, and I have no fucking idea what to do with that.

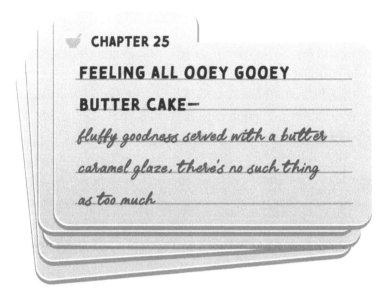

## CHAPTER 25

## FEELING ALL OOEY GOOEY

## BUTTER CAKE—

*fluffy goodness served with a butter caramel glaze, there's no such thing as too much*

The late morning sun filters through the lace curtains, drenching my bedroom in diffused warmth. I stretch under the fluffy comforter, dragging the backs of my hands across my eyes and readjusting my pillow under my head. Spence is already downstairs, too amped about Christmas Eve to stay asleep. But after a whole week of 3:30 wake-ups, I'm luxuriating in rubbing my legs under the fluffy comforter like a cricket.

Maybe it's getting a proper night's sleep, or maybe it's what happened last night with Wilder, but things don't feel so heavy this morning. And as my thoughts drift to the bakery, the crushing weight of emotions that were tied up in a big fat bow of grief are noticeably diminished. Instead, the ache is replaced with a tentative curiosity, like extending a hand to a wild dog, hoping it will lick your fingers but not totally convinced it won't bite your head off. I find myself wondering if I did decide to stay, if maybe Wilder was right, if I could reclaim some of my joy baking here. And maybe, just maybe, I could reclaim some of my joy with him. Just the thought sends my stomach tumbling over itself, my cheeks warming and my fingers touching my lips as I remember the feeling of his kiss.

Maybe I could just stay for a little while and test it out? I don't even have to commit to a full year, maybe just a trial period to see if I could make it work?

My God. Who even am I? Did someone drug me with optimism? For a flash of a second, the old fear seeps in, the voice that tells me that it'll all crumble into a steaming pile of shit that will break everything I love, but I'm too cozy in my bed and drunk on the memory of our embrace to allow it to bear any real weight.

Instead, I reach for my phone, ready to text Liv and find out how her night went. But when I see my front screen, there's already a text waiting from Wilder. And maybe it's just the hopefulness of the holiday morning, but a flutter arises in my chest.

> Wilder: Making breakfast for the
> cousins. Thought you might need to
> see this.

Below his words is a picture of him holding a plate of croissant French toast. If the croissant bit weren't decadent enough, it's stuffed with whipped cannoli filling replete with mini melting chocolate chips, topped with fresh raspberries and a raspberry reduction syrup. My stomach growls right on cue, as though it were wailing in longing.

Also in the picture is the signet ring he's worn since his sixteenth birthday with a Buenaventura B embossed on it. And for a split second, I remember how I secretly thought one day I might have a piece of jewelry with a B on it, too.

Me: I'm not sure if I hate you for
teasing me like that or if I'm in
awe of you. Maybe both.

And to my delight, it only takes him seconds to respond.

Wilder: I'll make it for you anytime.
Just say the word.

I stare at his text for a long moment, smiling at the offer like a goon.

Me: Be careful. If all your
cooking is that glorious, you
might never get rid of me.

It feels a little reckless, but good reckless, and safer than last night because it's text banter, not soul-searching looks and carefully articulated references to past heartbreaks.

Wilder: That's the idea.

My heart thumps so hard that I sit up, heat spreading through my middle like hot tea on a cold night. My eyes flit to my vanity drawer, in which there are many notes of me and Wilder talking to each other this way. And even though I'm old enough to know that it doesn't fix everything, maybe things don't need to be fixed the way I once thought. Maybe they need to be healed, and maybe that healing isn't a solitary action the way I've always imagined.

Also, flirting is good for the soul. That's got to be a truism, right?

> Me: Okay, Wilder. Show me
> what you can do.

For about thirty seconds, there's no chat bubble and no response. I'm about to close out of the text when his reply pops up.

> Wilder: With pleasure, Madeline
> DeLuca.

My pulse goes haywire. Does he know those are the same words he used in that note when we were teens; is that why he said them; is that why he hesitated? I immediately dismiss the idea. Of course not. It was a million years ago. I almost laugh at myself for thinking it, but a wisp of worry seeps in as I realize once again that my feelings for Wilder aren't neatly contained, that I'm not driving this emotional bus, rather I'm a reckless passenger balanced precariously on a seat, halfway out the sunroof with a drink I'm hoping not to spill.

Spence appears in the doorway, and my ponderings fizzle out, bringing my awareness back to the fact that it isn't just my heart I'm responsible for, but my son's, too.

"You're up!" he says, all enthusiasm.

"I'm up," I reply with a too-big smile and swing my legs out of bed. "Thanks for letting me sleep in. I really needed that."

He shrugs. "Sleep is like your favorite thing. And besides, I want you fully rested for all the sugar we're gonna eat today."

I laugh, standing and grabbing him in a hug, kissing the top of his head. "Is that right?"

"I mean, yeah. Tradition is tradition," he says with a grin.

I pause, giving it some thought. Because even though this holiday season has been a divergence from our usual, it's still very much ours; Haverberry didn't (as I feared) kill Christmas. "Ya know what?" I say, "I just saw a picture of a truly over-the-top breakfast, and now I'm thinking maybe we should make some super gooey cinnamon rolls with an obscene amount of frosting. Maybe pair them with a broccoli and cheddar quiche?"

Spence practically vibrates with excitement. "Oh my god, yes! Get dressed. Eat your coffee or whatever. I'm helping!"

And that's pretty much how the morning and afternoon go—making all our favorite treats and then eating them on the couch while watching Christmas movies. My mother pops in here and there to sample something and (specifically and only) address Spence, telling him that it smells good and he's turning into quite the baker. She's not as icy as yesterday, but it's also clear there's no easiness between us. And while part of me wants to talk to her, tell her I'm thinking about staying, another part of me is worried that it'll spark more unpleasantness. So I put it off, telling myself I'm waiting for the right moment when Spence is preoccupied.

But as we get ready for the Buenaventura's Christmas Eve party and no such opportunity arises, worry begins to seep in. We haven't discussed the sleigh ride, and I know Spence is really looking forward to it. Hell, I am, and I can't help but feel like it would be a shame if we all missed it because Mom and I can't find a way to make peace.

I leave Spence in the bathroom where he's spiking his hair and walk down the hall, lightly knocking on Mom's door, hoping she'll be wearing her signature red dress and that it'll be a nonissue.

"Come in," she says. Only instead of finding her seated in front of her vanity doing her lipstick, she's tucked into her bed with a book.

My pulse takes off like a bullet. "Mom?" I say, my voice betraying my shock, "It's six forty-five," hoping her staunch adherence to timely arrivals will jolt her into action.

"Yes, I know," she says, placing her book on her lap. "But I've had a headache all day, and so I've decided to stay home. I've already called ahead and explained that you and Spence will be going without me."

I stand there for a couple of baffled seconds. My mother not going to the benefit was one thing, but her not going to the Buenaventura's Christmas Eve party is unthinkable. She made me go the year I got my tonsils out and could only sip foods through a straw. She went the year she got food poisoning and could barely get off their couch because she was so nauseated.

"Please do tell them I send my regards," she continues like she didn't just flip the universe upside down. "And compliment them on their decorations, which I'm certain will be lovely as always."

But I just can't get past the obvious. "You've never missed a Christmas Eve party. Ever."

"Yes, well, things change," she says.

I suddenly feel a little queasy, like I've missed all the signs that would indicate my mother was experiencing some sort of emotional distress. "If this is because of me—"

"I just told you I have a headache," she says, and I feel the wall between us rise by a foot, me straining on tippy toes to see the other side.

"But the sleigh ride," I say, my thoughts a tangle.

"Yes, well, we'll do it next time," she says, and my stomach sinks. Maybe it's the look on my face or the fact that I'm hesitating, but her eyebrows momentarily push together. She smooths them, of course, and picks her book back up. "You better be going; punctuality is politeness."

Only I don't move. I can't. The guilt has glued me in place. "Mom, I know what we said was . . . I know that I hurt you," I start, my thoughts trying to cut a pathway through my heart's chaotic pounding. "I know you didn't want to talk about it yesterday. I know we've never been good at that. But I don't want you to miss something you look forward to all year because of me. If you want me to stay home, you can go with Spence. I just—"

"My decision has nothing to do with you," she says calmly.

"Is it about the will and Liv, then?" I ask, plowing forward, realizing there might be a layer of embarrassment I hadn't considered. "Because I can promise you that was just between us. And even she advised me against it."

"As I said, this is not about you." My mother frowns and her tone is clipped, indicating that I'm reaching the end of her patience.

My shoulders slump, resigning myself to yet another failed communication. And for a bright hot second, I get angry about it, wanting to shorten my tone and tell her it's been grand trying to talk to her, that it's no wonder we were never close when I was younger. But the instant I think it, I know it's stingy, that if Wilder had been half as reactive with me last night, then we would never have actually talked, that I would never have cried, something it turns out I needed so badly that my entire world has shifted as a result, like one of those pull tabs in a kid's book— the same image, just transformed. And that's when it hits me, the big fucking obvious thing I never considered. For a moment I'm so shaken that I struggle to even my breath.

"Is it Dad?" I ask, his name catching in my throat. "Is it because he isn't here? Are you hurting?" My voice wobbles. I've never asked my mother this and now that I think about it, I'm deeply ashamed. How could I not? And even though I know the answer lies somewhere in the abyss of things we never discuss, it strikes me that this is the core of our problem, that while we voice our anger, we never actually look at what's causing it—the pain that we trade back and forth like collector cards, hoarding and preserving so that we may point to it years later in pristine condition.

She exhales, and for a fraction of a second, I recognize the grief on her face. But it vanishes just as it appears. "No, Madeline, I told you I have a headache. And talking like this is only making it worse." But her tone has lost its normal cool. It's burgeoning on upset, and it breaks my heart.

"Mom—" I say, my voice gentle, but this time she talks over me.

"Now please, close the door on your way out; I'm going to retire early."

Even though I want to press further, I hear the plea in her voice, the demand that I give her space, and I know it would be wrong to force her into a conversation she isn't ready to have. So, I nod and make my way out of the room, her unspoken grief shining a light on my own and forming into a throbbing ache in my chest. Because just like my mother, I've spent this past year turning my head, telling myself I'd deal with my feelings later, at some more appropriate time—a time that never seemed to come until last night. As much as I loathe to think it, we are more alike than we let on, never wanting to show weakness, guarding our inner selves with steel traps and iron fences.

My breath hitches, and for the first time in what feels like forever, I want to cry for my mother. For all that we never were and all that we'll never be if we don't change something. And while I stash that thought away, push it down so that I can carry through with my night, I don't seal it off. I let it be, that blazing sadness, the small stuffed animal with arms outstretched that no one hugged, and I tell it to wait, that I'll be back, that it's not hopeless. Because I no longer believe it is.

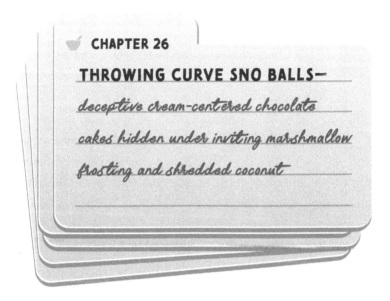

## CHAPTER 26

### THROWING CURVE SNO BALLS—
*deceptive cream-centered chocolate cakes hidden under inviting marshmallow frosting and shredded coconut*

The Buenaventuras' party is like a dreamy holiday card: Crimson handmade Santas and pillared candles lining their fireplace mantles, two trees—an enormous one in their foyer that has a two-story ceiling to give it space, and a smaller family one in their living room. Candelabras fitted with pine-scented beeswax circled in holly and old rocking chairs draped with fake fur blankets and needlepoint pillows depicting snowy scenes.

The sheer number of guests is jaw-dropping. It's as if they invited the entire town and then some. Practically everyone I've ever known from Haverberry stands in the Buenaventuras' spacious rooms sipping mulled wine and eating puff pastries stuffed with goat cheese. Matt, his sister, and their dads, Jenna and her mom, Raff and his mom and dad, and on and on. It's like flipping through an old photo album of my past, each complete with its own set of memories.

"Wow," Spence says, which pretty much sums it up. "This is awesome."

And while I might have disagreed with him yesterday, somehow the anxiety I've been experiencing in Haverberry is dulled, like an old wound that only aches in the rain.

"You said it, kid," I agree.

He stops abruptly, pulling on my arm. "Holy cow, is that real?" He points to a three-foot, tiered chocolate fondue fountain in the dining room surrounded by fruit and confection and currently circled by a pack of children. "Sorry, but you're on your own. I'm gonna need to get into that."

"Go for it," I say with a smile that he doesn't see because he's already gravitating toward it like a flame-drunk moth, not hesitating as he joins the group.

I've always admired that about Spence, his ability to confidently slip into social situations without an introduction. I asked him about it once and he just shrugged and said, "People are people, Mom." And while I'd like to agree with him in theory, I've never actually felt that same species-level bond.

I make my way through the living room, saying friendly hellos and meeting people's smiles, caught up in the holiday warmth, which is when I spot Liv near the living room window that looks out over the pond in their backyard. She's got a tumbler in one hand and the other is resting on a beautiful girl's waist whose tight curls tumble over her shoulders and down her back. And my heart swells. Liv did it. We both did. Maybe that plan wasn't so cockeyed after all.

"Claudette?" I say, walking up to them with a big smile, giddy over what her presence means for Liv. "I've heard so much about you."

"Subtle, Maddi. Real smooth," Liv says, even though she's

clearly beaming under her cynicism. "Remind me to always recruit you as my wingman."

"Ah, always so shy," Claudette says to Liv with a Haitian accent. "And why shouldn't your friends recognize me? I hope you gave them all such a detailed account." While I've never heard the word shy used in conjunction with Liv, I'm not sure she's wrong when it comes to matters of the heart.

Claudette winks at me, and instead of reaching out to shake my hand, she leans forward, kissing both of my cheeks. "Such a pleasure to meet you."

"Same!" I say, a little drunk on my lack of emotional heaviness—a lightness that has been so markedly absent these past few weeks that I almost forgot what being comfortable in my own skin feels like. Also, I'm instantly charmed by how easy these two are with each other, how even though I just met her, I can tell Claudette is a good match for Liv.

"My God," Liv says, eyeing me suspiciously. "It's like someone stuffed you with sunshine and dipped you in sugar." She raises an eyebrow at me. "Did you get laid?"

"Liv!" Claudette and I both object at the same time.

"What?" Liv says innocently. "I just want to know if I should be planning a DeLuca-Buenaventura union. 'Cause I have some pretty epic bachelorette ideas."

"No, I did not sleep with Wilder," I say with an insuppressible smile.

Claudette glances from Liv to me. "Oh!" Claudette says with recognition. "You're dating Liv's brother? How wonderful. Isn't he gorgeous?"

I nearly choke on my breath. "Uh, no, um, we're just work colleagues . . . friends."

"And my brother isn't gorgeous," Liv corrects her. "He's

decent with above-average hair. But what I want to know is why you're blushing like that, Maddi?"

"I'm not blushing."

"You're as scarlet as the tree skirt," she says, taking far too much enjoyment in the whole thing.

"Enough about me," I say, changing the subject with a whisk of my hand. "Tell me about yourself, Claudette. Believe it or not, you're the first of Liv's girlfriends that I've ever met. Very exciting stuff."

Claudette grins, her whole face lighting up. "I'll admit, it was no easy feat taming this wild woman."

"I want to hear all about it," I say, leaning in conspiratorially.

"Here we go," Liv says, shaking her head at both of us.

"Did you know," Claudette says, lowering her voice like she's letting me in on a secret. "That she wakes up early *every* morning she's in the city to walk to my favorite deli and bring me breakfast in bed?"

I fake shock. "No! Liv . . . that sounds dangerously like hopeless romanticism."

"For everyone's information," Liv says, "I feed Claudette because she's vicious in the morning, not because I'm a good person."

Claudette pinches Liv's cheek. "Isn't she cute?"

"The cutest," I agree.

"I should never have introduced you two," Liv protests.

Only my laugh gets cut short when I spot Kate across the room talking to Mrs. Buenaventura. Liv follows my gaze. While I'm sure it doesn't mean anything—she was probably invited by Wilder's parents, like the rest of the town, not by him personally—my last interaction with Kate is still too clear in my mind not to feel a pang of nerves.

"I know," Liv agrees, eyeing Kate in a way that says she finds her wanting.

Mrs. Buenaventura leans into Kate with a laugh, placing a hand on her arm like they're best chums, upping my pang to a more pervasive unease. I want to ask Liv the particulars, but I think the better of it—getting confirmation that Kate is close with her parents is not going to make me feel any calmer.

Liv must see it on my face because she diverts. "So," she says. "I want to hear all about what happened last night. Wilder wouldn't breathe a word and instead walked around all day lit up like Rudolph's nose. But first, how about we get you a drink?"

As if he sensed we were discussing him, Wilder appears next to us in black slacks with shiny shoes, a white button-down, and a dark hunter-green sweater with wooden buttons, his hair freshly washed and wavy, a couple of pieces sneaking their way down his forehead. And when he looks at me, I swear my stomach leaps in the air, bottoming out on its way back down.

"I'd be happy to get you something, Maddi," he offers, staring at me as though he would close the distance between us if we weren't in a room with other people, and like he's considering doing it anyway.

I swallow, taken aback by the intensity of his gaze. "Sure," I agree, unable to look away even though I'm certain Liv is reading into it. "I'll, uh, go get it with you."

Liv chuckles lightly and Claudette elbows her in the ribs. "You two have fun now," Liv says, wagging her eyebrows at me like she's a sixteen-year-old boy with a filthy mind.

I give Liv a halfhearted glare over my shoulder, which only seems to increase her enjoyment.

Wilder offers me his arm and I take it, slipping my own through his elbow and resting my fingers lightly on his forearm as we walk away. I can feel the heat of him under his sweater, and it suddenly occurs to me that I didn't hesitate in moving toward him the way I would have twenty-four hours ago. And with each step, I vacillate between enjoying his proximity, my heart warmly firing in my chest, and the bright little stomach flips that remind me of alarm bells—my body trying to warn me that I've crossed my own boundary line and am no longer on protected land.

As though he could sense my floundering, he pulls his arm in reassuringly, bringing me in with it, leaning down to speak to me like he's sharing a secret.

"I've been thinking about you," he says, and my heart plays my ribs like a drum solo.

"Is that so?" I manage, enjoying him more than I should.

I can smell the lingering fireplace aroma on his clothes, mixed with a heady almond scent of clean soap, and it's all that I have not to lean in closer. I almost laugh. Get it together, Maddi. Twenty-seven-year-olds aren't supposed to lose their minds over one kiss; that's just not how it works.

"There's something I want to show you," he says, a smirk pulling up the corners of his mouth. "Unless you want to grab that drink first—"

"The drink can wait," I say too quickly, and his smirk graduates to a grin. Perfect. What's next? Maybe I should just strip naked and crawl seductively across his parents' carpet since subtlety clearly isn't my thing.

"Wonderful," he says, and leads me through the foyer where I catch a glimpse of Spence down the hall, animatedly telling a story and surrounded by young people.

Wilder leads us through the doorway into the library, which is well populated like the rest of his house, but feels strangely intimate, a room Wilder and I spent more time in than any other. The fireplace is lit, the couch across from it strewn with navy and maroon pillows, and the mahogany shelves that line the walls tower above us.

"I found something the other day," he says, leading us around the people and to the window on the far wall that I sometimes climbed through when we were teens. "Something I had completely forgotten about. To tell the truth, I'm surprised no one found it. But then again, my parents never did use this room much."

I watch him as he opens the drawer in a small reading table and pulls out a folded piece of paper. He stands there for a moment, turning it over in his fingers.

"I, uh, wrote this after that fight we had on the beach, the one right before prom," he says, and hands it to me. "I carried it around for a week in my pocket, then stashed it here." He chuckles lightly at the memory.

My heart forms long reverberating beats as my fingers catch the edges of the paper and unfold it. I want to respond, but my thoughts are swimming, suspended in the ether and not forming into words. I look down at the note, his handwriting a perfect reflection of him—elegant and messy—and I read.

Mads,

I've written you so many notes that this one shouldn't be any different, but somehow it's nearly impossible to get out. I just need to tell you that you've been right about everything—that I didn't say enough, that I wasn't being totally honest with you, that there were pieces of our story you were missing. And that when I told you that I wanted you, that I thought of you every night before I fell asleep, I was actually underplaying it. You are and probably always will be the most pervasive thought in my mind. And while I know this note isn't enough, I can never seem to tell you these things in person. It's like there's some barrier between us now, one I know I'm responsible for and I don't know how to break through.

Forever yours,
Wilder

I look up at him, my hand unsteady and my pulse thrumming, scanning my memories like a hazy dream, picking out moments here and there. "Why did you never give me this?" I ask, my voice barely audible above the general din.

"I've wondered the same thing more times than I can tell you."

But in a way, I understand perfectly. I, too, was overly aware of our divide with no idea how to breach it. While part of me is turning to molten liquid at the fierce sentiment his words invoke, the other part is searching, trying to make sense of what he's sharing. "You said there were pieces of our story I was missing?"

"Yes," he says, his face taking on a more serious expression, and even though there are other people in the room, laughing and socializing, it's like we exist in a vacuum, he and I, our world crystal clear and everyone else a blur on the periphery.

"That day on the beach," I say, remembering the piece of our conversation that broke things in a way we never recovered from. "I accused you of breaking up with me because your mother told you to."

"You did," he replies, and I can see the sadness on his face like a neon sign. "And you were correct."

I stand there, feeling both vindicated and gutted, knowing

that I was right and that there was something else going on, something playing behind the scenes that he was keeping from me.

"And you listened?" I hear the discord in my voice, the old rejection bubbling up. Because even after all these years, what happened with Wilder doesn't feel like history, but something alive that merely fell into a deep slumber like a fairy-tale princess, surrounded by thorns so thick it was impossible to get to.

"I felt I had no choice," he says, opening his mouth to continue, but I'm faster.

"No choice but to shut me out and never explain the truth?" I say before I can consider it, bringing us back to the starting point, to the first flood that slowly eroded the landscape of our relationship.

He pauses, but not because we're wading through old arguments; it's something else. "Actually," he says, looking more unsure than he did a second ago. "Yes."

I stand there trying to understand, drenched in uncertainty. I feel my face tightening, my eyebrows pushing together.

He shakes his head at himself. "In some youth-driven logic, I thought I was making things easier for us both with a clean break, if you can imagine."

"But why Wilder? Why would you listen to your mother?" I reply more forcefully than I intend, probably catching the attention of people around us, but I don't bother to check, still singularly focused on him.

He opens his mouth, but before he responds, his eyes flick to the side, momentarily popping the bubble we created. And when I follow his gaze, I see what he's looking at, or rather who is standing not six feet away from us, and I instantly feel ill.

Mrs. Buenaventura trails off at the end of her sentence, which is something about how Wilder is always tucking himself away in this library. And I have no doubt in my mind that she heard what I just said because her mouth pinches shut.

*When I arrive home from the bakery, I head for the living room, where my mother is mid-phone call. So I make myself quiet, something I've grown good at these past few months, as I pluck my notebook off the coffee table.*

*"No, I didn't know that," my mother says with an edge in her voice, catching sight of me and signaling for me to sit down on the couch. "I really do apologize. I can't imagine how put out you must be." Pause. "Yes, yes, I know . . . Of course . . . I'll tell her."*

*It's the* I'll tell her *part that stops me short.*

*My mother clicks the phone onto its receiver on the end table and turns to face me. The disconcerted look on her face combined with her compensating tone only leads me to one conclusion as to the subject matter.*

*"Do you know who that was?" she asks.*

*"Mrs. Buenaventura," I say, not as a question but a statement of fact, because she wouldn't look this put out if it were anyone else. "Jake and Wilder got into a fight last night at prom."*

*"Maddi," my mom says like she's exhausted, brushing her perfect waves back from her face. "How could you not tell me this? Why am I always being blindsided by the things you do?"*

*"Things* I *do?" I repeat back, confused. "You mean things Wilder and Jake do?"*

*"The fight wasn't about you?"*

*"It was about me, but what does that matter?" I say, my defensiveness on the rise. "If it were about this couch, would you be blaming it?"*

*"Really, Madeline," she tsks, not like she's mad, but like I'm wearing her out. "An entire week of suspension is a serious thing. It's no wonder Hannah is upset."*

*"Suspension?" I repeat.*

*My mother nods. "It's a mark against Wilder's permanent record."*

*For a split second I do feel bad, but I shrug it off. There are only so many things I can be responsible for and Jake and Wilder fighting like roosters is not one of them. "Still, not my fault."*

*"Maybe not," she concedes. "But Hannah and I think it best if you and Wilder stay away from each other for the time being."*

*Whatever semblance of calm I once possessed vanishes. Being forbidden from talking to him feels like I'm some sort of social pariah who's corrupting the fine folk of Haverberry with her wanton ways. "Hannah and you? This is what you think of me? That I'm some bad influence who should be banned?"*

*She exhales audibly. "We're not saying this is anyone's fault. But you must admit that every time you two are together there's some sort of altercation. We think it would be better for both of you to have some space," she qualifies, lifting her hand in the air like she could pacify me with it. "Just until things settle down."*

*I scoff. "You mean just until we go to college on different continents? What happened to all those years of pushing me toward the Buenaventuras like they were the social North Star?"*

*Her face tightens like a corkscrew. "I understand that you're upset. Maybe we should discuss this when you've had a moment to realize the reason in it."*

*Now my face cinches. Because once again we're back to me being the problem—not the forced separation, not what it implies, but some innate failing on my part to see logic. "Tell me, Mom, do you actually agree with this or are you just too afraid to disagree with the all-powerful Mrs. Buenaventura and stand up for your own daughter? Afraid you might lose your invite to bridge?"*

*"Madeline DeLuca," she says like a warning, and I know I've crossed a line, that I've pushed her too far, but I don't care. "You will stay away from Wilder Buenaventura and that is final."*

"Wilder," Mrs. Buenaventura says to her son after a strained beat. "I wonder if I might borrow you a moment."

"No, I'm sorry, but it'll have to wait," Wilder says so decisively that some small part of me feels bolstered.

"I really wasn't asking, dear," she says like she has no intention of walking away.

The other larger part of me, however, feels nothing but dread. The fact that there's a beautiful, civilized party currently underway would be reason enough for most people to awkwardly defuse the tension, but not Mrs. Buenaventura, who has never once shied away from having an argument, public or not—not that I have any real leg to stand on in that department.

"And I wasn't negotiating," Wilder says back, not meanly, just as a statement of fact.

I gulp.

Mrs. Buenaventura looks from Wilder to me and back again. "So be it," she says, appearing friendly enough, except that her undertone is steely. "I thought I'd let you know that I had a conversation with Kate's mom. As you know, Kate's going to help us redecorate our offices since your father will be shifting things to make room for you. She was planning on traveling next week, but things have changed, and I'd really like the two of you to meet up right after the holidays and go over the space together. It's time you took your place in the office like we discussed."

Her words explode into the air like a bomb, shining a spotlight on all the insecurities that exist between me and Wilder in one go. Kate is redecorating their family offices? Did Wilder know? And really, how hard is Mrs. Buenaventura working to interfere with whatever's happening here, 'cause it feels like she's putting in overtime. Not to mention Wilder just admitted that he broke up with me because his mother asked him to, and now here she is not so subtly telling him she has different plans, ones that obviously do not include me. I find myself defensive of her invasion into this moment, aware how fragile the tether is that links me to Wilder, not wanting our connection to be trampled before it even gets a chance to take root.

Wilder's expression darkens. "I've changed my mind, I'd like that private word," he says, and gestures toward a less populated spot near the fireplace. "Forgive me, Mads. I'll only be a minute."

She follows him and I'm left awkwardly standing there, clutching his note and the feeling it represents. And it's damned uncomfortable. I shift my weight, refolding the paper and chewing on the inside of my cheek.

I look out into the room, trying to find something else to focus on to keep my doubts at bay. But as my eyes flit over the happy crowd, they land on Kate—wine glass pinched elegantly between her forefingers, staring straight at me. I feel the discord in my bones, and know before she even lifts a tapered heel to step in my direction that things just took a turn for the worse. Did she hear my conversation with Wilder? Did she hear his mother?

Only I don't make a run for it; maybe I fear that if I leave this room everything will go irrevocably sideways with Wilder, or maybe it's my pride, not wanting to signal to Kate that she makes me nervous as hell, but whatever it is, it lives securely in the realm of bad ideas.

"Maddi," she says, rolling my name across her tongue like this situation wasn't vying for a place among Dante's levels. "I owe you an apology."

For a flash of a second, I'm taken aback. Kate's apologizing? To *me*?

"My behavior in the market was inexcusable," she continues.

And I hear myself mumbling a nervous, "It's fine." Which really, it's not, but I'm so hyped up that all I have is rote response.

Also, I hope that by giving her no more than a few words we might end the conversation here.

"I appreciate you being so generous," she says, and for a second, I wonder if I misjudged her—well, not misjudged exactly, but maybe she's not supervillain evil, just a malevolent side kick? "It's just that . . . Well, I'm sure you've heard that Wilder and I have an intense relationship? That this isn't the first time we've broken up? And I probably shouldn't be telling you this, but I feel I owe you an explanation. Wilder didn't just break up with me, he called off our engagement."

Whatever blood was in my cheeks makes a fast escape, my unease ratcheting up to a thousand. "I, um, I'm sorry to hear that," I say, because there is literally nothing else to say. They were *engaged*? I hate being caught so unaware. Why didn't Wilder tell me this? Why didn't Liv?

Kate nods into her wine glass. But before she replies, I catch Mrs. Buenaventura's voice through the crowd. "You can't truly be encouraging this nonsense, Wilder." Which I can only assume is about me or the bakery or likely both. And it doesn't escape my notice that people are glancing over their drinks at her and her son.

I don't hear Wilder's response because Kate's speaking again. "I offered yesterday to take a step back from working with his family, but he didn't seem to think that was a good idea, said he liked the idea of us working together . . ." She trails off with a sigh, like she's giving it some thought.

My heart beats violently in my throat. Yesterday? He was telling her he wanted to spend time with her yesterday? The same day Wilder *kissed* me? And the sick feeling that follows only makes me mad at myself. What am I doing right now? Why am I tangled up in this? I'm standing here convincing myself that Wilder's somehow pining for me, meanwhile he's getting engaged every two seconds, flitting from girl to girl, never able to live up to commitment, just like all those years ago.

As if Kate could hear my doubts, she says, "But you know how Wilder is, so hot and cold. I seem to remember him telling me you two had a lot of push and pull to your relationship as well?"

She looks directly at me now, watching for my reaction, which I'm not doing a very good job of masking. In fact, I think I'm nodding? Because her words ring true.

"And anyway, Wilder says you're going back to California?" Kate continues when I don't respond, and it feels like I'm unraveling—is this what he's been telling her, that I was going away? I doubt myself even more.

She glances at her wine, swirling the red liquid. "Besides," she says, and this time when her eyes meet mine, she seems focused, "everyone knows that Mrs. Buenaventura would never let her son work at that bakery long-term. No offense, but I give it two months tops before he abandons it in favor of his family business."

It's like she's inflicting tiny cuts, slowly bleeding me out, the warmth leaving my fingers and toes first, making me dizzy and unsure.

I want to shut her down, slam the drawbridge on this conversation, but my confidence has taken a real blow. Which is when she adjusts the hem of her sleeve and a gold bracelet shakes out with a calligraphy charm on it. I instantly recognize it as the Buenaventura family B. My stomach takes a nosedive that is so dramatic, I touch my middle to mitigate the fall.

Kate follows my eyeline to her wrist and smiles. "Isn't it beautiful?" she says, holding it out for me to see. "I think it was Wilder's great-aunt's or some such?"

Of course, it's a family heirloom.

"You done?" I say briskly, because I don't want to do what Kate does, veil my insults and poke at her insecurities. It's clear that whatever is going on between her and Wilder is not only complicated but isn't as over as he made it seem. And I want no part of that mess, of Wilder's emotional vacillations, never deciding what he really wants.

"I'm sorry?" she says like she's not sure why I'm reacting. "If I upset you, I didn't mean—"

"Yes, you did mean to. And fine. You're hung up on Wilder. I get it. I spent a lot of time that way myself. Hell, maybe I still am. But I'm not playing whatever game this is." My tone is clear and direct.

The instant I admit I might still have feelings for Wilder, the façade of civility disappears as though I just vowed to marry him myself. She raises one perfect eyebrow like she's taking aim, her sugary sweetness gone. "You want honesty? Okay fine. How about this? You're a temporary distraction from his childhood." Her words are silky smooth with an aftertaste of poison. "Even then everyone knew the only reason he kept hanging out with you was because he felt bad for you. Poor lost pregnant Maddi. Do you really think it's any different now? Can't pay your rent. Can't get along with your mother . . . or anyone really? It's no wonder he tells me he has to handle you with kid gloves, that he pities you. And come on, do you really think the Buenaventuras would ever allow it?"

Her words slice right to my core.

And to make matters worse, Wilder's mother raises her voice. "You need to think about your family. About building a future worthy of you. And this . . . this is certainly not it."

Kate looks so satisfied that it snaps my tentative grip on my temper.

"Screw you, Kate," I fire back too loudly, earning me

shocked glances, but I've blown way past caring. "You might be upset about Wilder, but that's no excuse to be a raging shit of a person. I'd much rather be lost and confused than whatever it is you are. And maybe you're right about Wilder's mother. She's always been petty and judgmental, which is probably why you two get along so well."

Kate winces, suddenly aware of the people around us who have stopped to listen. And to make this steaming turd of a situation worse, Wilder and his mother are headed our way, likely having heard the last of what I said. Mrs. Buenaventura stares at me like I'm a monster. And while I don't feel like a monster, I do feel like a fool. A supreme idiot who thought things might be different this time. But Wilder didn't know what he wanted as a teen, and it seems he still doesn't.

And I shit you not, Kate's chin shakes. "You'll have to excuse me," she says, doing a very good impression of fragile innocence.

Mrs. Buenaventura reaches out for her. "Kate honey, wait."

But she's already turning away, hand to mouth, cutting a dramatic exit through the room.

I stand there, stunned, seeing all of it stretched out before me like a bad soap opera—Kate's Oscar-winning performance, Mrs. Buenaventura's disapproval, my own mother bound to agree with her, pitting me against Wilder's family once again, and him ultimately choosing them. And I'm angry, angry that I let myself get ensnared. But the worst part is, I'm still standing here, hanging onto the hope that I've gotten it all wrong.

Mrs. Buenaventura's expression turns stark. "I was going to appeal to you, Madeline, to talk some sense into my son, but I can now see that's never going to happen."

"Enough," Wilder says brusquely. "Do not insert yourself here."

"What would you have me do, Wilder?" she replies. "Sit

back while you board a sinking ship? And be honest, how much of your sudden desire to take over the bakery is simply to spite me? Do you think you're doing Maddi or yourself any favors by pretending otherwise? Sell the place like you advised Eleanor and take your position by your family as you agreed."

And that's it—the moment I realize I'm a profound idiot for believing him.

Wilder meets my eyes. "Maddi, it's not—"

"What it sounds like?" I say, humiliated and shrinking. "Did you or did you not tell my mother to sell the bakery?"

Wilder's hesitation is all the confirmation I need.

*Sell the place like he advised Eleanor?* Those words devastate me, thoroughly eviscerating the sweet moment Wilder and I shared last night. All the things he said about how he only ever wanted to be at the bakery now feel cheap and distorted. And it's too much. Ten straws too many for this camel.

"I think I should go," I say, already turning away from him, my cheeks flushed and my heart hammering long betrayed beats.

"Maddi," Wilder says, but I don't stop.

He follows me, catching my elbow just as I enter the foyer. "Wait."

*Wilder finds me by accident two days later, while I'm sitting on a stool at Tony's countertop bar with a fountain soda, waiting for my to-go order of pizza. He walks in with a group of friends, laughing as they choose a four-top—not sulking at home under his mother's watchful eye like I imagined him to be. And seeing him so at ease, while I've been at home crying, hits me like a two-by-four to the head.*

*Which is when he spots me. But instead of looking relieved to have an opportunity to clear things up, he visibly pales. It takes him a long conflicted second to push himself up from his seat. And his reluctance stings so brightly that I curl in on myself, swiveling my stool forward so he can't see my face.*

"Maddi?" he says, stopping next to me.

"You're not grounded, huh?" I say, because I'm trying to understand why he wouldn't at least try to explain what happened to me himself.

"No," he says, a twinge of guilt in his voice. "I, uh, I'm sorry I haven't called," he starts like he can hear my thoughts. "I thought we might talk in person. I just haven't seen you."

His lame excuse makes me constrict even further.

"I don't know if your mom told you—"

"She told me," I say curtly, looking at the blackboard pizza menu instead of his face. "So don't worry about explaining. You can go back to your friends."

"No, I want to explain," he says, and even now I want to believe that he wants to be here next to me, which only makes me more upset with myself.

"The thing is, my mom is real worked up right now. You know how she gets. I think if we just give her a couple of weeks, she'll forget all about it. But if I fight her on this, it'll become a thing. Trust me."

I hear myself laugh like I'm somewhere outside my body, viewing the cynical look on my own face. "Okay, Wilder. Great. Let's do that."

"I know this sucks," he tries again. "But it'll all work out. Everything will go back to normal in like three weeks tops."

Now I do look at him. "All work out?" I say, trying to fight my instinct to hold onto his words, breathe life and meaning into them. "Back to normal? What about our relationship is normal to you, Wilder?"

He opens his mouth, then closes it again.

"Tell me, why did you ask me to dance at prom?" I say, trudging forward, too wrapped up in my own crumbling world to stop.

"I thought . . ." He stumbles, his expression looking conflicted.

*And for once, I don't try to romanticize it or cling to fanciful ideas. Right now, I see us clearly, and there's nothing romantic about us.* "Did you do it because we're such close friends? 'Cause if we're being honest, we're not. Did you do it because you still have feelings for me? Except no, you asked Elaina to prom without so much as a heads-up. Did you do it because you and Jake have some stupid turf war over me? Yes, yes you did."

"You can't seriously think that," Wilder says briskly.

"Can't I? What about that argument in front of the school about Jake asking me to prom? Or you almost kissing me when you knew I was dating him? Or a thousand other things," I say, and as his expression grows more conflicted, my hurt grows. "I'm not saying it's entirely your fault. I definitely played my role, so desperate for you to still care about me that I let you come back over and over again. But you know what? I'm done. As much as it truly pains me to say this; our mothers are right. We're no good for each other."

*I know people are staring at us, and that for the five millionth time this year, Wilder and I will be everyone's favorite gossip. Hell, our families will probably have a bullet-pointed cheat sheet of everything we said before we even get home. But right now, I don't care. My heart is aching. My stomach is turned. And I have zero fucks to give, because as far as I can tell, there's nothing left to salvage, and the sooner I accept that, the sooner I can move on.*

"Mads, please—" *He exhales in exasperation, but I cut him off.*

"I think you should walk away now," I say, my voice quieter than before. *I slide off my stool, collecting my purse and my drink, not willing to wait for the rest of my order and risk crying in front of Wilder.*

*But Wilder's not walking away, he's staring at me like I just ripped the rug out from under his feet.* "Look, I know things have been weird between us. And I know that's my fault. But listen, Mads—"

*I brush past him. As I do, he catches my hand.*

*"Let go of me, Wilder," I warn, fighting the feeling that I'm drowning.*

*"I can't," he breathes, and the jumble of emotions those words invoke slam into me like a giant wave, threatening to pull me under and scrape me raw.*

*"Why is it that every time I try to extricate myself from you, you find some way to pull me back in? Let me go, Wilder. Let. Me. Go."*

*As he drops my hand, I know the days of us pretending things were okay are gone forever. We'll go to college, move away. The Maddi and Wilder of our childhood, a unit so infallible that I couldn't imagine a world without him, no longer exists.*

I shake my head. "Don't, Wilder," I say, my heart straining with the effort, because I can't unknow the things Kate and his mother said. I saw the truth of them on his face. "I can't go through this again," I manage through a voice thick with emotion, handing him back his note. "Or rather, I won't."

"If you'll just let me—"

"Explain?" I say, fighting to keep my heart in my chest. "To what end? So that we can fall back into the same pattern we used to occupy—push and pull, hot and cold?" I choke a little on Kate's words, hating them for the truth they hold. "It's not a good idea. For either of us."

His face falls. "Maddi, please, don't walk away again. Just hear me out."

It's the *again* that kills me. "You're blaming me for—" I swallow, my voice lodged firmly in my throat. I don't know whether it's the hurt or simply that I feel upside down, but I know I need to draw a line, a hard one that leaves no possibility of falling back into his gravity, circling around him and destroying myself in the process. "I'm going back to California, Wilder. You keep the bakery. Or sell it. I don't care." The words are bitter in my mouth, a lie I desperately need to believe. "But I'm done here. I was a long time ago. I just needed to realize it again."

And I walk away. I don't cry or yell, I just look for my son and lead him out of the house without fanfare. When Spence asks me what's wrong, I say that I want to get some rest so we can wake up extra early and open presents. What I don't say is *so I can pack up the car right after.*

**CHAPTER 27**

**COMMUNICATION IS KEY**

**LIME PIE—**

*turning tart limes into sweet goodness*

When I get home from the pizza place, my fight with Wilder still vibrating through me like an aftershock, I make the mistake of slamming the front door, not thinking that my parents might be in the living room.

"Madeline?" my mother says, which is the exact moment I realize I'm not carrying the pizza that I told her I'd pick up for dinner.

I squeeze my eyes shut for a second in the foyer, lifting my face to the ceiling before making my way to the living room doorway.

My dad lowers his book, pulling down his reading glasses, and my mom tilts her head.

"I, um, didn't get the pizza," I start, my lips suddenly dry, wishing I'd stuck it out at Tony's a few minutes longer so I wouldn't have to have this conversation. "Wilder was there and—" I'm about to explain, tilt the truth until I think she'll accept it.

"Did something happen?" my mother says, her tone hesitant.

But I'm exhausted from spinning narratives, trying to put a

rosy glow on things that don't deserve it. And just like with Wilder, I give up trying. "We got into a fight."

My mother deflates, and her eyes flick to the phone, telling me that in this moment she isn't considering what I might be feeling, but rather whether or not Mrs. Buenaventura is going to call her about it. "Oh Madeline," she sighs. "We literally just discussed this."

My shoulders inch up toward my ears. "It was unavoidable."

"Was it, though?" she asks like she's not convinced.

"What's that supposed to mean?" I say, now back on the defensive, a position that's grown all too familiar.

My mother spreads her hands. "Just that every time something like this happens, it's always someone else's fault. Never your own," she says, her voice even-keeled as though she has ceased to be shocked by my behavior. Heat warms my cheeks and my shoulders transform into earrings. "And it always seems to take place at maximum volume. I'm certain the entire pizza place got an earful?"

I glance at my dad, but he just sits there frowning and listening to my mother. "Ah, now we're coming to what you really want to know," I say, the hurt tightening my voice, wanting to lash out in return. "How badly did your daughter embarrass you this time? What sort of a mark did she make on your pristine reputation? Be honest, Mom, that's what you've cared about this whole time. Not what I might be feeling or how hard it might be, but about yourself and what people think of you. You're selfish."

"Madeline," my mother says with a bright tone of shock. "That's completely inappropriate."

Which is when Dad decides to chime in. "Madeline, take it down a notch."

I look at him, his frown carved deeply into his mouth and his eyebrows pushed together. "Of course you're on her side. You're always on her side."

"This isn't about sides," he replies.

*But it is. He doesn't stand up for me when it comes to Mom. He won't tell her to back off or to give me a break. Ever.*

*"I think you'd better go up to your room," my mother says. "Before I decide that grounding is in order."*

*"Grounding?" I say with a hurt laugh. "Isn't that my life anyway? What friends do I have? Where do you see me going exactly?"*

*"The bakery," she says, and it steals the breath right out of my lungs.*

*"You wouldn't," I reply, just above a whisper.*

*"I would and I am," she says. "I'm sick and tired of fighting with you like this. Things are difficult enough without this house becoming a boxing ring. I told you to stay away from Wilder. I warned you there would be consequences. One week and no bakery."*

*I look at my dad, who hesitates. And I feel his reluctance like a slap. When it becomes apparent that he's not going to say anything, I feel myself giving up, shutting down and closing in.*

*"I truly hate you," I say to my mom. "I only wish that I could embarrass you more."*

*Her face visibly pales. "And now it's two weeks," she says.*

*My dad opens his mouth, but he only closes it again.*

*I stare at my dad, my chin shaking. "I don't know why I ever thought you were different. You're just as awful as Mom."*

*"One month," my mother says, and I have to press my lips together to keep from crying.*

*I turn around before my breath can hitch, blinking away the moisture that's congregating in my eyes, and I run up the stairs.*

*Only I stop when I get to the landing, my steps faltering with my dad's brusque tone, wondering if it means he's mad at her? But all he says is that he's leaving to retrieve the pizza.*

*And that's it. No discussion of them stripping me of the only thing I had left, no regretful remorse.*

*So I close myself in my room, pacing across my rug, hands drawing worrying circles over my ever-growing belly. Bitterness and grief well up inside me, fracturing me from my center like a windshield struck by a perfectly angled pebble.*

*I feel myself slipping into a dark place, and I know with certainty that what I said to Wilder is true—things will never return to normal. I look down at my belly, at the baby inside of it.*

*My lip still quivering, I say, "I promise you, baby, that you'll never feel like this. That you'll always know that I love you. I'll tell you a thousand times a day if I have to."*

*And that's the moment everything changes.*

*I know I can't stay, that if I do, I'll not only be sealing my own fate to some dismal unhappiness but sealing my baby's as well. That if my child grows up in this house, in this town, he'll get constant reminders that he's a shameful disappointment, that he'll be told however subtly he's the reason my life didn't work out. Maybe I can't save myself, but I can save my kid.*

*I'm packing my bags before I even fully make the decision, grabbing the checks for the account that holds my college savings. Even though I don't know where I'm going yet, I know I'm leaving. And as much as I'd like to think differently, I know in my heart that if I go far enough, my parents won't come after me. Maybe they'll even be glad.*

I lay in bed, staring out the window at the faint light that tints the black sky a deep indigo. It's only six forty or so, but I've been up for hours, just like the morning I left all those years ago. I carefully swing my legs out from under the covers and run my hands over my face.

Having given up on passing back out, I creep out of the room, not wanting to disturb Spence. I leave my phone on the bedside table, where it's been off since I left the party last night. I know Liv probably texted. Maybe Wilder did, too. But I'm not ready to deal with that yet, not if I want to get through Christmas morning with the appropriate amount of enthusiasm for Spence's sake. For a moment there I thought I was getting a second chance, that just maybe I could carve out a piece of happiness in the wake of past hurts. But Wilder is still Wilder, I'm still me, and my mother is still my mother.

My biggest regret is getting Spence's hopes up. It's for the best, I tell myself, thinking about Jake coming by later this afternoon. He'd inevitably disappoint Spence. But even that thought, one I was adamant about a couple of days ago, isn't landing and I find myself doused in guilt, like an overstuffed closet that finally hit its limit.

I walk quietly through the house, happy that it's mostly dark and that I don't have to face the world yet. I figure I'll line up three of my mother's tiny coffee mugs like shots and douse myself in caffeine while prepping an over-the-top comfort breakfast of frittata, homemade hash browns, and I Wish I Never Let Wilder Kiss Me Bread Pudding made with bittersweet chocolate, fresh tart raspberries, and vanilla coconut whipped cream.

Caught up in my menu, I walk distractedly into the kitchen, flipping on the light and startling so intensely that I yelp as I register my mom seated at the breakfast table.

"Merry Christmas," she says with the same nonplussed tone one might use for *there's a cold front coming in.*

My hand flies to my chest, attempting to quell the spike of adrenaline. I think *trick or treat* might be more appropriate for someone lurking in the dark, but I know better than to say it. "What are you doing down here so early?"

"I thought I might watch the sunrise," she replies, glancing out the window that overlooks the backyard, her tone hinging somewhere between melancholy and pensive.

"I was just going to grab some coffee," I say, rethinking my breakfast prep. "I'll be out of here in a minute."

She nods, and something about her expression strikes me as vulnerable, like I caught her before she had a chance to put her face on. I move to the coffee machine, and she looks back toward the window. Only as silence descends, it's not the easy coexisting that you share with family and friends, it's the type that pulls the air taut and strains your forehead. It's as though our conversation from last night hangs between us, and not only that but the mess at the party she has yet to hear about, plus the fact that I need to tell her I'm leaving.

I retrieve my baby cup of coffee, and the weight on my shoulders presses firmly down like it might actually push me through the floor. I consider leaving the kitchen to collect my thoughts, give myself space to work up to the conversation(s) I know I need to have with her, but I find myself hesitating. I'm not certain if I leave that I'll return, and I likely won't get an-other opportunity like this after Spence wakes.

I wet my dry lips, pulling the hot cup to my chest, figuring the only way to do this is the Band-Aid approach. *Mom, I caused a giant scene, prepare to hear about it for the next couple of weeks and turn red with embarrassment, Mrs. Buenaventura officially hates me, and by the way, I'm leaving and disappointing everyone just like you predicted. Merry freaking Christmas.*

But before I can get a word out of my shit confession, my mother starts speaking.

"You know," she says, still looking out the window, "your father and I used to watch the sunrise every Christmas morning."

My internal machinations stop abruptly like she threw a stick into the wheel spokes of my thoughts.

She sighs. "He'd wake me up early with an offering of hol-iday tea. 'You're gonna miss it, El, if you stay asleep any longer.

Today is the day to watch the world come alive.'" She shakes her head at the memory. "I'd always grumble that I could watch the sunrise perfectly well from my bed, but he wasn't having it. He'd insist we go downstairs. And here, on the kitchen table would be a warm treat just out of the oven and a present—something to start the morning properly, he'd claim."

My heart squeezes so intensely that I find myself off-balance, my voice only one notch above a whisper. "He'd leave a pastry on my bedside table for when I woke up," I say, realizing I'd forgotten all about that Christmas tradition, packed it away with the rest of the things I knew I couldn't keep when I left.

She nods, giving me a sad smile. "Would you like to join me?" she asks, and now I'm really thrown. My mother doesn't do vulnerable; I'm fairly certain she's made of steel and wire instead of soft malleable flesh. So to see her like this in her bathrobe, eyes heavy and untouched by makeup, with her heart on her sleeve, rattles me.

"I would," I say after a beat, sinking into the seat across from her at the breakfast table.

We sit there for a long minute, looking out the window at the purples and pinks dusting the tops of the trees in our backyard, and remembering Dad. And the lump that forms in my throat is so insistent that I can't think past it, can't imagine how I'm ever going to tell her what I need to without feeling like an awful person. I press my lips together, trying to swallow, to normalize my breath.

But as if she could hear my worry, she asks, "How was the party last night?"

I freeze, immobilized by an onslaught of guilt.

Her forehead scrunches in confusion at what I'm sure is an overwhelmed expression on my face. "Madeline?"

But I'm afraid to speak. Afraid to tell her that for reasons unbeknownst to me, my presence always seems to incite an altercation, a loud one. And that this time it included her closest friend, leading me to want to flee Haverberry once more.

"Did something happen?" she asks, and her tone already betrays that she knows it did, that in some way she expected it.

But instead of taking offense like I usually would, my face crumples, my head bending toward my cup. "I don't want things to always be this way," I say. "I just don't know how to do it, ya know? I don't know how to change things."

Only instead of waiting for me to collect myself, she reaches her hand across the table, laying it on top of mine.

"I'm afraid you got that from me," she says, and the kindness shatters me. Without warning, I'm crying, my shoulders vibrating, and my grip on my coffee slackening.

I look up at her, trying to reel myself in, finding it hard to take a breath. "I wish things were different. God, I wish that so much," I say, my voice so garbled I have to wonder if she heard me.

She sighs, making her appear even wearier. "Why don't you tell me what happened?"

"You're not going to like it."

"Why don't you tell me anyway," she says.

And after a second of hesitation, I do. For the first time ever, I talk to my mother about Wilder, past and present. I tell her about the kiss and about wanting to stay. I tell her about Kate and Mrs. Buenaventura, about how hopeful I'd been when I went to that party. She asks questions here and there, but mostly she just listens, refilling my coffee cup when it empties, and bringing us cookies from the containers Spence and I filled yesterday.

When it's all said and done, when my cheeks are dry and the sun is shining, she gets up. "Excuse me a moment," she says, and walks out into the hall.

But when she doesn't return right away, I move to the doorway, wondering what could be so pressing, not confident she took everything I told her well. I know it was a lot to process, that there were sections that were particularly hard for her to accept, especially the ones about Mrs. Buenaventura. So, when I hear her pick up the phone off the foyer mail table, my heart sinks.

I close my eyes, exhaling and leaning my weight on the doorframe, and just as I expected, she says Mrs. Buenaventura's name into the phone.

"Hannah? I'm glad I caught you. I don't want to interrupt your holiday celebrations, but I wanted to clear the air from last night."

It's a stake to the heart. Only this time, I stupidly didn't see it coming. It felt like she was listening, that for the first time, she was seeing me, even if she didn't fully understand. I suppose it couldn't last—this moment of peace with my mother. I just also didn't expect her to wipe it away as though she were sliding her arm along a fully set table, crashing all the plates to the floor.

"Yes, that's what I've heard," she says after a moment.

I hang my head in my hands, defeated, my temples starting to pound. Part of me wants to go back to bed and hide under the covers, vow to never be hopeful again, and remind myself that it only ends in heartbreak.

"I think you owe my daughter an apology."

My head flies up. Wait, what? I can't have heard that correctly.

Another pause. "Do not get me started on Kate, that snake. She should count herself lucky Madeline didn't ambush her after her performance in the holiday market."

This is not happening. I'm hallucinating. Have to be.

A long minute passes, and I find myself leaning forward, straining to listen even though my mother isn't speaking.

"What you said was inappropriate and you put her in an

untenable position," she continues. "Now I understand you don't want your son to work at the bakery and I'm sorry you feel that way. But do you really think that we can control them? It worked for naught when they were seventeen; do you really want to wage that battle again and lose? I lost my daughter for nine years. Don't make the same mistake I did."

My eyes are so wide that I wonder if I've stretched them permanently out of shape. I almost creep into the hallway just to double-check that it's really my mom saying these things.

"No, I'm not telling you what to do with your son. I'm telling you what not to do with my daughter. And truly Hannah, I don't care if Jesus is sitting at your dining room table waiting for his eggs, this is important, and it needs to be said."

My hand clamps over my mouth, glad that she can't see my face.

The phone clicks onto the receiver a moment later, and when I hear my mother headed my way, I run back to the table and sit down, bracing my empty cup like a prop. My mother takes one look at me and raises her eyebrow.

Only she doesn't bring up the fact that she just fought her best friend for me. All she says is, "You hungry?"

And I realize at that moment, that we're not going to have some cuddly reconciliation where she tells me she's on my side and everything will be okay. That's just not her, and for once I don't need it to be.

"Actually, yeah," I say, standing up from the breakfast table and putting my cup in the sink.

She nods, moving toward the fridge. "I was thinking about making your dad's favorite omelet," she says, "the one stuffed with grilled mushrooms, caramelized onions, and cheese. Maybe some fried potatoes?"

"That sounds perfect," I say, relinquishing my own menu

in favor of hers. "I'll go wake Spence up so he can de-grumble and then . . . I can help you prep if you want?"

She gives me a small smile. "That'd be nice, Madeline," she says slowly, and as I turn around, my eyes fill, only this time from happiness.

Once again, I feel the bright spark of hope glowing among the embers, promising a fire if I provide the wood. And I do. I pile it on. Log after log as we open presents and curl up on the couches under throw blankets to watch *Miracle on 34th Street*. For the first time since I was little, I don't feel that itch to escape her, to hold up my shield to block whatever she might throw my way. I just keep thinking about how she said she lost me, that she made a mistake. And on more than one occasion I have to discreetly dab my eyes, overwhelmed by how I interpret those words as an adult, as a parent who knows that it's impossible to get everything right.

The morning and afternoon pass too quickly, my heart growing like the Grinch's. I hold my son tight; I laugh with my mom. I would never have imagined it possible, but it's a pretty perfect Christmas . . . that is until Liv shows up.

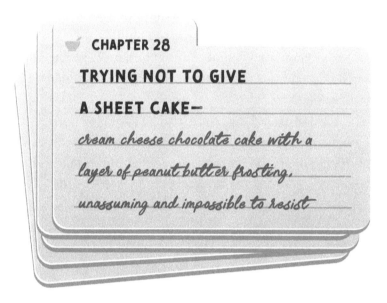

## CHAPTER 28

## TRYING NOT TO GIVE

## A SHEET CAKE—

*cream cheese chocolate cake with a layer of peanut butter frosting, unassuming and impossible to resist*

Liv's Aston Martin slides into our driveway with a purr like a sleek puma. I exchange a glance with my mother, and I know by her nod that she understands I need a minute in private.

"Spence," she says, not missing a beat. "I just remembered I forgot a couple of stocking stuffers in the closet upstairs. Want to come find them with me?"

"Most definitely!" my nine-year-old says at the prospect of more presents, launching himself off the couch.

As soon as they leave the room, I race to the front door, hoping to get out there before Liv comes in. I forgo a coat, slipping outside just as Liv places one high heel in our driveway.

She retracts her leg back when she sees me, instead leaning over and pushing the passenger door open from the inside.

"So, you're alive?" she says, giving me a look as I slump into the seat next to her and click the door closed against the chilly air. "Well, that's a relief. 'Cause I wasn't sure after I texted you five thousand times with no reply."

I wince at her words. "I turned my phone off after I left your house last night."

She grunts like she can't argue with that decision.

We fall into a momentary silence, and I pull at the edge of my sweater. I was hoping to get through the rest of the day without incident, not that I haven't been thinking about my fight with Wilder. But it's one thing to think about it and another to have Liv shine a spotlight on it.

"Liv, no offense, but what are you doing here?" I ask, turning to face her. "It's Christmas Day. Not that you're not welcome, you always are, but what about Claudette? What about your family? Don't you have a hundred cousins and aunts at your parents' right now?"

"Claude is taking a nap. I swear that woman was a house cat in her last life. And my family?" She shakes her head. "I know I shouldn't have just shown up here on a holiday . . . sorry about that, but I didn't want you skipping town before I said my piece."

I sigh in anxious resignation because her concern is legitimate; I'd been planning on leaving first thing, or at least that was the plan before I talked with my mom. I consider telling her as much when she puts her car in reverse.

"Hang on, where are we—"

"Nowhere," she replies. "I just think better while driving."

I nod because that actually works for me—keeps Spence from peering through the windows at us. She takes my nod as agreement and reverses onto the quiet street.

"I know showing up here is a little aggressive," Liv starts. "And, I mean, aggressive is basically my MO, but I'm actually not trying to put you on the spot like you might think. I just couldn't not come. Again. Like a bad repeat of ten years ago."

For some reason, this startles me. "Liv . . . you were in college when I left."

"Yeah, I know. But that shit with my brother went on for months." She frowns at the memory as we cruise through the fading light that dapples the winter streets. "And . . . he used to call me about it, about what was happening between you two. My point is that I wasn't blissfully unaware like you might have thought."

I stare at her, unsure how to respond. Wilder is such a private person that it never occurred to me he might discuss the details of our relationship with his sister.

She shifts gears as we slow for a stop sign. "And in all my infinite teen wisdom, I thought that staying out of it was the best thing for you both."

"I really don't think there was anything you could have done," I say, because I can hear the guilt in her voice and because if I were her, I probably would have stayed out of it, too.

"I could have called you," she says. "I could have invited you up to Yale for a weekend, gotten you out of this place for a moment of fresh air. I mean, fuck, you were basically my younger sister. I think I liked you better than Wilder. And when I heard you left Haverberry, I thought you'd be back. But you never returned, and the time went so fast. All of a sudden, it felt impossible to reach out to you, like my absence was too big to apologize for."

I look at my hands, remembering those early days in LA and how isolating they were. "I wasn't mad at you."

"Well, I'm mad at me. And I'll be damned if I repeat that. So here I am on Christmas afternoon, pissing my mom off and leaving her scintillating mulled cocktail hour," Liv rolls her eyes, "in order to make sure you're okay."

We hit a pothole at the end of Liv's sentence, one of those crater-sized ones that shaves a couple of years off your life.

"Fucking New England potholes," Liv breathes. "Going to give me an eye twitch." She pats her steering wheel like she could comfort her poor car.

"All you can do is pray and clench your butt cheeks," I offer, referring to both potholes and my present situation.

She laughs and the mood eases slightly, some of the tension being gobbled up by humor.

Until she says, "Here's the thing . . . I'm not going to beat around the bush," and I know without a doubt that this conversation just took the turn I feared. "I'm here for me, but I'm also here because I think you should talk to Wilder. Alone. Without my mother and Kate fucking things up. My God, do I wish I knew what was happening in that library last night."

I stare out the window, tensing. "Liv, I don't think—"

"I know Wilder screwed up. I know better than anyone, well, besides you that is. And I'm not making excuses for him. But I also think that you're going to want to hear what he has to say. And that if you don't, you're always going to wonder if things might have been different."

I give her the side-eye because I'm sure she's aware that she's speaking directly to my doubts. It's no wonder she studied law—the entire bar-certified population probably wept when she changed professions. "Look, I get what you're trying to do, but it's just . . ."

She waits for me to find my words.

"I don't trust him," I reply. "I just don't. And nothing he says is gonna change that."

"Mads—"

"Liv," I say, this time cutting her off. "I appreciate you coming to see me, and everything you said. You and I? We're good. I'm glad you're back in my life. But me and Wilder?" I shake my head. "He was engaged to Kate two weeks ago. I mean, if that doesn't indicate that I shouldn't get involved, I don't know what does."

She cringes a little. "Believe me, I know it all looks bad. But you also have to understand that Mama Buenaventura has made it her mission to curate his position as the male Buenaventura heir or something equally barbaric. And maybe I give him too much of a break on this one, but you remember our never-ending stream of nannies. Wilder wasn't like me, he didn't box up his heart and write fuck you on the flap, he was always trying to win Mom's favor, make her proud so she'd notice him, and I don't think he ever really unlearned that behavior. It took you coming along to—"

I cut her off, her words hitting me harder than she realizes. Because as a parent I see it differently than I did as a kid, and I don't want my sympathy for the neglected child that Wilder was to draw me back in. "I get what you're trying to do. I know you care about your brother and that you want what's best for him. But truly, what's best for both of us is to stop trying to patchwork something that fell apart years ago. We'll just wind up hating each other."

Liv opens her mouth, but I start speaking again before she can continue to pull at my heartstrings. "Now, as much as I love you, I do have to get back to the house. Jake is coming by soon to see Spence."

Liv exhales long and loud. But she takes the next turn onto my street. "Okay, I respect your decision. And I'm gonna butt out. All I'm saying is that if you *do* want to talk to him, I mean if you change your mind, he's not at my parents' house."

This, of course, gets my attention. He's not at his parents' house on Christmas? "Where is he?" I ask, hating myself a little for not being able to resist.

A hint of a smile appears before she erases it from my view. "He's at his house . . . alone. I guess whatever happened last night between you two devastated him, made him not want to be with my mother. And good for him. It's been far too long since he's drawn a line with her." She steals a glance at me to make sure her words are landing, and I wish I could say they weren't. "I'll give you the address. He gets spotty reception there, so he doesn't always see texts."

"I don't need—" I start as she pulls into my driveway.

"31 Winter Street," she says before I can get out my objection.

She pulls to a stop in my driveway, and I give her an objecting look.

"Merry Christmas, Mads," she says with a grin, leaning over to hug me. "I'm glad we did this."

I lift an amused eyebrow. "Uh-huh," I say, opening the door. "Me, too, I think?"

She laughs as I step out into the driveway. "Say hi to your mom and Spence."

I grumble a little as she pulls away, vowing to block out the things she said about Wilder, especially the part where he's spending Christmas alone. But as the day winds down, my thoughts keep drifting back to him. I'm positive he wasn't devastated. Liv was probably exaggerating. Had to be.

But . . . what if she wasn't?

Ugh! SHUT UP, brain!

When Jake finally shows up (an hour late), the phone rings. While my mother answers it, I excuse myself and head up to my bedroom to have a minute alone. To stare at my suitcase, as it were, the one I was so intent on packing not twelve hours earlier. Because the question of leaving, the one that I've been struggling with since I first read my dad's will, has been buzzing in the back of my mind all day. But before I have a chance to really agonize over it, there's a knock.

"Madeline?" my mother says, and I tell her to come in.

She, too, looks at my suitcase. "I wanted to give you this . . . before Christmas was over," she says, holding an envelope between her hands.

On the outside is my name written in capital letters, the way my dad always printed, and the sight of it sends my pulse skittering into chaos.

"Your father," she says and swallows, "had this awful dream about three months before his heart attack." She stops, rubbing her thumb along the envelope in a way that tells me this is hard for her, which only unsettles me further. "In his dream, a truck drove into the bakery and killed him." She looks at me meaningfully.

My eyebrows push together in confusion. "Wait, hang on . . . You think the dream was a premonition?" I ask, not able to hide my surprise—my mother isn't one to give credence to anything she can't see.

"Not at the time," she admits. "But he did. When he woke up, he wouldn't stop talking about it, about how real it felt. As you might imagine, I argued with him about it. But he wouldn't let it go. Two weeks later, he went and changed his will, wrote that addendum about the bakery."

Her words hit me like a right hook, spinning my head and rattling my vision.

Mom takes a breath. "He tried to talk to me about it, but it only made me angry." Her voice catches slightly, and she takes a moment to even it out. "Then he put this letter in the safe. Told me to give it to you a year after he died. I was so mad at him for going on about his death, that I almost burned the thing."

I stare at the letter, struggling to breathe. I don't ask her why she never told me because the answer is obvious by the look on her face—that after fighting with him about the validity of it and being proven wrong, she felt it her duty to honor his last wishes.

"Anyway," she says, lifting her chin to stave off a sniffle. "I wanted to give it to you before you left." She glances at my suitcase once more.

There's no judgment in her tone this time, no veiled insult about my maturity, and it gets me. I have to clear my throat in order to speak.

"Thank you," I say as she hands it over.

She nods and leaves the room, neither of us composed enough to talk about it further. And for a solid minute, I stare at my dad's penmanship on the envelope, frozen in place on my rug. For a passing second, I think maybe I shouldn't read it; maybe I should wait until Spence is asleep, until I'm not so confused, until I have time to process, until, until, until . . . But when does that moment come? When do things get so perfect and calm that you can deal with all the broken bits? Never, that's when.

So, I do it even though I don't want to, even though I'm terrified, even though part of me is trying to launch a defense about why my dad didn't tell me about his dream. But I know why, because I wouldn't frighten Spence with that if the dream had been mine.

My hand shakes as my finger catches the back flap, pulling it free and breaking the seal. I slide the paper out with care, like there might be a piece of my dad inside. And as I unfold the letter—stationery I recognize from his desk at the bakery—I brush my eyes with the back of my hand.

*Madeline,*

*I'm a simple man, and I often get things wrong when it comes to other people's emotions. But just the same, here it goes, the sloppy version that I hope you'll be able to understand.*

*I don't know if you remember, but a short while before you left you were making lemon rose cupcakes in the bakery and you asked me if I wanted you there. The question threw me at the time because I didn't think you ever doubted that. I've thought about that conversation a thousand times since. And I know that this is far too late, but I'd like to answer that question now.*

*Yes, my darling girl, I've always wanted you at the bakery. From the moment I met you in the hospital until the day I die and even after I will feel the same. I built it for you, just as my great-grandfather built his for his children. And there isn't a day that goes by that I don't wish you were here rolling and kneading beside me.*

*But I also want you to know that I don't blame you for going. That while I selfishly want you here, I understand. My only true hope is for you to be happy.*

*With love,*
*Dad*

I stare at his letter, my heart strangled in the grip of his words as tears cloud my vision. I pull it to my chest, immensely grateful he had that dream and the forethought to write me this letter. And although his message addresses something much deeper, I can't help but wonder why he didn't try to explain his addendum, why it was so important for him to write it in the first place. Maybe he knew how much I once loved this place and wanted me to give Haverberry another shot? But that doesn't explain why he gave half of the bakery to Wilder. Or why he waited a year for the addendum to take effect. Although, that part I understand better. An allotment of time for grief. Because everyone knows things gradually get easier, and that at first your heart wants to scream so loudly that the stars cover their ears. No one is prepared to think clearly in the wake of it.

I sit on my bed, clutching his letter, the sound of my pulse thrumming in my temples, and I glance at my phone, wondering once again about Wilder's part in my dad's decision. Because even though we spoke about the bakery that night on the beach, I never asked Wilder flat out about the addendum and if he knew why my dad set it up that way. And the longer I stare at Dad's note, the more the need to know grows stronger, becomes some visceral ache. My dad did this all with intentionality. He thought he was going to die and the last thing he did was write this note and that addendum. He was trying to tell me something or show me something. Logically, it somehow involves Wilder, and if I don't know the reason, Wilder certainly must.

All of a sudden I'm standing, walking toward my phone, my desire to understand so pressing that I've abandoned caution and my tempered plan of not getting riled on Christmas.

I carefully fold Dad's letter back up, slipping it in the envelope and placing it gently on the bedside table, followed immediately by hastily disconnecting my phone from its charger and pressing the on button.

As expected, there are about a million notifications from Liv. But there's also one from Wilder time-stamped at 4:36 a.m., suggesting he slept about as well as I did. I click it open, pushing past the bright pang of anxiety.

> Wilder: When you're ready, I'd still
> very much like the opportunity to
> explain, to fill you in on things I
> should have years ago.

I refresh my screen, thinking there must be more because

no one would write such a short and cryptic message after last night. But that's all there is. One sentence.

"Great," I breathe, shaking my head. He knows I won't be able to ignore this, that I'll wonder about it until I finally cave. I growl at the text, ready to blast something back, but think better of it.

Liv said he had bad reception. And there's nothing worse than having a tense conversation in shoddy, delayed fragments.

"My God, Liv totally played me," I say, half in awe. I don't know how she knew, but she definitely did. And before I can think of all the reasons I shouldn't, I stuff my phone in my back pocket and leave the room. At the top of the stairs, I hesitate, but I'm too hyped up on emotion over my dad's letter to reconsider. Because if I do leave Haverberry tomorrow, it has to be with a clean slate. I'm not leaving things unsaid, dragging my burning disappointment to California only to find out ten additional years down the line that I didn't know the half of it.

No. Not again. Not this time.

I stop in the living room, where Spence and Jake are playing with a remote-control car that scales the walls.

"Hey, Mom! Look at this," Spence says, and makes the thing do a loop around my mother's sconce.

"Very cool. Just be careful with Grandma's breakables," I say, giving him a meaningful look, and plucking my purse off the coffee table.

"I will," he says like he's far too mature to be reminded.

"Going somewhere?" Jake asks.

"Yeah," I say, and reflexively hesitate, which shifts Jake's expression to something less smiley, as though my hesitation can only mean one thing—Wilder—and as it turns out, he's right. I clear my throat. "Yes. There's something I need to do. I'll be back soon."

Jake opens his mouth to say something, and I can already see it's going to be an objection.

So I cut him off. "You got him, Jake?"

"Yeah, of course," he responds, and tries to go on, but once again I cut him off.

"Great. There are drinks in the fridge and more sweets than you could ever eat in the kitchen. Spence can show you. See you both soon," I say, and turn around, putting a kibosh on Jake feeling he can chime in on my relationship with Wilder. And I make a decision here and now that the next time we're alone, I'm going to tell Jake to nix the flirting, that communication is important, and that I don't want anything said or done that interferes with our ability to co-parent. Spence comes first. Always.

## CHAPTER 29

## LIFE IS AN ILLUSION CAKE—

*it looks like an old shoe, but is actually a triple vanilla bean masterpiece with layers of custard, thinly sliced strawberries, and a whole lotta yum*

Driving through my snow-covered town, I'm feeling good about myself, like maybe I'm finally handling the gray areas, clarifying my relationships in a way I couldn't when I was younger. But as I turn onto Winter Street, my confidence falters or rather gets swallowed up by all-consuming anxiety that I'm making the wrong choice. It's better to know, I tell myself. I can't wonder about this forever. I won't. If I don't do this, then one day he'll send another cryptic text and I'll be reeled in all over again. Just the thought fires me up.

No more push and pull, Wilder. This is where it ends.

My rant is abruptly halted, however, as I spot a wrought iron post on the edge of the road with a wooden sign displaying the number thirty-one. I slow my car, turning into the dirt driveway, a little surprised by it. Why does Wilder live out here on the edge of town anyway? I half expected him to live on Maple Street near his parents in some imposing house with snooty shrubs, the kind that are manicured within an inch of their lives and pointed out to guests for how difficult they are to grow. I snort, feeling justified in my assessment of him. But I'm distracted from my thoughts by the loss of light as the tall trees on either side of the driveway blot out the moon. Only a handful of seconds later, they open up, revealing a large yard and a cozy lit-up house.

As I register what I'm looking at, my stomach bottoms out. I lean forward over my steering wheel as though those couple of inches will explain what I'm seeing. The walls to Wilder's house are made of old cobbled stone, the roof is thatched, rising high up in slanted peaks, displaying four puffing chimneys, and the windows are the kind with the small diamond panes that open outward from the middle.

"Stop," I say in disbelief, so thrown that I almost forget to hit my brake. My car jerks to a stop just before a stone walkway leading to the front door.

I'm out of my car in a split second, barely remembering to close my door behind me as I stare up at the house, taking in the nuances of the stone walls near the soft amber glow of the windows and the wrought iron lanterns perched beside the door.

Wilder Buenaventura lives in an English cottage . . . in Haverberry. A goddamn perfect English cottage exactly like the one I described all those years ago when he asked me about my dreams. No, not like what I described; it's actually far better than what I imagined.

STOP. Don't even think it. That's not what this is. It's simply a coincidence. A big fat very specific coincidence.

Before I collect myself, Wilder opens the front door.

"Maddi?" he says, looking more shocked than I do, which is certainly a feat.

"Wilder," I say back, faltering, hands on my hips, realizing I'm straining my neck to gape at his house—a house he did not invite me to. I drop my arms, trying to reclaim the frustrated determination I had a moment before, but come up short. "Liv, um . . . she gave me your address?"

Earth to Maddi—he should be on the defensive, not you. It's technically his fault you've ambushed him and his stunning house on Christmas . . . right?

For a second his thrown look remains, but then he trades it for something softer, gesturing to his arched door. "Would you like to come in?"

"I, um." For the love of God, stop saying *um*. "I came here to ask you a question."

He watches me a moment, obviously registering my awkwardness—I mean, I'm basically broadcasting it with a cabaret line. "Come, I'll fix you something hot to drink. It's freezing out here."

I want to say no, that I prefer to have this conversation in the bitter cold, a perfect reflection of my bitter heart, but even I recognize how dramatic that is. Against my better judgment, I walk through his charmingly arched front door with wrought iron accents, past a stone wall that I swear is two feet thick. There's no grand foyer or empty hallway, just a rustic bench situated under handmade coat hooks that leads right into his living room. He offers to take my coat and scarf for me, but I hang them up myself.

Despite the fact I'm doing my darnedest to look steely, I feel my eyes widening in awe. I don't meet Wilder's gaze, too embarrassed that he'll be able to tell I like this place an indecent amount. Only, I can't stop myself from ogling his living room. It's the perfect size, big enough to fit two oversized couches in front of a stone fireplace, but small enough to feel inviting. The lamps are antique, the coffee table has uneven edges where the wood is knotted, and rustic beams run overhead, framing a large arched doorway leading into the dining room and the kitchen beyond it.

"Can I offer you a hot chocolate?" Wilder asks, watching me as I walk around the room, taking in the faux fur throw blankets and perfectly worn navy and maroon Oriental rug. Weirdly, he looks just as uncomfortable as I do, maybe even more so.

"Herbal tea, if you have it?" I reply. Hot chocolate feels too familiar; no one can be properly annoyed while drinking it. It's bad enough I'm staring at my dream house belonging to the one person I decidedly stopped dreaming with a long time ago; I don't need any extra lures to confuse things.

He smiles, not his usual confident grin, but something more unsure like he hasn't fully processed that I'm here. "I think you'll recall that I'm half British and that I'd be shaming my people if I didn't keep copious amounts of tea on hand at all times. So name your preference and I'm sure I'll have it."

"Anything. Anything works," I say, stammering a little and he nods, heading for the kitchen.

I then set to mentally reiterating all the things he's kept from me these past couple of weeks and reminding myself that this house isn't what I think it is. When he comes back, I'm still standing in the middle of his living room, staring at the crackling fire and arguing with myself.

He places two steaming mugs of tea, which smell of cinnamon and apples, on the coffee table. "Please, make yourself comfortable."

He scratches the back of his neck and I fidget with my sweater sleeves, both of us making an unsmooth go of sitting on the couch. And as I sink into the far too comfortable cushions, I frown. It's all too polite and hesitant for my present state of unrest, and it only agitates me further. When I imagined this interaction in my head, it most definitely didn't include admiring his house and sipping tea on his couch.

I turn to face him, and his shy expression spirals me further. Is he doing this on purpose? Does he realize it's impossible to be mad at someone who looks shy? You have not bested me, Wilder. I will not fall for this again. You can take your cottage and shove it right up your—

"I'm glad you're here," he says, and I attempt to swallow. He scratches the back of his neck . . . again. "I was worried you'd leave without me getting to explain." He pauses. "Not that I wouldn't have flown to California in that case."

I stare at him, my confusion turning to shock. "You would have flown . . ." I trail off, increasingly flustered and trying not to be flattered. This isn't how this is supposed to go. I'm supposed to be formidable, nail him with my tough questions, and suss out the truth before making a striking and fiery exit. I rub my forehead, trying to clear my head. "Don't, Wilder," I say, trying to remember all the things I wanted to ask him. "I don't want to hear that."

His eyes widen like I've caught him off guard, and the momentary disappointment that flashes across his face makes me feel bad.

"This is what I mean," I say, gesturing at him and his endearing expression. "You don't get to look like that after you encouraged my mother to sell the bakery. How am I supposed to believe anything you said?"

Wilder's eyes meet mine like he knew this was coming and he's ready for it. "I know how that sounded, believe me, but it wasn't an accurate portrayal of what happened. It was shortly after your father passed and your mother was overwhelmed. I never encouraged her to sell; I merely said that I understood her desire to. Which is how I started working at the bakery while she got on her feet."

While his answer sounds downright generous, that's the thing about Wilder—he's kind, just not when it comes to commitment. How many times did I return to him in our youth because he said something that I needed to hear? Yet it didn't change a thing.

I shake my head. "You still lied to me."

He sighs, deflating. "Believe it or not, I thought I was doing the right thing."

Bingo. All the frustration and hurt I felt a half hour before comes back tenfold. "You thought you were doing the right thing by playing me and Kate off one another?"

"What?" he says with emphatic shock, his eyebrows jumping up his forehead. "No. I'd never do that."

I give him a look like *oh, come on.* "And what about when you told me you cut all contact with her?"

"I did cut contact with Kate."

"So you weren't talking to her the same day that you kissed me? Telling her that you liked the idea of her working for your family?"

He hesitates. "Is that what she told you?"

Now I pause, embarrassed by how much I care. This isn't the conversation I was after. I wanted to ask him about my father and the addendum. Ask him if he ever heard about the dream. I got jumbled somehow, got my signals crossed and knotted. "It doesn't matter," I start, but he cuts me off.

"It does matter," he says in all seriousness. "Because I said no such thing, especially not to Kate. I did however speak to my mother and tell her that if Kate was redecorating the offices, I wouldn't begrudge her the job but that I also wouldn't be involved in the process. It was part of the reason I was so annoyed when she brought it up last night."

I stare at him. "Were you or were you not engaged to Kate a few weeks ago?"

Wilder falters.

"That's what I thought," I say, knowing I've caught him, only not feeling happy about it the way I imagined.

"It's not as simple as you think. Yes, we'd talked about engagement, or rather our families had, but it wasn't official. No rings were exchanged."

"Just a bracelet?" I quasi-hate the way I feel saying it, as though it somehow betrays that I once secretly hoped for something just as symbolic.

"That would be my mother inserting herself again," he says with a hint of frustration, signaling that what Liv said earlier was true. For a brief second, I waver. But there is no good situation with Wilder where his mother is actively rooting for someone else, evidenced by the fact that he broke up with me once just because she asked.

I shake my head, hating that I'm getting worked up over this, but unable to hit the brakes. "I wish you told me yourself, Wilder. I felt foolish last night. Hell, I feel foolish right now. You don't just call off a potential engagement and then kiss someone else. And if you do, it's not meaningful. It's a rebound. I did this once with you when we were teens, and I really, really don't want to do it again. Not when so much hangs in the balance."

"And what if I told you that the last thing you are is a rebound." His expression is so sincere that I scowl at him.

"I'd say I don't believe you. And again, it doesn't matter. This is what we do. This is what we'll probably always do—back and forth, push and pull; there is no happy ending for us, Wilder. And that's why I left last night, to put an end to it before we fell headfirst into our terrible pattern."

"You're wrong."

"Excuse me?"

"You're not wrong with the way you remember us. But you were never at fault. I was the problem."

I hesitate, surprised he just owned it like that, but before I can get out a retort, he continues.

"I told you last night that there were pieces of our story you were missing. And there still are. Yes, my mother wanted me to break up with you—"

"Which you readily listened to," I clap back.

"Yes, you're right. But what you don't know is that I thought I was doing what was best, making a hard decision so that you wouldn't have to."

"Oh, come on—"

"There was a mistake in the deed for your dad's bakery," he says quickly, probably sensing I'm about to stand up.

I close my mouth, the conversational one-eighty leaving me dizzy.

"A measurement error," he continues before I get my bearings. "The property line of your father's bakery is actually four inches smaller than anyone thought, which my mother only discovered when she set out to remodel the property next door and had an appraiser come in."

My eyebrows push together, trying to understand. "What does this have to do with anything?"

"Everything," he says with meaning. "Because at the time my mother was already harping on me about college, about going to Oxford and taking over the family business. But of course, you and I had planned to go to—"

"Vassar and the Culinary Institute," I say, suddenly catching on to what he's implying and feeling a little breathless.

"Right," he says, and turns fully toward me like he needs me to see that this is important. "And the less I budged on that decision the more insistent she got. My mother began to see you as the root of the problem. So, when she found the deed error, she didn't just correct it the way she might have a year earlier.

Instead, she brought it to me. Explained what a huge expense it'd be if your dad had to tear out that wall and rebuild—the wall that supported all the hookups for the sinks and housed the brand-new custom ovens."

My mouth opens, my throat suddenly tight. "He spent his savings putting in those ovens."

"I know," he says, and my chest feels so heavy that I fear my ribs will crack from the pressure.

"Your mom . . ." My voice is so low it's only a notch above the crackling fire. "Told you to break up with me and go to Oxford or she'd ruin my dad's business?"

"Yes," he says, and all the air whooshes out of me. "If I did what she wanted, she'd redraw the deed. That was the deal. The push and pull . . . It was my fault. I couldn't seem to stay away from you, and occasionally my self-control would slip, and I'd tell you how I really felt. Those girls I dated in high school? Asking someone else to the prom? I was literally doing everything in my power to distract myself from you and still I failed."

It's as though he just inserted a missing piece into the clock of our past, the gears finally clicking into place. Every time I asked him to explain himself, he'd shut down. Every time it seemed like we were getting closer, he'd pull away. He'd tell me he cared, and then shut me out again. "How could you never tell me this?"

He sighs. "At first, I thought I had to keep it from you. That if you knew the truth, we'd never stay away from each other, no matter the consequences. I thought my mother would eventually figure it out and your dad and the bakery would take a huge hit, one my mother so clearly explained they wouldn't recover from. That bakery was your life, Maddi. It was your dad's. I couldn't let that happen."

I swallow, the implications of what he's saying overwhelming me.

"And as time went on, I didn't tell you because I thought you hated me, justifiably so. I even convinced myself that you were better off without me, that knowing would only hurt you more." He rakes his hand through his hair.

"What changed?" I manage, my world spinning.

He shakes his head. "Honestly . . . I don't know. But about a year and a half ago something shifted. My parents asked me to come back to Haverberry to start learning the family business. And it didn't sound like the worst idea. I was in a bad spot. I'd broken things off with my fiancée in France six months earlier and given up my bakery in London. I was lost." He scratches his eyebrow. "After I came back, I stopped by the bakery to see your dad. He said I was welcome there anytime. And I thought, yeah, actually, that sounds nice. It'd be a perfect break from everything else."

I look briefly at my hands in my lap, remembering a time when I felt the same.

"It started as a once-in-a-while thing. I'd drop in on your dad in the early morning and help him get things ready for the day. Or sometimes he and I would work on a new recipe in the evenings." He glances toward the fire like he's remembering. "We didn't talk much, about things that weren't baking, that is. And I appreciated that. It was the one place I could just be. Most days we worked in companionable silence."

I nod sadly, because just hearing it makes me remember the comfort I once found in moving quietly around my dad, trading ingredients and commenting on cake decorations.

Wilder pulls his gaze from the fireplace and looks at me. "Then one day, he brought you up, asked me why I never talked about you. It took me by surprise, like someone reached into my chest and shook my heart awake. I don't know why, I really don't, but I told him the truth."

It takes me a second to catch his meaning. "About the deed?" I say, my voice betraying my shock. "Does my mother know—"

He shakes his head. "Your father thought it best to keep it between us. Thought your mom and mine might lose their friendship over it."

I press my lips together, biting back my response that maybe they should. But the moment I think it, I feel bad. My dad was trying to protect her; can I really begrudge him that? Then it hits me: "So that's why my dad left you half the bakery? He was settling the debt of the deed?"

But instead of nodding, Wilder looks shy again. "Actually . . . no, that wasn't it."

Wilder leans over the arm of the couch and opens a tiny drawer in the end table. Only what he pulls out of it stops my breath. A letter, just like the one my mother gave me, only with Wilder's name on the envelope instead of mine.

"When did she . . ." I start, my voice trailing off as he hands it to me.

"The day we read the will," he says, answering my question even though I can't seem to get it out.

I hesitate before opening the envelope, not sure what I'm going to find in there or that I'll be able to keep it together in front of Wilder.

He leans his elbows on his knees, looking down at his hands. "If you prefer," he says gently, "I can give you a minute alone—"

"No," I reply, not even sure why I'm so adamant about it. This would certainly be more comfortable without him, but in a way, it also feels like the easy way out. If he's brave enough to tell me all of this, to show me his letter, then I'm brave enough to read the thing in front of him.

I exhale, steeling myself and sliding the letter out, written on the same stationery that mine was.

*Dear Wilder,*

*I know this must all come as a shock, and I know what you're probably thinking, that I'm attempting to repay you for saving the bakery. But no. It's something much simpler than that and much more import-ant. You've been a true friend to me, and I like to think I've been one to you. It's my parting wish to give you the one thing I think you need—a chance to tell the truth. I don't know what you'll do with it, but I do hope you'll make it count. Trust me on this; life is short and it's precious and you don't want to look back one day like I am now and realize it could have been different.*

*Be well, my son,*
*Charles*

I look up at Wilder, stunned into silence, and return his letter, my hand unsteady. My dad wanted to give Wilder a chance to tell me the truth? That's why he stuck us in that bakery together, figuring eventually we'd have to talk about it?

I take a deep breath, running my hands over my face. This, of all things, was not what I was expecting. Did Dad know how badly I needed this? But the answer is obvious. Of course he knew—he orchestrated an elaborate plot just to give me the opportunity to heal. And the thought makes my chest rise and fall a little faster. Whatever doubts I had about my relationship with my father are suddenly gone; he wanted me to be happy.

"I know I've botched this," Wilder starts. "And that I made you feel like I was keeping things from you. But I don't want you to think those things were motivated by my feelings for Kate or that I was in any way trying to keep her on the line. Kate and I were bad for each other. We were the same kind of broken, trading in our own happiness for our families' wants, and we bonded over it. But we never had that connection, the thing that makes things more. She's likely more bothered that I embarrassed her than she is that our relationship ended." He takes a breath. "And my mother? She wants me to fit into her image of what a Buenaventura should be, willing to sacrifice my happiness to do it. It just took me a long time to see that, or maybe to accept it. After that party last night, I realized there was no appeasing her unless I let her direct the entirety of my life—my job, my marriage, even my interests—which I'm not going to do."

I remember what Liv said about Wilder always trying to get his mother's attention, fighting for her love. And for a second, I want to reach out to him, place my hand on his arm in a comforting way. It never occurred to me how much of a struggle this whole addendum business has been for him.

"I'm not . . ." I say, flustered. "I don't know what to say."

"You don't need to say anything. I know it's a lot. And I know you must be reeling. I'm just relieved you gave me a chance to explain. After last night, I wasn't sure you'd ever speak to me again."

I open my mouth and close it. My world has tilted too many times in this conversation for me to even know how to proceed. "Which is why you were going to fly to LA?" I'm not even sure why I say it, maybe because I want it to be true, or maybe because for once I really want to know what it is that exists between us, for better or for worse.

"Yes," he says, looking at me like he's never been more serious. "I should have gone years ago. Hell, I should have gone after you the moment I realized you'd left."

"Wilder—" I start and stop, breaking eye contact with him.

"I knew if I showed up in LA all those years ago that I probably wouldn't leave, that I'd stay there with you and the baby."

He laughs a sad laugh. "If you can believe it, I was jealous at the time because Spence wasn't mine. Still am."

My heart misses a beat. Wilder wishes he was Spence's father?

"But if I had gone to LA, my mother would have destroyed your dad's bakery, probably burned down the town in some misguided effort to get me back. I thought you'd hate me if you knew the truth. I hated myself. But now? No hesitation. If you and Spence would have me, I'd follow you to the end of the earth."

My heart pounds inside my chest, sloppy and far too loud. The fact that he included my son, that he recognizes I put him first, means more to me than I could ever say. I search for words, for any response that makes sense, but nothing comes.

And he's not done. "Your father and the bakery helped me find myself when I was lost, helped show me what I truly want."

He smiles at me, and I feel it move through me like electricity. His waves fall lightly on his forehead, and his eyes stare intently into my own. But I don't get up the way I thought I would. I just stare right back at him, letting him know I'm listening, that this is important to me, too.

He glances briefly at the living room. "That's when I started building this house."

Bright specks of light form in front of my eyes. "Hang on . . . you *built* this?"

He nods, the same uncertainty from when I first arrived reappearing on his face. "Had the stone shipped over from the UK."

I immediately try to convince myself that this isn't really happening. He didn't build it because of me. He just stole my very good idea. Or maybe he became attached to the architecture in England and decided to flaunt his wealth by literally shipping it across an ocean? He probably doesn't even remember that conversation we had on the bench all those years ago.

"Why would you do that?"

The smile that appears on his face is gentle, a fragile thing that embodies far too much hope. "I thought that'd be obvious." His eyes meet mine. "When I designed it, everyone assumed that I missed England," he says, pausing. "But really, I missed you."

My breath screeches to a stop, my body temperature shooting up a thousand degrees. This isn't a situation I was prepared for. This isn't a situation anyone is prepared for. Who would ever predict that their first love and mortal enemy would build their dream house? Just the mere thought makes me faint. I touch my forehead, begging my body to settle down so that I can make sense of it all.

"I built this place for you, Maddi, because I wanted you to have a piece of your dream," he continues, and my heart takes one final beat before it nosedives into his atmosphere, positive I'll knock myself out when I hit land and not really caring.

I feel my eyes welling before I can stop them, feel my whole heart lifting in a standing ovation. "Wilder . . ." I start, truly moved. "It's beautiful. It's more than beautiful."

The smile that spreads across his face is so bright that I lean closer.

"But how can I . . ." I trail off, not knowing how to accept something like this, to embrace a gesture this big.

"Slowly," he says. "If you decide to give me the chance, we'll go at your pace. Whatever you need. Even if what you need is to be somewhere other than Haverberry."

My eyes widen at the thought. "And leave this perfect cottage?" I say, aghast.

He shrugs, but his eyes twinkle. "This is just a house. A cozy one for sure, but you're far more important."

Suddenly all the roadblocks that seemed so impossible—his mother, Kate, my family, all our past hurts—lose their power.

They don't disappear, but they're diminished, dulled to the point that I don't fear them the way I used to. And in their place, something else springs up, something softer and hopelessly optimistic.

"I want to stay," I reply, the words slipping out so easily that I'm not sure I was the one who said them. "Here in Haverberry. With you."

And just like that, the air between us is charged, sparking like the wild end of a severed cable.

"You do?" he asks, his eyes searching mine, his body leaning ever closer. I can almost hear his heartbeat, see the pounding in his chest.

I nod, my hand reaching for his, tentative and curious. He wraps his fingers around mine, lifting my palm to his mouth and slowly kissing it, the heat from his lips spreading along my skin. In that instant, the remnants of hesitation drain out of me, pooling on the floor by my feet as though someone pulled a plug. And this time, as he leans toward me like a question, I lean in to meet him.

I feel Wilder's smile as his lips find mine, matching it with my own. He moves his hand through my hair above my ear, sliding it behind my neck, his other arm wrapping around the small of my back. He pulls me into him, pressing our bodies together, his hot breath dancing on my tongue. And unlike the last time we kissed, when I was afraid of what I might feel, of what it might mean, I don't hold back. Because that barrier, the one we built as teenagers and could never seem to breach, is finally gone. And all that's left is heat and anticipation, a connection so intense that it steals my breath and fills my body with electrified warmth.

Wilder carved out a place in my heart all those years ago, one I couldn't seem to fill no matter how hard I tried. And feeling him this close, drinking in his smoky scent, is like returning home, willingly tangling myself up in him, in this town, in the bakery.

I pull back, breathless and beaming. "Wilder," I say, tracing a finger along his perfect jaw.

"Maddi," he replies, his expression filled with awe.

We stay like that for a long time, looking at each other, holding hands, just being. And it's so wonderful that I resent the movement of time, the clock on his far wall that tells me it's getting late.

"I want to stay . . ." I start, wishing minutes were hours.

"But it's Christmas?" he offers.

"Exactly," I reply with an exhale. But then it occurs to me that Wilder isn't with his family and that if I leave, he'll once again be spending the holiday alone. So in a moment of inspired optimism, I add, "I'm wondering . . . would you like to come with me?"

Wilder's eyebrows rise. "Are you offering to take me home for the holidays, Miss DeLuca?"

I grin. "Yeah, I think I am. I mean, yes. I want to."

He smiles, a full reckless smile that breaks my heart into operatic singing. "There's nothing I'd like more."

Just a couple of days ago, Wilder's enthusiasm would have made me nervous, and the idea of letting him spend time with Spence would have had me out of sorts. But this feels intrinsically right, like salt in the ocean or warmth from the sun. For once I know what I want, and even though it's not going to be simple, in a way it is, because the things that truly matter, the ones you wouldn't trade anything in the world for, are the ones that require the most faith.

## CHAPTER 30

## THERE'S ALWAYS ROOM FOR ICE CREAM CAKE—

*with those crunchy chocolate nibs between the layers, some things are so wonderful they stand the test of time*

As Wilder drives, his fingers laced through mine, I'm surprised I still fit in my body, convinced I might actually burst from happiness, a feeling I haven't had in this town in more than a decade. Things seem possible again in a way I can hardly explain. I'm still me, Wilder is still Wilder, and Haverberry is still Haverberry, but right now it all looks different. It's lit up, or maybe I am. Perspective is a funny thing. To think the entire world shifts when our thinking does is its own type of magic.

We turn into the town square and an idea suddenly dawns on me. Before I can talk myself out of it, I tell Wilder to drive onto Periwinkle Lane. I tell him to stop half a block down in front of a peachy Victorian, and I get out with a too-big grin. Then I race up the walkway and knock before I can think of all the reasons this is crazy.

The door opens and Mr. Hamza stands on the other side,

his beard much whiter than I remember. "Madeline?" he says with confusion written on his brow.

"I know I shouldn't have just shown up here. I'm so sorry if I disturbed your evening. But I was hoping . . . just hoping that I might convince you to bring out your horse-drawn sleigh again, whenever it's convenient? Tomorrow, the next day—I'll take anything I can get. And I'll pay you anything you want. Bake you a thousand pies. See, the thing is, my dad proposed to my mother in a horse-drawn sleigh and—" I pause, trying to keep my emotion from overflowing. "We missed your ride this year. I just know it would mean the world to my mother if we got to do it."

Mr. Hamza smiles at me, reaches out, and gently pats me on the head like I was still twelve, a gesture I find oddly comforting. "Yes, Madeline. I can do that. In fact, if it works for you, you all can meet me in town in an hour."

"Really?" I say too loudly, half misty and half elated. "Thank you so much! You don't know what this means."

He gives me a small grandfatherly smile. "I've been giving your parents that ride for the past twenty years," he says. "Your father was a good man."

I nod at him, not trusting myself with words, and after a good deep breath, I say ten more thank yous, vowing to bring him a whole mess of pastries after the holidays.

Only when I return to Wilder's car, instead of his guessing what I was doing, he stares at his phone with a frown.

"Everything okay?" I ask as I get in his passenger seat.

"Yeah, I mean I think so," he replies, looking up from his screen. "It's my mom."

My good mood stutters. "Oh."

"It's nothing for you to worry about," he says reassuringly, but recalibrates, shaking his head and sighing. "No, that's not exactly it. The truth is she feels bad. Says she'd like an opportunity to apologize in person . . . to us both."

My stomach jumps out of the plane with no parachute. I open my mouth, but he's faster.

"Which is something I'd never ask you to do. I just didn't want you to think I was keeping anything from you. The only way we work, the only way we've ever worked, is with total and complete honesty. I know I come with a trying family dynamic, and I never want you to feel uncomfortable or attacked the way you did last night at my parents' house." His declaration takes me by surprise, throws off my initial resistance.

For a long moment I consider it, thinking about my struggle with my mother and how much miscommunication we've had over the years. "No, I mean, yeah, I'd be open to it. I'm not promising we'll be best friends, but I've learned the hard way that hearing people out is important."

Only instead of replying, a smile slowly inches up his face and the look he gives me is one of absolute fascination.

"What?" I say, not sure what to make of his expression.

"You," he says. "You're just more than I'd ever hoped for."

I laugh, a little thrilled by his admiration. "Well, before you praise me too much, fair warning that I come with baggage, too. And speaking of which . . . I think Jake might still be at my house."

Wilder glances at me, turning back onto the street with a shrug. "The only thing I really care about is that Jake is good to you and Spence," he says like he means it, and I let the conversation end there, no longer shying from the complications in my life, but taking them head-on.

Wilder parks his car in my driveway and we find Spence, my mom, and Jake in the living room.

Jake takes one look at Wilder and shifts uncomfortably. My mom, however, wears a self-satisfied smirk.

"I have a surprise," I announce, which has Spence drop his controller and give me his full attention. "It's in town in about forty-five minutes."

Spence, of course, is over the moon. My mother lifts a questioning eyebrow, and Jake looks like he doesn't know how to react.

"You're welcome to join us, Jake," I say, not because I think it'll be comfortable, but because I don't want to give the weirdness and the rivalry any more life. We all need to learn to coexist.

Jake hesitates, his eyes flicking to Wilder like he's going to say yes just on principle. But something changes his mind; I don't know if it's Christmas cheer or a moment of maturity, but he sighs and says, "Thanks, but I think I'll sit this one out. I was thinking I might take Spence out tomorrow, though, if that works for you, Maddi?"

Spence looks from his dad to me.

"Anytime, Jake. I hope you'll come by often, now that Spence and I will be living here."

Surprise ripples through the room. Spence jumps up with a "Whoohoo" and Jake grins. But it's my mother who gets me. Her chest fills with air and the smile on her face is so genuine that my heart swells.

*◦◦◦◦◦*

Soon enough, Wilder, Mom, Spence, and I are all bundled up, standing in front of the bakery, Spence bouncing for all he's worth. The air has a delicious scent, like fresh pine and shaved ice, and even though it's quite cold, it feels full of potential, like Santa himself might drop by for a chuckle and a cookie.

Many believe somewhere in their being that they can move a coin with their mind, if they just think hard enough or put the right energy behind it, that they will in fact realize their superpowers. But few ever think that way about a broken heart or mending grief. I never believed that if I leaned in, I could make things better. And I see now that isn't true, that we always have the power to change, in small ways and momentous ones.

Mr. Hamza appears in the square just as he promised, his horses dappled gray and his sleigh lined with velvet. I turn to my mom.

Her breath catches and her hand presses over her heart, her eyes filling with tears. She doesn't speak right away, not that she could be heard over Spence's enthusiastic squeals. But the look of gratitude she gives me is everything I hoped for.

"Thank you, Madeline," she says. "It's not often someone gifts you a second chance."

Every once in a while, there's a moment that stands out. It doesn't need to be big or shocking or even noticeable to anyone but you, but for reasons untold, that moment is captured in the amber of your heart. And this moment, here with my family, my hand snug in Wilder's, feels like something I might remember for all my days. The unexpected warmth of it. Our collective second chance.

# ACKNOWLEDGMENTS

Whoever said writing a book was a solitary endeavor clearly never met my amazing support system. Without them, this story wouldn't exist.

First and foremost, I have to thank my real-life love story—my husband James Bird and our son Wolf—for inspiring me to create fictional characters just as swoon-worthy as they are.

To Sandra Mather, who always believes in my dreams, thank you for being my ultimate rom com mom and never letting the baked goods run out.

Of course, I could never write a book without a little help from my furry friends. To my cats, Smeagle, Princess, Bear, Mortimer, and Duncan and my loyal pup Banana—thank you for cuddles, kisses, and a healthy dose of inspiration.

And then there's my incredible agent, Rosemary Stimola—the fairy godmother of my publishing dreams. Without her, this book wouldn't have found its way into the world, and my heart would still be pining for a happily ever after.

ACKNOWLEDGMENTS

To the incredible team at Blackstone Publishing—Dan Ehrenhaft, Celia Johnson, Lydia Rogue, Cole Barnes, Josie Woodbridge, Sarah Riedlinger, Ananda Finwall, Amy Craig, David Baker, and Katrina Tan—thank you for bringing this book to life.

Last but not least, to my fellow writers, critique partners, and chosen family—Kit Vincent, Kerry Kletter, Jennifer Niven, Emily Henry, Lana Harper, Jilly Gagnon, Chelsea Sedoti, Nic Stone, Kali Wallace, Audrey Coulthurst, Jeff Zentner, Angelo Surmelis, and Bri Cavallaro. Thank you for holding my hand through the tough parts, cheering me on through the good, and always reminding me that love is worth fighting for.

And to my readers and FAMB members—you're one of the premiere joys of writing. I hope this rom com makes you laugh, swoon, and feel all the feels. Thank you from the bottom of my heart!